NOT ONE MORE DAY

A Nurse's Transformative Journey *from*
Victim and Violence *to* Compassion and Confidence.

Candice Morrow, RN

This memoir is a reflection of my own personal experience. I have written it to the best of my recollection, though time and trauma may have shaped certain details. I have tried to recreate events, locales, and conversations from memory of them. Names, locations, identifying characteristics, and sequences of events have been altered or combined to protect the privacy of people involved. Any resemblance to persons living or deceased beyond those explicitly mentioned is purely coincidental.

This book contains themes of domestic abuse and trauma, which may be distressing to some readers. It is not intended as a substitute for professional advice or support. If you or someone you know is experiencing abuse, please seek help from a trusted resource or professional.

The views and opinions expressed in this memoir are solely my own and do not reflect those of any organization, institution, or individual mentioned.

Copyright ©2025 Morrow & Co. Media, LLC

All rights reserved.

Hardcover ISBN-13: 979-8-218-61521-5
Paperback ISBN: 979-8-9991910-0-7

This book may not be reproduced or transmitted in whole or in part, in any form or by any means electronic or mechanical, including photocopying, scanning, recording, or any information storage or retrieval system, without prior permission in writing from the author.

DEDICATION

To my sons

You are part of this journey, and this memoir is as much for you as it is me. I hope these pages bring understanding, healing, and a reminder that love should never hurt, and no one deserves to suffer in silence.

This book is dedicated to anyone who has ever felt silenced, afraid, or alone in pain. May these pages remind you healing is possible, your voice matters, and you are never alone.

TABLE OF CONTENTS

Foreword		9
Preface		11
Acknowledgements		13
Chapter 1	Hidden Metal	15
Chapter 2	No White Picket Fence	20
Chapter 3	Aunt Gen and Uncle Willis	27
Chapter 4	Slow Learner	33
Chapter 5	The Love Bomb	37
Chapter 6	What's Wrong With Me?	43
Chapter 7	An Overwhelming Challenge	51
Chapter 8	Sudden Changes	64
Chapter 9	The Blue House	69
Chapter 10	"Seek Help from Your Church"	75
Chapter 11	"You Should Go To College"	82
Chapter 12	My Name Is Candy	87
Chapter 13	"Go to The Police"	94
Chapter 14	The Envelope	101
Chapter 15	The Mechanism of Action	113
Chapter 16	I'm Going to Kill You	126
Chapter 17	The Blue Convertible	136
Chapter 18	Playing Dead	143
Chapter 19	Quiet Determination	153
Chapter 20	A Woman in Uniform	162
Chapter 21	Breakfast and a Bullet	172
Chapter 22	Jets and Jail	178

Chapter 23	A Sense of Purpose	187
Chapter 24	Unmasking Deceit	202
Chapter 25	The Mornings After	216
Chapter 26	My Name is Candice	235
Chapter 27	Reclaiming My Life and Career	249
Chapter 28	Death, Documents, and Deception	263
Chapter 29	An Unexpected Visitor	280
Chapter 30	I Have a Voice	291
Chapter 31	Molly & Me	296
Chapter 32	Divorcing My Family	316
Chapter 33	Goodbyes	333
Chapter 34	This Is *My* Life Now	**343**

| Afterword | 349 |
| About the Author | 355 |

FOREWORD

When you're a plastic surgeon, you invariably wind up talking a lot about transformation. That transformation is a process of taking what was broken, scarred, or hidden and reshaping it into something strong, whole, and visible once more. Plastic surgery is not just about external appearances, it's about reconstruction and renewal.

Similarly, *Not One More Day* stands as a testament to transformation. A survivor of intimate partner violence (often called domestic abuse or domestic violence), author Candice Morrow endured both physical and emotional pain yet managed to escape and become an advocate for herself and others.

At the hands of her abusers, her world was one of fear, isolation, and self-doubt. Led to believe she was worthless and the cause of her own suffering, Candice suffered guilt and shame that left scars as deep as the physical wounds she also suffered.

But her narrative inspires as it details the resilience of the human spirit despite overwhelming adversity. It is a reminder that while the past may leave its marks, those marks do not have to define the future.

By her own admission, breaking free of codependency meant cultivating the inner strength to overcome intimidation and reclaim her sense of self. Helping her along the way were the unforeseen allies, some with names she recalls vividly and others who were present only fleetingly, but all contributed in some small or profound way to her success. These angels, as she calls them, underscore the immense value of human kindness and connection.

Each achievement along her road to recovery—be it graduating from nursing school, raising two children, running a business, or creating an endowment—enabled her to more clearly realize what mattered to her and why she was deserving of joy.

Even after escaping it, the internalization of abuse can have an indelible impact on an individual's ability to trust, hope, and feel safe again. Candice shows us the possibility of recovery even after years of being an undeserving victim. Her personal as well as professional successes, coupled with her capacity for compassion, support the notion that one can not only survive but actually thrive in the aftermath of walking away.

In the latter part of her career as a registered nurse, Candice has largely served as an educator, teaching countless clinicians the techniques to effectively perform in their practices. Her memoir serves no less a pivotal role in potentially shaping the future trajectory of women who find themselves in a life like hers once was. She has turned her pain into purpose, reminding other victims that strength can be found within, and the damages suffered do not have to become defining.

In a world where silence often surrounds domestic abuse, this book shatters that silence. Hers is the story that others need to hear, so they can reclaim their narrative, overcome, and find joy again. It is a beacon of hope for anyone who has ever felt trapped, voiceless, or unworthy. It is a reminder that healing is possible.

Kristin A. Boehm, MD, FACS
March 26, 2025

PREFACE

I was looking forward to a long-awaited trip with my dear girlfriend Julie, a trip we'd been planning for almost a year. Five days before, I found myself behind the wheel of a Tahoe SUV, driving across North Dakota from Bismarck to Minot for two aesthetic trainings, when powerful straight-line winds suddenly picked up the vehicle. In an instant, I was airborne. I screamed, gripping the wheel, and braced for the worst—until a soft voice whispered in my ear, *"Take your hands off the steering wheel and your foot off the brake. I've got you."* Terrified but compelled by the voice's calm insistence, I obeyed.

The heavy Tahoe twisted through the air, then landed gently, as if cushioned. The voice I heard wasn't just anyone's—it was Aunt Gen's. Though she had passed, I felt her presence with me. She was my protective angel that day. Miraculously, I walked away with only a scratch on my elbow and a scrape on my ankle.

That near-death experience shook me to my core. My life could have been cut short in a matter of seconds. As I sat in the quiet aftermath of the accident, reality hit me: *Now* was the time. It was time to tell my story.

I had tried to write it once before, years ago. I remember sitting at the dining room table, writing out three painful pages before crumpling them up and tossing them in the trash. The weight of those memories was simply too much. The pain of revisiting my past, of putting those words onto paper, was more than I could bear. I wasn't ready then.

This time, though, was different. I was determined to make my journey matter for myself and for other women who might find hope in my story. I wanted my pain to serve a purpose, to show others that survival and healing are possible, even after the darkest of days.

I've spent the past two years writing every single day, with weekly calls to my writing coach to help me stay focused and grounded. Some days I could barely manage a single paragraph; on others, I'd sit for eight hours, letting the memories flow as much as I could tolerate. Reliving those horrific moments with the perspective of a healthier mind has been an act of emotional endurance, torture at times, but necessary. Every sentence written, every tear shed, brought me one step closer to finishing. And knowing my story might bring hope to others, that it could help someone feel less alone in their pain, is what kept me going.

I knew I wanted to write an in-depth, detailed account of my experiences. A story that didn't gloss over the truth but laid it bare in all its complexity.

Throughout this process, I've grieved deeply for my younger self, mourning the woman I once was, wishing she had the tools, the knowledge, and the support to have seen things more clearly. But while I can't go back and save her, I can honor her by telling the story she was once too afraid to tell.

The time is *now*. Because my story matters and because I've finally found the strength to tell it.

ACKNOWLEDGMENTS

To those dear souls who lifted me up, who pushed me forward, who told me I had to keep writing, even when the memories were too heavy and the words too painful to bear, I thank these angels from the depth of my being. Your support helped me find my voice.

To my writing coach, Mari Ann Stefanelli, I thank you for the countless hours you spent gently guiding me through every line of this memoir. Your steady support and thoughtful insight helped bring my story to life with grace, clarity, and compassion.

To my editor, Jennifer Lawler, I'm deeply grateful for your keen editorial expertise and unwavering support, which were instrumental in the final shaping of my memoir.

CHAPTER 1

Hidden Metal

It was a beautiful summer Saturday morning. I woke and opened the curtains in my bedroom. Sunshine flooded the room as the air-conditioning unit kicked on. As I gazed at the tree-filled courtyard from the balcony, my gut clenched. Placing my arm on my stomach, I gave myself an awkward hug. *Oh no, God. Please, not today.* It was as if I had a sixth sense when something bad was about to happen. It wasn't a gift. It frightened me. I knew something was coming, I just didn't know how bad it would be.

Richard would be here soon.

I brushed off the dread and checked on my boys. Ben, eleven, and Jason, eight, were still sleeping in their shared bedroom, their faces peaceful in the soft morning light. I went downstairs to make myself a cup of tea, savoring a quiet moment to myself.

Richard and I had been together for nine years, married for five. After countless failed attempts, I had finally succeeded in leaving him. I'd been living in this townhouse for about nine months, trying to make a fresh start. It was a fragile, tentative peace, one I'd fought hard to create.

But only six months after my escape, he'd tracked me down, reappearing like he'd never really left. His phone calls now were remorseful, his voice softened with apologies. "I'm in therapy now," he'd say, pleading with me. "I've changed. I'm different now. I love you. No one will ever love you like I do. I'm not drinking anymore."

I was confused by this shift in his behavior. As I sipped my warm black tea, my thoughts wavered between logic and lingering hope. I was still finding my footing, struggling to navigate life and society on my own. I'd been cut off from society for so long, trapped in his prison. I wanted to believe him, to trust that maybe this time would be different. But the rational side of my brain kept telling me, "No, you've come this far. Don't go back." The words were soft but insistent, even as old emotions tried to draw me in.

Why do I take his calls?

I have no other choice. I'm exhausted. I can barely pay the bills. He'll help financially. This is a good thing. He's a body with some money. It will be different this time. He says he's changed. He says he won't hit me anymore.

Then why does my stomach hurt so bad?

The doorbell startled me, breaking the quiet stillness. Richard had said he'd come for breakfast with me and the boys, something he'd rarely shown interest in doing before. I opened the door and greeted him, trying to keep my voice steady. "Good morning, come on in."

"How are you?" he asked, reaching out as if to embrace me. I stepped back, creating a small, safe distance.

"The boys are still sleeping," I said, keeping my tone casual, "but I thought I'd make breakfast when they wake up. Is that okay with you?"

"Sure, that's fine," he said, seeming more relaxed than I'd expected.

"Could I make you a cup of tea?"

"No, I'm fine, but thank you."

The easy conversation made me hopeful, but my stomach was still in knots.

"I'm going upstairs to change and get ready for the day," I told him, hoping for a few more quiet minutes to gather myself. But instead of waiting, he followed me, an unwelcome shadow at my heels. My stomach clenched tighter as I crossed the landing and glanced at the boys, still asleep in their twin beds.

I walked into my bedroom, and Richard sat down on the edge of the bed, his gaze fixed on me as I brushed my teeth in the bathroom.

"I'm so happy we're back together. I haven't had a drink in thirty days now."

I kept brushing my teeth. I didn't like looking at him. *Where did he get the idea that we're back together?*

As I walked past him, he reached out and groped my ass, a familiar invasion that made my skin crawl.

"Please don't grope me. I don't like that," I said, forcing myself to meet his eyes, disgust evident in my voice.

In an instant, his demeanor changed. He stood up, his body tensing as he arched his back, puffing out his chest like he was gearing up for a fight.

"I will do whatever I want to do with you, cunt, and you…will…obey…me." His voice was a snarl, his eyes dark and bulging with anger.

Before I could react, he drew back his arm and swung, his fist slamming against my body. His fists cracked against my face, my arms, my torso. Like fireworks, pain exploded inside me, again and again.

"You're too ugly for anyone to love," he spat, his voice filled with venom. He swung again, punctuating each blow with a slur.

"You…are…a…bitch. Whore. Slut."

I crumpled and curled into a fetal position, my hands shielding my head as he swapped his fists for his feet, unleashing kick after kick. I struggled to protect myself, desperate not to scream, desperate not to faint, desperate not to wake the boys, but the pain was a beast that swallowed me. Each blow stripped away whatever hope I had clung to.

It will be over soon.
He will stop hitting you.
Just protect yourself so you don't die.

Grabbing my hair, he yanked me upright, his rage mounting. He pulled me with one hand, and with the other, overturned the entire dresser, sending its large mirror crashing to the floor. Glass shattered across the carpet. His dilated pupils obscured the color of his eyes, becoming terrifying black holes. Then he came at me again, dragging me across broken shards that sliced deep into my skin. A nerve in my right foot stung. Cuts covered my body.

Then he stopped.

He sauntered over to the bed and sat against the headboard, breathing hard yet eerily calm.

"I will kill you if you don't obey me. I will kill your family. I will take your children and you will never see them again. You are nothing without me. Will you obey me now, bitch?"

I stared at him as my bloody, bruised body shook uncontrollably. *How could I have possibly ended up in this mess once again?* Shame and anger engulfed me for believing he could have changed.

A whimper behind me broke into my thoughts, and I turned around. My sons stood in their bedroom doorway, eyes wide and filled with a fear no child should ever know. Their small faces were pale, their shoulders slumped. They looked so much older than their years. The weight of what they'd seen crushed me. Then a fire ignited inside me, burning through my fear. I turned back to Richard, meeting his gaze directly, and screamed, "No, I will not obey you anymore!"

"Oh, is that so?" he sneered.

He reached under the bed and pulled out a sawed-off shotgun.

My stomach dropped. *Where did that gun come from?*

"You're going to die, and your children will watch you die," he said, his voice low and steady, pure hatred in his eyes.

He raised the shotgun and aimed the barrel between my eyes, his finger on the trigger.

You're going to die.

Unable to move, I held my breath as I stared at the shiny, rough edges of the gun barrel.

He pulled the trigger.

CHAPTER 2

No White Picket Fence

When I was growing up, we lived in a nice, middle-class neighborhood, in a modest ranch-style home with three bedrooms and two baths. On the outside, we were a typical family. My older sister and I shared one bedroom, while my younger sister and brother shared another. But there was no white picket fence, the symbol of safety, warmth, and the promise of a loving home, where parents gently tucked their children into bed with a goodnight kiss on the forehead. Beneath the surface lived something far colder, something that left no soft place to fall.

The walls of our house, though outwardly unremarkable, held the weight of countless battles fought behind closed doors. My father's words were a constant reminder of the silence we were forced to uphold: "What happens in this house stays in this house." It was both a command and a warning.

My father, David, was a short, slim man who reminded me of a Caucasian Sammy Davis Jr. He always had a cigarette in his right hand, and every night and all day on the weekends he wore a path to the refrigerator, pulling out one can of cheap beer after another and drinking it. He worked for General Motors and always drove the latest model.

My mother, a stay-at-home mom, was a miserable soul. She loved her Valium, always chasing it down with a glass of wine or a beer. Her hair color changed like the wind; it could be pink one day and white the next, depending on the month and her mood. And yes, pink hair was a thing in the fifties.

I lost count of how many times they were divorced and remarried.

They fought mostly about money. Both were examples of the cliché "keeping up with the Joneses." Getting further and further in debt.

Though we seldom ate dinner together, when we did the table was a battleground, a fragile stage where tempers ignited and chaos reigned. One evening remains vivid in my mind. My father, seated at the head of the table, and my mother, to his left, were screaming at each other, their voices sharp and cutting. Suddenly, my father stood up, his face contorted with fury, and placed his hands under the table. With one violent motion, he flipped it over, sending the pot roast, mashed potatoes, and carrots flying in every direction, painting the walls in a mess of food and shattered glass.

I stared, transfixed, as mashed potatoes slid down the wall, leaving greasy yellow streaks of butter in their wake. Milk pooled on the floor around the broken glass. The gravy boat had hit a wall and splattered its contents in every direction, dripping onto the chaos below.

My mother shot up from her chair, her foot slipping on the scattered food. She steadied herself, reared her arm back, and tried to strike my father, but he was quicker. He grabbed her arm mid-swing, snarled, "You bitch, you better not hit me," and shoved her to the floor. With a roar, he lunged at her, pinning her in the mess of food and glass. They locked in a brutal struggle, my father striking her face and body as she swung back at him, her voice filled with rage as she screamed, "You bastard, get off me." Their insults and profanities filled the room.

My brother Asser and I stood frozen, staring at each other, our clothes smeared with remnants of the meal. Mashed potatoes and bits of carrots spattered my red-striped glasses, blurring my vision as I tried to comprehend what was happening. Asser's wide eyes reflected the same fear I felt.

My older sister, Jane, broke her paralysis, instinctively jumping onto my father's back. She slipped on the slick floor as she tried to pull him away, her voice breaking as she screamed, "Stop! Get off her! Stop, Dad! Stop hitting her!"

My younger sister, Sue, stood motionless, her wide eyes glistening with fear, her face and clothes smeared with food.

They finally stopped, the chaos subsiding into a tense, heavy silence. My father stood, breathing hard, his face flushed with anger, while my mother pulled herself off the floor, her hair disheveled, her cheeks streaked with smeared gravy. None of us moved at first, too stunned to do anything but stare at the wreckage around us.

Then, as if nothing had happened, they ordered us to clean up the mess. No apologies, no acknowledgment of the violence, just barked commands to gather the broken glass, mop up the food and spilled milk, and scrape the food from the walls. We moved robotically to obey. The room smelled of a ruined dinner, a reminder of how quickly everything could fall apart in our house.

After they argued, the silence was always deafening. They wouldn't speak for weeks, each retreating into their own corners. My father would escape to the garage, spending hours tinkering on his antique car, the clinking of tools and the hum of the engine the only sounds marking his presence. My mother, on the other hand, took her anger to the kitchen, slamming cabinets and rattling dishes. The tension was palpable, hanging heavy in the air, and we, the children, tiptoed around it, careful not to ignite another spark. Their silence spoke louder than their shouting ever did, a constant reminder of the simmering unrest that defined our home.

None of my siblings, including myself, knew what it was like to have compassion for one another. Love, empathy—any emotion other than fear was foreign to us. We were taught to suppress our feelings, to bury our emotions deep where no one could see them.

Growing up, we were not close. We were each fighting our own battle to survive. Holidays, even Christmases, were never the warm, joyful occasions they were meant to be. Such days felt more like an obligation to endure rather than a celebration to enjoy. There were no hugs, no *I love you*, and no laughter.

* * *

When my father was angry, his rage was terrifying and unpredictable. He would grab me and throw me around the living room like a football, his strength leaving me helpless and bruised. Even in his rare moments of playfulness, his actions were more torturous than kind. He would pin me to the floor, kneeling on my chest with his knees pressing against my ears, and tickle me relentlessly. At first, I would laugh out of reflex, but laughter quickly turned to panic. I would gasp for air, thinking I was going to die.

My mother was abusive as well, in her own cruel and calculated way. If we said or did something she didn't like, she would demand punishment in the most demeaning way: "Put your hands down by your side so I can slap your face." It felt unnatural, almost impossible, to obey. Every instinct screamed for me to raise my hands to protect myself, but she demanded submission.

The abuse began when I was so young I thought it was normal, a part of childhood everyone endured. My world was so small, so isolated, that I couldn't comprehend that life could be any other way. I was painfully trusting, assuming what I experienced was just how life was meant to be.

The trauma found ways to manifest. I began sleepwalking, wandering the house in the middle of the night as though searching for a way to escape. Sometimes I would find myself trying to crawl into the clothes dryer, drawn to its small, enclosed space, maybe seeking some sense of safety or control. Bedwetting became another silent cry for help, a physical expression of the fear and turmoil I couldn't put into words.

A frightening incident happened during a family vacation in Canada, one that still haunts me. In the middle of the night, in a deep sleepwalking state, I got up and wandered into the water, wading in up to my waist. I was completely unaware of what I was doing, lost in a fog of unconsciousness. It wasn't until the next morning, when I woke up with my pajamas soaked from the waist down, that I realized what had happened. The realization terrified me, but I never told anyone. I learned to keep things to myself, hiding them out of fear of being punished or ridiculed.

One morning, while I was getting ready for middle school, my mother stuck her head into the bedroom I shared with my sister and demanded, "Are your beds made?"

I froze, panic gripping me as I thought, *She's going to find out I wet the bed again.* My bed was clearly unmade, the covers still bunched up, hiding the truth.

"Why haven't you made your bed?" she snapped, her voice sharp and accusing. "What? Did you wet the bed again? You wet the bed again, didn't you?" Her words cut through me.

Before I could protest or explain, she marched over to my bed and yanked the covers back. There it was, a large yellow stain in the middle of the sheet. Her eyes burned with frustration and disgust, and I wanted to disappear.

That moment, like so many others, left me feeling small, broken, and helpless.

Standing at the foot of my bed, I kept my eyes fixed on the floor, my stomach twisted in knots.

What is she going to do to me?

"Oh, so you want pity? I'm going to give you pity," she sneered. "Take your sheets off your bed and go hang them outside on the clothesline. I want everyone to see you still wet the bed and how lazy you are that you can't get up at night to go to the bathroom. Your brother and sisters don't wet the bed." Her words stung like a slap. The humiliation was suffocating. "Now hurry up so you can get to school on time."

My hands trembled as I stripped the damp sheets from my bed, the large yellow stain glaring back at me like a brand of shame. I walked to the back door, grabbing the basket of clothespins, my head hung low. Outside, as I clipped the stained sheets onto the clothesline, the voice in my head wouldn't stop.

What is wrong with me?

I'm just stupid.

I have to do better.

What if all the neighbors see these sheets and know they're mine?

Another thought, crueler still, whispered back. *Who cares if they find out? They probably already know I'm stupid.*

All day at school, I couldn't stop thinking about the sheet flapping in the wind for everyone to see. When I got home, the first thing I did was walk to the back door, dreading what I might find. Sure enough, there it was, still on the line, the yellow stain in the center catching the afternoon sun as it swayed in the breeze. I stuffed my tears down, the way I always did, telling myself to be stronger, to hide the hurt.

CHAPTER 3

Aunt Gen and Uncle Willis

The only solace I had during these turbulent years came from my great-uncle and my great-aunt. They were from my father's side of the family. Each year, they invited us to spend two unforgettable weeks at their motel. I affectionately called them Aunt Gen and Uncle Willis and they were my everything.

They owned a charming place in Florida in St. Petersburg Beach (now known as St. Pete Beach), called the Alicia Motel, which had direct access to the sparkling shoreline. The motel boasted at least fifty guest rooms, some with small, well-equipped kitchenettes. The grounds were a sight to behold, with neatly trimmed grass and perfectly manicured shrubs that created an atmosphere of quiet elegance. At night, the walkways glowed softly with small landscape lights, and the intoxicating scent of the ocean breeze seemed to follow you everywhere.

I cherished those two weeks every summer. Those visits brought me a sense of freedom and peace, temporarily lifting the weight of our daily struggles. My parents, for once, would be on their best behavior, refraining from their usual arguments. I felt so at ease that I wouldn't sleepwalk or wet the bed.

I was drawn to Aunt Gen and Uncle Willis, captivated by their loving and gentle relationship. They never raised their voices or spoke harshly about one another.

Our journey there was an adventure in itself, all six of us crammed into our Chevrolet Biscayne, sticky with the heat from having no air-conditioning, making the long drive from Michigan to Florida.

Sue, being the youngest, sat in the front seat between my parents, while Jane, Asser, and I squeezed into the back seat. Since I was the runt, Asser and Jane tried to force me to sit in the middle so they could have the window seats, but I fought hard for a spot by the window. Most of the time, I managed to win.

If my maternal grandmother decided she wanted to join us, the trip became even more of an ordeal. She was a large woman, and her presence meant four of us crammed together in the back seat. With all the windows rolled down, the wind blew hot, suffocating air into the car, as the temperature soared to ninety degrees or more. It was absolutely miserable. The drive took approximately twenty-four grueling hours, made worse by the fact that the majority of the journey took place on two-lane roads. In the late 1950s and early 1960s, interstate highways were still in their infancy.

My father always insisted we drive straight through with minimal food and bathroom stops. "I'm going to stop at this gas station to get gas and I want all of you to go to the bathroom, so we don't have to stop again," he would say in a stern voice and put the fear of God in us. Of course, he didn't understand, or maybe didn't care, that four children never need to use the bathroom at the same time. If it wasn't time for him to refuel, my mother would hand us a bottle and tell us to use it. Peeing in a bottle in front of everyone crammed in the back seat like sardines was humiliating. I'd sit with my heel pressed into my bladder to keep from peeing in that damn bottle, until I thought my bladder would burst. I'd cling to the desperate hope we'd reach a gas station soon and he'd have to stop, but the waiting always felt endless.

No one in the family talked to one another unless it was absolutely necessary. Hours would pass in complete silence, the atmosphere heavy with tension. God forbid we had music playing; there was no such thing as listening to the radio to lighten the mood. I would pass the time sitting by the window daydreaming, letting each billboard spark my imagination. When we passed a motel, I craned my neck to see if anyone was swimming in the pool, wishing with all my heart that it could be me splashing and playing in the cool water, instead of sweating it out in the miserable car.

Meanwhile, my parents wouldn't talk to each other unless they were screaming at each other. They would argue literally about everything. If my father said the sky was blue, my mother would say it was yellow. Then the name calling would begin.

I knew we were getting close to the motel when the road narrowed and I could see water glistening on both sides. The sight of it made my heart race with excitement. *You're almost there,* I'd tell myself, my legs bouncing uncontrollably. *Just a little longer and you'll finally be free from this sardine can.*

When we arrived, we all leaped out of the car and begged to go swimming. Their motel was situated directly on the Gulf of Mexico. We had the ocean to swim in and a pool we could use at the motel next door. We had finally escaped the car ride from hell!

"Please, please, please," we implored, hopping around.

"Yes," my mother finally said, "but only after we unpack the car."

We couldn't unpack the car fast enough. As soon as the bags were out, we tore through our suitcases, threw on our bathing suits, and bolted to the ocean. For two glorious weeks, we would swim from sunup until sundown, our days filled with laughter and freedom. Aunt Gen even taught us how to do ballet in the ocean. She was a synchronized swimmer, and watching her graceful movements felt magical.

She and Uncle Willis were never able to have their own biological children, and they poured their love and joy into playing with us and teaching us.

One of our favorite games was playing "restaurant" with Aunt Gen. We'd sit at the bar in her cozy kitchen, and she'd put on an apron, transforming into a waitress.

"May I please take your lunch order, ma'am?" she'd ask with a big, playful smile.

"Yes, I would like a peanut butter and jelly sandwich, please," I'd respond, trying to sound fancy.

"And what would you like to drink?"

"Iced tea, please," I'd reply, barely able to keep from giggling.

"Here is your sandwich, ma'am."

My eyes would light up with joy. It was perfect. The crust was trimmed away and the sandwich cut into triangles. It made me feel so special.

After lunch, she'd brighten our day even more by saying, "Are you kids ready to go to the toy store to pick out your toy?"

Our trip to the toy store with Aunt Gen was pure magic. She only had one rule: we could pick out anything we wanted but it had to be just one toy. We respected that and felt lucky to have the chance.

She drove a big white Cadillac, and her tiny stature behind the wheel always made me smile. She was so petite, she could have been mistaken for a child driving that massive car.

As we rode along, I couldn't help but think how much she and

I were alike. I would catch myself staring at her in admiration. I often felt like she could have been my blood relative. Deep down, I wished my mother could be more like her: gentle, kind, and full of love. Aunt Gen had a way of making everyone around her feel cherished. In her presence, the world seemed brighter.

Aunt Gen and Uncle Willis were very comfortable financially, and my father was obsessed with the idea of inheriting their money after they passed away. Around them, my parents would transform into the picture of a loving couple, holding hands, laughing, and pretending they adored one another. During our visits, there was no yelling, no spanking, no pulling hair, none of the chaos that usually defined our family. They worked hard to project the image of the perfect family, doing everything they could to ensure they stayed in Aunt Gen and Uncle Willis's good graces.

My father, however, was fiercely protective of his perceived claim to their fortune. He wasn't about to let any of his children get too close to them, for fear they might consider leaving money to someone other than him.

"I don't want you bothering Aunt Gen and Uncle Willis," he'd warn us sternly. "They're very busy and can't be bothered with you."

This was very confusing to me, because they loved playing with us and being around us. But it taught me not to ask them for anything.

As each trip came to an end, Aunt Gen and Uncle Willis would take us all out to dinner, a tradition that should have been a highlight but was often overshadowed by my parents' behavior. Before we left for the restaurant, my father would give us a stern lecture.

"You will eat EVERYTHING on your plate! And don't be asking a bunch of questions. NO exceptions! This is very expensive, so don't waste food or their time!"

This would terrify me. *If I don't eat everything on my plate, they won't love me, and Aunt Gen won't want to play with me anymore. I have to make sure I eat everything on my plate. I don't want to make Mom and Dad mad.*

The pressure I felt was immense, and the dinner, while delicious, was tainted by my constant fear of doing something wrong.

The next morning, after our staged performance at dinner, we'd pile back into the stifling car from hell for the grueling twenty-four-hour drive home. As the motel disappeared in the rearview mirror, I held my toy close while my heart ached. I didn't want to leave. I felt safe there, far away from the dysfunction that waited at home. The return trip felt worse; the sense of peace was already fading into a memory.

CHAPTER 4

Slow Learner

School was always a struggle for me. I couldn't concentrate or stay engaged no matter how hard I tried. Reading even a single paragraph felt like an impossible task. My mind would drift before I reached the end.

Teachers told my mother I was just lazy and refused to pay attention, and soon I was placed in what my teacher referred to as the *slow learners'* class. At home my parents called it the *stupid kids'* class, reinforcing the belief that my struggles were purely my fault. They thought all I needed to do was focus more and the problem would resolve itself. It wouldn't be until after nursing school that I was finally diagnosed with ADHD and dyslexia, two conditions that would explain why I had struggled for so long.

One evening, while my mother was washing dishes and Jane and I were drying, my father sat nearby, delivering a passionate speech to Jane, who was fifteen at the time.

"It's really important that you continue to get good grades in high school so you'll get admitted to a college," he said, looking directly at her. "Your grades are really good. This is how you're going to get ahead in life. You're so smart. I think you would make an excellent nurse. You should plan on going to nursing school after you graduate from high school."

Jane beamed. I stood there drying each dish carefully so I wouldn't make too much noise. I didn't want to miss a word he was saying.

"Do you really think I would be a good nurse, Dad?" she asked, her voice full of hope.

He went on to praise her, listing all her accomplishments and saying how proud he was of her. I just stood there taking it all in, my heart sinking with each word. *What about me?*

Without thinking, I blurted out, "Dad, am I smart enough to be a nurse?"

He didn't even hesitate. "No, you're too stupid to go to college."

His words hit me like a slap. *Why am I not smart enough? Why am I not good enough to be a nurse?* I kept asking myself, but no answer came, only the ache of knowing what he believed.

At the time, being labeled as stupid crushed any aspirations I might have had for the future. I believed the best I could hope for was to get married, have children, and rely on a husband to take care of me. Dreams of a career or independence seemed out of reach, something meant for people far smarter than I thought I could be. My worth was limited, and that belief would haunt me for years to come.

* * *

During my senior year in high school, I lost my virginity to my boyfriend Scott. Soon, I became pregnant.

One day I stood at my locker, grabbing my books for the next class, when a group of girls walked by. As soon as they saw me, their voices dropped to whispers, but not low enough that I couldn't hear.

"I heard she was pregnant," one of them said, her tone dripping with judgment.

"I would leave school if I got pregnant."

"Can you imagine walking these halls, nine months pregnant?"

"That's just disgusting. She's a slut," another chimed in, as if I wasn't standing right there and couldn't hear their entire conversation.

Their words stung, but I didn't turn around to confront them. Shame and embarrassment washed over me. Shortly after that, I left school for good—three months before graduation.

At the time, my parents were divorced and I was living with my father and brother. When I told my father I was pregnant and dropping out of school, he barely reacted. "Okay," he said flatly, taking a long gulp from his beer can. It was as if he'd always expected this to happen.

My mother didn't seem to care, either. She was too consumed by her own Valium-induced haze and alcohol dependency to offer any guidance or support. Hell, she never even taught me how to use a tampon, let alone contraception.

Scott's parents were furious, and their disapproval only added to my sense of shame and guilt. Despite this, Scott and I married early in 1968, six months before Ben was born.

I carried more than just the baby during those months. I also carried the guilt of knowing Scott had to drop out of college to marry me, fulfilling what he felt was his obligation. His decision made him eligible for the draft, a constant shadow looming over us. And just before our son was born, he received his summons. We spent most of our short marriage apart. Thankfully, Scott never left US soil and was spared from combat during the Vietnam War, but the weight of it all, our rushed marriage, the draft, and the baby, strained our relationship.

Looking back, I don't think I ever truly loved Scott the way a wife should love her husband. I think we cared for each other, but it wasn't the kind of love built on maturity or understanding. At the time, I didn't even know what love was supposed to feel like. I was searching for validation, for someone to tell me I was pretty, smart, and a good person, things I couldn't believe about myself without someone else's approval. I also wanted desperately to escape the dysfunction of my parents' home.

Scott and I weren't able to keep our marriage together. Our divorce was finalized before Ben was two years old.

CHAPTER 5

The Love Bomb

Not long after Scott and I separated, one of my friends and I decided to go out for some drinks and dancing. When we arrived at the bar, it was still early, and the place was pretty quiet, but we didn't mind. The DJ was playing 60s and new 70s music in the background, loud enough to create a fun vibe but not so loud we couldn't hear each other. We hadn't seen each other in some time, so we chatted girl stuff.

While we talked, I noticed a table of four men across the room. They were drinking, laughing, and clearly having a good time. One man in particular caught my attention because he kept staring at me. I wasn't sure why and I couldn't help but glance back at him a few times, my curiosity piqued.

When my girlfriend excused herself to go to the ladies' room, he rose from the table and swaggered over to me with the kind of confidence that immediately caught my attention. Slimly built and strikingly handsome, he had dark brown hair that fell softly against his forehead. His smile was the kind that could light up a room.

"You are the most beautiful woman I have ever seen," he said, his voice smooth and full of charm. "My name is Richard."

I was so flattered and taken by surprise that my stomach did flip-flops. Was this handsome man really talking to me?

He gently extended his hand. "Would you like to dance?"

I was completely captivated. Without a second thought, I reached out and placed my hand in his, letting the moment sweep me away.

"What is your name, beautiful lady?" he asked, his voice warm and inviting.

"My name is Candy," I replied softly, still feeling a mix of nervousness and excitement.

As the slow song played, he pulled me close and held me tightly. My head rested against his chest, and I caught a whiff of his cologne. It smelled so good, comforting and familiar. I took a deep breath, savoring the moment. It had been a long time since anyone held me this way, and I felt a sense of safety I'd been craving.

As we swayed back and forth to the music, he whispered words that both flattered and unsettled me.

"I can't believe I found you."

"You are never leaving me."

"I have to have you in my life."

Though his words were beautiful, they also made me uneasy. They felt intense, too soon, and I questioned their sincerity. How could a stranger feel this way about me? Was this too good to be true?

"I can't live without you," he said.

In that moment, I blurted out, "I have a baby boy who is one and a half years old." I was reluctant to tell him I was in the middle of a divorce, worried it would scare him off.

He pulled away just enough so he could look into my eyes. His gaze was steady, sincere, and filled with an intensity that made my stomach flutter. "I don't care. I need you in my life."

His words hung in the air, wrapping around me like a blanket of reassurance. I wanted to believe him, to trust that he meant every word, but a small voice inside of me whispered caution. How could someone I had just met feel so strongly about me? Was this real?

Still, with his eyes locked on mine and the music surrounding us, I couldn't help but feel a flicker of hope, hope that maybe, just maybe, this could be real.

My girlfriend came up to us while we were still dancing and said that she was ready to leave. "Do you want me to drop you off at your place?" she asked, her voice cutting through the music.

I glanced at Richard, unsure of what to do. He looked at me earnestly and said, "I'll make sure you get home safely. Please don't leave me."

Something about the way he said it made me feel secure. I turned to my girlfriend and said, "No, I'm going to stay. Richard will take me home." She seemed fine with the decision, giving a slight nod before heading out the door with a few friends she'd just met.

Richard and I continued to dance and talk. Our conversation deepened with every song and every shared word. Time flew by, and before we knew it, the bar lights flickered on, signaling closing time.

When he took me home, he was the perfect gentleman. He walked me to the door, kissed me softly, and asked for my phone number. I didn't hesitate; I gave it to him that night, my heart full of hope and possibilities.

As I lay in bed afterward, I envisioned a future with him: a loving husband who adored me, children playing in a big backyard, and a beautiful home filled with laughter. In that moment, I believed I had met the man who would make all of those dreams come true.

* * *

My relationship with Richard moved quickly, too quickly, in hindsight. There was no real courtship, just a few dinners out. Before I knew it, we were in deep. He called me constantly, sometimes six or eight times a day.

The phone rang again. "Hi, beautiful. How are you?"

"I'm fine," I said, trying to sound casual.

"Have you made your decision to move in with me yet? It's just plain torture being away from you," he said, his voice full of longing. "I want you with me every day. I've never felt like this about anyone I've ever met."

I hesitated, my stomach a mix of butterflies and knots. "Yes, I've been thinking about moving. I just need to get my things in order first."

"What things do you need to get in order? I can help you."

"No, I'm okay. I just need to make sure I have everything taken care of."

It was flattering, almost intoxicating, to hear him say how much he missed me, and how deeply he felt for me. But beneath the excitement, there was something else, a nagging uncertainty I couldn't quite explain. Part of me was thrilled that a man could love me so much, yet another part whispered that it was all happening too fast, too intensely. I couldn't decide whether his relentless pursuit was a sign of genuine love or something else entirely.

Is it possible for a person to fall so deeply in love in such a short time? Why am I feeling reluctant to move in with him? He loves me! Could he be selling me his dream of how pretty I am and how he can't go on with his life if I'm not in it?

Despite my misgivings, we moved in together about a month after meeting in the bar. Desperate to feel loved, I didn't waste any time. But as my son and I settled into Richard's dark, dingy one-bedroom apartment, I couldn't ignore the gnawing feeling in the pit of my stomach.

The apartment was cramped and unkempt. I scrubbed every inch of it from top to bottom, making sure it was clean and safe for my baby. I tried to focus on creating a home, convincing myself that this was the right decision.

After a couple of weeks of living with Richard, I felt restless. This internal conflict left me reluctant and unsure, torn between the allure of his charm and the nagging feeling that something wasn't quite right. Deep down, I felt I needed some space to make a clear and thoughtful decision about building a life with Richard.

Confused, I visited my mother to ask for help. When she opened the door, her expression was a mix of surprise and irritation.

"What are you doing here?" she asked curtly.

"I need to talk to you," I said. "Can I come in?'

We sat down at her kitchen table, and I nervously began to explain my situation. "I recently met a man. And he says he loves me and can't live without me. Scott and I aren't officially divorced yet, and I just want to make the right decision. Should I try and get Scott back or should I stick with this man that I barely know?"

Steeling myself, I continued on, asking, "Can we stay with you for a while? We just need a safe place until I can sort things out. Please?"

Her expression hardened into disgust. "What? No, you can't move in with me."

"Mom, please!" I begged. "I'm desperate and I just need a few weeks, maybe two weeks."

"No," she said coldly. "I won't have you disrupt my life." She stood up abruptly, walking toward the front door, motioning me to follow. She opened the door and without a hint of remorse, said, "You get out of here. Go back to Scott where you belong." Then she shut the door in my face.

CHAPTER 6

What's Wrong With Me?

When I met him, Richard worked as a salesperson at a tire store. He had a knack for convincing anyone of anything. His confidence in his schemes made him dangerously persuasive, and I often found myself questioning where the line was between charm and manipulation.

One evening a few months after I'd moved in, Richard came home with big news. He'd been promoted to a management position and was being transferred to North Carolina to manage a new tire store. His excitement was palpable as he begged me to move with him.

"It will be great, I promise," he said, his eyes bright with possibility. "We'll find a nice apartment, and I'll make enough money so you won't even have to work."

I couldn't respond right away. Part of me wanted to believe him, to trust that this move would bring us closer, maybe even offer the security I craved. But another part wondered if I was walking into something I couldn't escape.

"Please, please move with me," Richard begged, his voice tinged with desperation. "I can't lose you, and this is a great opportunity for me. Will you come with me?"

His words hung in the air, heavy with expectation. I knew deep down I didn't really have any other choices. My mother had slammed the door in my face, leaving me nowhere else to turn.

Reluctantly, I nodded. "All right," I said, my voice barely above a whisper. "We'll move with you."

The words felt final, like the closing of a chapter I wasn't ready to end. Feeling scared and anxious, I began packing up all our belongings, each item reminding me of the uncertainty ahead. Within days, we were on our way to North Carolina, my heart pounding with both fear and the faintest hope that this move might finally bring the stability I longed for. I wanted to feel safe, valued, and supported, free from fear and chaos.

We found an apartment quickly and got settled into our new surroundings. Ben and I were mostly isolated within the confines of the apartment walls. Richard took the car to work every day, leaving us without transportation. When Richard was home, I took the car for grocery trips, and even then, I always brought Ben with me. I wasn't sure whether it was safe to leave him with Richard.

One evening not long after we moved, Richard didn't come home straight after work. I'd spent the day preparing a nice dinner, pot roast with potatoes and carrots, because I knew it was one of his favorites.

It was dark when he finally burst through the door, staggering. The sharp smell of alcohol filled the room. His eyes were glassy and unfocused as he glared at me.

"What happened?" I asked.

"You bitch, what's wrong with you? Why are you so pissed off?" His words were slurred and venomous, and I was shocked into silence. I'd never seen this side of him. Sure, he could be sarcastic and rude at times, but this? This was something else entirely. My heart raced as I stayed quiet, unmoving. *Just stay calm.*

"So what if I went drinking with the boys?" Richard spat, his voice rising with every word. "I work hard so you have a nice place to live, and I should be able to drink when I want to."

I stayed silent, trying to maintain an expressionless poker face. *Let him rant*, I told myself. *Just stay quiet.* But his anger grew. He took a step closer. My back pressed against the cold edge of the kitchen sink. He was too close. The acrid smell of alcohol on his breath made my stomach churn.

Then, without warning, he slapped me. The crack of his palm against my face was deafening, and the force sent me stumbling to the floor. Pain erupted in my cheek, sharp and searing, and I clutched my face, tears stinging my eyes as I looked up at him in disbelief.

Why did you hit me? What did I do? The questions screamed in my head, but I didn't dare voice them.

Don't say anything, I told myself, pressing my hand against my burning cheek. *Just keep quiet. Maybe he'll calm down soon.*

He immediately dropped to his knees, his voice breaking. "I am so sorry. I didn't mean to hit you. Please forgive me. Don't leave me. I will never hit you again. I don't know what came over me."

I just sat there on the floor, staring at him, my face throbbing with pain. His words blurred together as he reached out, pulling me close. He cradled my head in his hands and rocked me back and forth, whispering over and over, "I'm so sorry."

After a moment, he stood up and held out his hand to help me up. I hesitated but took it, the warmth of his touch a strange contradiction to what had just happened. He led me to the bedroom, his grip firm yet oddly tender. My skin crawled as I realized what he wanted. Sex. But fear held me hostage. If I refused, would he hit me again?

Lying down on the bed, he motioned for me to join him. I moved mechanically, my body tense as he kissed me, the sour scent of alcohol heavy in the air. His hands began to explore my body, and despite my resistance, my body betrayed me, responding to his touch.

This is wrong. He just hit me, and now he wants this.

But another part of me whispered, *Just give in. It'll be over faster.* I kissed him back.

"I love you so much," he murmured, his lips brushing against my ear. "I'm so sorry. I will never hurt you again."

His arms tightened around me, his hold suffocating yet oddly comforting. For a fleeting moment, the warmth of his embrace made me feel safe, as though maybe, just maybe, things could change.

If I can just be better, quieter, kinder, less of whatever it was that upset him, maybe he won't hurt me again.

Afterwards, he rolled over and almost immediately began snoring.

I lay there, staring at the ceiling, motionless, numb, but my mind was spinning, tangled in confusion and shame. I felt like I'd just been sexually assaulted, used for his pleasure while my emotions were left discarded.

You don't make love after you've hit your partner. Or do you? Is this normal? The questions gnawed at me as I tried to make sense of what just happened.

Maybe he really does love me.

Maybe if I was a better person, he wouldn't hit me anymore.

The truth weighed heavily on me. I had no high school diploma, no family to turn to, no friends to confide in. I had Ben, my sweet toddler, to protect.

The isolation felt crushing, leaving me with no real options. *Maybe*, I thought desperately, *if I get pregnant, he won't hit me anymore and he won't leave us.* The thought lodged itself in my mind like a tiny spark of hope.

* * *

Not long after moving to North Carolina, I did become pregnant. We'd never discussed marriage, much less having children. That wasn't unusual for us, though. Richard and I never talked about anything in depth. Our relationship functioned on an unspoken arrangement: I would be a stay-at-home mom, and he would work outside the home, handling the finances. My attraction to Richard wasn't rooted in love or shared dreams, it was about security, about the hope that he could provide the safety I desperately needed.

One evening, Richard came home from work in an unusually good mood. This seemed like the perfect time to tell him. My nerves were raw, and my hands shook slightly as I prepared dinner. I wasn't sure how he would react, but I had to take the chance.

We sat down for dinner, and as I was cutting up Ben's food, I said as casually as I could, "Richard, I think I'm pregnant."

For a moment, there was silence, and I braced myself for the worst. But then Richard jumped up from his chair, a broad smile spreading across his face. He hopped up and down, clapping his hands like a child who'd just been given a long-awaited gift.

"Really? Are you sure you're pregnant?" he asked, his excitement almost infectious.

"I still need to make an appointment with an OB, but I'm pretty sure," I said cautiously. "I'm having some morning nausea, and my breasts are sore."

Richard beamed. "I'm so happy we're having a baby. I can't wait."

His reaction was such a stark contrast to the Richard I'd come to fear that I felt a flicker of hope. Maybe this would change things. Maybe being pregnant would keep him from hitting me. For the first time in a long time, I dared to believe things might get better.

But as we finished dinner and the evening wore on, doubt began to creep back in. What if this happiness didn't last? What if it was just another fleeting moment of peace before the storm? I couldn't shake the nagging thought that somehow, I was the problem. My father didn't love me, and he hit me. Richard said he loved me, and he hit me, too. What was wrong with me?

As my pregnancy progressed, so did Richard's drinking. His absences became more frequent. He disappeared for days at a time, without warning or explanation. I spent those long hours sick with worry and fear, my stomach tied in knots so tightly that even basic tasks felt impossible. By now, I was completely trapped in the prison of his control.

One day, we decided to spend the afternoon at the apartment complex pool. It was a rare moment of calm, and I let myself relax a little as I played with Ben in the water. Richard lounged in a chair nearby, sipping beer. A male resident sat down at the edge of the pool and struck up a casual conversation with me. He asked how old Ben was and mentioned that he had a son about the same age.

Richard noticed us talking, and his mood shifted instantly. His face darkened, and he shouted, "Get out of the pool now! We're going back to the apartment." His voice was loud enough to make everyone at the pool stop and stare. Humiliated and caught off guard by his public outburst, I quickly got out of the pool with Ben, packed up our towels, and followed him.

As soon as Richard shut the apartment door behind us, he turned to me with a cold, furious glare, the "evil eye" that I had come to dread.

"What were you doing flirting with that guy?" he snapped, his voice full of hate.

"I wasn't flirting with him," I said, trying to keep my voice calm. "We were talking about our children. What's wrong with you?"

"You're acting like a fucking whore," he spat. "You're pregnant, and you think it's okay to flirt with some guy at the pool? You're a fucking cunt."

"Richard, I wasn't flirting with him," I said again, trying to defuse the situation. "I'm sorry if you think I was."

Before I could say another word, his hand shot out and slapped my arm so hard that I stumbled and fell to the floor. Ben began to cry, his little face red and terrified. As I struggled to stand, Richard swung again, this time aiming for my torso. He had become an expert at hitting me in places where the bruises wouldn't be visible: my arms, legs, stomach, even feet. The force of the blow made me gasp, but I stayed silent, knowing any protest would only make things worse.

Finally, he grabbed the car keys and stormed out, slamming the door behind him. Once again, I was stranded, left alone to pick up the pieces, comforting Ben, soothing my aching body, and trying to hold back the flood of tears.

This wasn't the life I had imagined, but by now, I didn't know how to escape it.

After being gone for a few days, he walked in the door like nothing had happened. The air around him carried an unspoken threat, a heavy reminder of the consequences of questioning him. If I dared to ask where he had been or why he left, I knew I would become his punching bag again. But this time something inside of me broke.

"I can't take this anymore, I'm leaving you," I said firmly, my voice breaking with both fear and resolve. He barely flinched, slumping on the sofa as if he couldn't believe I had the courage to say the words out loud.

"No, you can't leave me," he muttered, his voice hollow. "I can't live without you."

But I didn't care. I was done with the endless cycle of violence and empty promises. As I lugged our belongings down the stairs to the car, each step felt like an act of defiance. I had no plan, no money, and no destination. Ben clung to me, and every aching muscle screamed at me to stop. But I couldn't, not when the thought of another child with this man, another life tethered to his rage, pushed me forward. I needed to leave, to find safety. But deep down I knew the truth. He would come looking for me, and I would never truly be free.

I collapsed on the living room floor, my body quivering with exhaustion, tears streaming down my face. Every ounce of strength I had left was gone, drained by the weight of my fear and the heavy loads I had carried downstairs. I barely noticed when Richard came over and knelt beside me. Gently, he pulled me into his arms, pressing my face against his chest. For a fleeting moment, I felt the warmth of comfort, but it was quickly drowned by the confusion and fear swirling inside me.

"Don't leave me," he whispered, his voice crackling with desperation. "I'll do better. I won't hurt you ever again. I'm going to stop drinking this time, I promise." His words wrapped around me like chains, pulling me deeper into the cycle I so desperately wanted to escape. I wanted to believe him, I always wanted to believe him, but the promises felt as hollow as the empty bottles he swore he'd leave behind.

CHAPTER 7

An Overwhelming Challenge

In the weeks that followed, Richard kept his promise to stop drinking, creating a fragile sense of hope. I clung to the possibility that this time things would be different.

In 1971, a few weeks before Thanksgiving, Richard walked through the door with an air of authority, delivering his latest announcement. "We're moving to Lexington, Kentucky." His tone left no room for discussion.

"What?"

"The company asked me to go to Lexington to manage a store that's not been profitable. I've decided we're going."

His decision was final, and he didn't seem to notice, or care, that I was nine months pregnant and about to have a baby any day. Panic swirled in my mind. What physician would accept me as a patient so late in my pregnancy? Where would my child be born? How was I supposed to pack up our belongings to move when I could barely manage my day-to-day tasks?

"Richard, what about the baby?" I asked, my voice small and uncertain. "I need a doctor to deliver the baby."

"You'll find a doctor," he said dismissively. "I'm not worried about that."

But I was. I was terrified. Yet, as always, I went along with whatever he said, suppressing my protests, swallowing my fear, and pushing aside my doubts. I felt I had no voice, no choice, no power over my own life.

Within a couple of weeks, three-year-old Ben and I boarded a plane to Lexington with everything I could cram in two suitcases. Utterly exhausted, I had packed up as many of our belongings as I could manage, knowing the movers would ship everything else in a few weeks. Richard promised to follow soon, driving the car with more of our things.

I kept telling myself, *Richard will take care of everything. Just hang in there. It will be okay. Tomorrow will be better.*

Ben and I arrived at the furnished month-to-month rental provided by the company. The reality of our situation hit me the moment we walked in: no car, no phone, no television. We were isolated in a city I'd never been to before. I was nine months pregnant, with no obstetrician, no plan for delivery, and a three-year-old child in tow.

My mind raced. *What if Richard doesn't show up? What if he gets drunk and goes to another state? Who's going to deliver my baby?*

The days dragged on endlessly, each one longer than the last as I waited for Richard to arrive. I tried to keep Ben entertained with the few toys I'd managed to bring. His restlessness mirrored my own. We walked to the grocery store to pick up just enough food for the day, but even that small outing felt like an overwhelming challenge. I was tired, scared, and desperate for reassurance that never came.

Richard finally arrived ten days later, breezing into the apartment like nothing was wrong. The very next morning he started his new job, full of energy and excitement, acting as if the world was at his feet. He didn't ask how we'd managed those ten days alone, or if

I was okay, or if Ben was struggling. He never seemed to notice the toll his decisions took on us—even worse, he didn't care.

The day the phone was finally installed at the apartment, I wasted no time. I dug through the phone book, searching for an obstetrician, my fingers shaking as I traced the names and numbers.

"I'm sorry, we can't take on a new patient this late in pregnancy," one after another said. My hope dwindled with each call until one number remained on the list.

With desperation tightening my chest, I dialed. The phone rang, and a woman with a soft, sweet voice answered. "Good morning, Dr. Smith's office. May I help you?"

"This is Candy," I said, trying to steady my voice. "I've just moved here from North Carolina and I'm nine months pregnant and I really need a doctor to deliver my baby. Please, can I make an appointment?"

There was a pause before she replied, her tone curious. "You moved here at nine months pregnant? Why would you do that?"

"I had no choice, ma'am. My husband was transferred here for work. Please, please, can I make an appointment? I'm healthy and I haven't had any complications during my pregnancy. I need a doctor to deliver my baby."

She sighed. "Were you seeing a doctor in North Carolina?"

"Yes, ma'am, I was," I assured her quickly. "I was seeing him monthly."

"Can you hold on for a minute? Let me speak to the doctor."

I clutched the receiver, my palms damp as I whispered, *Please, please let this doctor say he will deliver my baby.*

After what felt like an eternity, she came back on the line. "The doctor said you can make an appointment to speak with him, but there is no guarantee he will take you on as a patient."

Relief flooded through me. "Thank you, thank you so much."

When Richard got home that night, I eagerly shared the news, hoping for some acknowledgment of my desperate situation. He didn't even look up, giving a disdainful wave. "See, I told you. I knew you could find a doctor. Nothing to worry about."

The following week, I arrived at my OB appointment. Ben was with me but Richard, predictably, wasn't; he said he couldn't come because of work. Sitting in the waiting room, I felt a wave of anxiety that I couldn't shake. My mind was filled with self-recrimination. *You shouldn't have gotten pregnant in the first place and you wouldn't be in this mess.*

Then the door opened. A middle-aged man with a kind smile entered. His white lab coat was embroidered with his name. He introduced himself, then sat down across from me and folded his hands. "Now, tell me why you would move to another state nine months into your pregnancy."

"I didn't have any choice, Doctor; my husband was transferred here with his company," I replied, the lie slipping out effortlessly. Richard wasn't my husband, but the truth felt too messy to explain.

Dr. Smith nodded but looked serious. "Do you understand my concerns about taking you on as a patient at this late stage of your pregnancy? It creates a significant liability for me. If something goes wrong, I'll be blamed. It's a risk I can't ignore."

"Yes, I understand," I said quickly. "But I've had an uneventful pregnancy. I'm healthy and so is the baby."

He glanced down at my records and sighed. "Your previous OB's notes do indicate a healthy pregnancy. However, I'm sorry, but I can't accept you as a patient. The liability is too great."

His words hit me like a punch to the stomach. Tears welled up but I forced them down. *You have to try harder,* I told myself.

Showing up at the emergency room in labor and hoping for the best was a terrifying thought.

"Please," I said, my voice breaking. "I have no other options. I promise I won't give you any problems. Please help me and my baby."

He sat quietly, his brow furrowed in thought. The silence stretched on, feeling like an eternity. Finally, he looked up at me, his face softening with concern. "Okay," he said with a sigh. "I'll accept you as a patient."

Relief washed over me so intensely I felt like I might collapse. "Oh, thank you. Thank you so much. You're so kind to do this for me and my baby."

He nodded. "We'll schedule your next appointment and make sure everything is in order for your delivery."

I grabbed Ben's hand, clutching it tightly as we walked out to the reception area. For the first time in weeks, I wore a genuine smile of relief on my face. The receptionist with the kind voice looked up from her desk, her own warm smile matching mine.

"Everything went well, I take it?"

"Yes," I replied, my voice filled with gratitude. "Thank you so much for fitting me in. I can't tell you how much I appreciate you."

She handed me a card with my next appointment written on it and then added, "The doctor asked me to pass along a few recommendations for pediatricians. You'll want to call them soon to set up an appointment."

I took the paper she offered, my eyes stinging with emotion. "Thank you. Really, thank you for everything."

I smiled again and felt a deep sense of gratitude toward this woman who had shown me kindness when I'd felt so alone.

* * *

A few weeks later, I went into labor. Panic gripped me as I woke Richard and he drove me to the hospital. When we arrived, he made sure I was admitted, but then he left to take Ben back home. My anxiety spiked as I watched him walk out the door. I didn't feel comfortable leaving Ben with Richard, knowing his temper and unpredictability, but I had no other choice. Fathers weren't allowed in delivery rooms in the seventies, but I doubted it would have made a difference. Richard wouldn't have wanted to be there anyway.

I couldn't help but feel abandoned. I was left alone, petrified, in a strange city, in a strange hospital, with a doctor I had practically had to beg to deliver my child.

Hours later, as the first light of morning broke through the window, Jason was born. He came into the world without complications, and as I held him in my arms, relief washed over me. *Thank God.*

And then: *You're now twenty-one with two children.*

I had been home from the hospital for about a week when the phone rang, jolting me from my haze of exhaustion. I picked it up and heard a voice I wasn't expecting.

"Candy, this is Mom, how are you? How's the new baby?"

I said nothing for a moment, shocked. Mom rarely called, and our contact had been sparse ever since she slammed the door in my face at the start of my relationship with Richard. What could she possibly want now?

"I'm fine, the baby's fine," I replied cautiously. "How are you?"

"I'd like to come see you and the new baby," she said abruptly.

Her words took me off guard. She had never bonded with Ben, had never been the grandmother type. She never referred to him (or any of her grandchildren, for that matter) as her grandchild. Now, out of the blue, she wanted to come for a visit.

"I'll only stay a couple days. I'll drive down this weekend, if that's okay."

I hesitated but didn't see any way to decline without creating more tension. "That's fine. I'll see you this weekend."

After I hung up, my stomach churned. I needed to ask Richard if it was okay for her to come. *At least while she's here he won't get mad or beat me. He would never show her this side of him.*

To my surprise, Richard agreed to her visit without hesitation. During her two-day stay, everything remained uneventful. She was polite, even pleasant, and Richard was on his best behavior, the picture of composure. There were no real emotions exchanged, no *I love you*, no hugs. She didn't bond with the boys, but she wasn't cold, either. I was still confused about why she came, but I had too many other things to worry about besides her intentions.

The evening after she left, Richard came home, slamming the door so hard the walls seemed to shudder. He stomped toward me, his face beet red, veins bulging in his neck. The sharp smell of alcohol hit me before his words did.

"Why do you treat me this fucking way?" he roared. "Why are you so fucking stupid? You're disgusting, look at you, you're fat! No one is going to love you! You're too fucking ugly."

My stomach twisted, but I forced myself to stay calm. "Richard, what's wrong? Why are you so angry?"

"Because you make me fucking mad," he shouted, stepping closer, his fists clenched at his side. "You push me away, bitch."

"When did I push you away?" I pleaded. "I'm doing everything I possibly can to show you how much I love you."

His answer was another barrage of insults. Then came the

breaking point: both the boys began to cry, their wails piercing the tension.

"It's okay, Jason. Mommy's here," I whispered, holding him tightly in my arms as his cries turned to hiccups. I reached out for Ben's blanket, handing it to him. "Here's your blanket, sweetie. Hug your blanket." Ben, overwhelmed and confused, wanted no part of his blanket and threw it across the room. His sobs grew louder.

Richard's face twisted in anger as he grabbed the keys to the only car we had. "I'm leaving," he bellowed and stormed out, slamming the door behind him.

I stood there, cradling Jason, who had finally quieted, and doing my best to soothe Ben. My mind raced with the same crushing thoughts that always came after these explosions.

He must be right. I need to do better. I have two boys; I must do better. I'm dependent on him. I need to help him love me, like he did in the beginning.

After giving the boys a bath and tucking them into bed, I sat on the couch, staring out the window. Richard still hadn't come home.

The street was dark except for headlights, each set of beams sending my heart into overdrive. *Please let it be him. Please let this be the car that pulls into the driveway.*

Every sound outside felt like hope and dread rolled into one. My thoughts spiraled.

Maybe something happened to him. Maybe he's not coming back.

I prayed, bargaining with God. *The next car that drives by, let it be Richard.*

But each time, the car sped past without slowing down.

As hour after hour slipped by, I realized it was going to be another long night of disappointment. He wasn't coming home. I curled up on the couch, paralyzed with fear, barely able to move. I was consumed by the crushing weight of abandonment.

For the next two days I could hardly eat, sleep, or function.

By the third night, I hadn't slept more than a few hours. The boys didn't know what was happening, but I was unraveling. In desperation, I cleaned the house from top to bottom, even rearranging the living room furniture, anything to keep my mind occupied, anything to make myself useful.

This is all my fault.

I'm not enough.

I have to do better. I have to make him stay.

With the boys down for a nap, I decided to pull out the secondhand sewing machine I'd taught myself to use. I couldn't afford new clothes, and Richard certainly wasn't going to buy me anything nice. So, I made my own.

Digging through my fabric stash, I found some navy blue material. It wasn't much, but I figured I could turn it into a jumpsuit. Something simple, but something that would make me feel pretty, for him.

The machine hummed steadily as I worked, the rhythmic sound soothing my restless thoughts. Within a few hours, the jumpsuit was done. I pressed out the wrinkles, slipped it on, and stood in front of the mirror. It wasn't perfect, but it made me feel hopeful.

Maybe tonight will be different. Maybe Richard will come home.

He did, but not in the way I hoped.

The door swung open, and he stumbled in, reeking of liquor. His eyes were wild, red, angry, and soulless. He staggered toward me, bumping into one of the living room chairs.

"Okay, bitch, I'm home," he slurred, like the past three days of silence hadn't happened.

I stood there, unable to move, heart pounding.

"What are you wearing?" he sneered, swaying on unsteady feet.

"I made this today," I said, softly. "I wanted to look pretty for you."

He squinted, leaning in closer. "You look like a fucking whore. Go take it off."

Something inside me cracked. His words should've gutted me. They usually did. But this time, they didn't. The fear I'd grown so used to feeling wasn't there. Instead, I felt something different. Something stronger.

I straightened my back, lifted my chin, and met his gaze head-on. "I'm leaving," I said firmly.

He blinked, confused. "What the fuck are you talking about?"

"I'm going out to get drunk, just like you."

His laugh was harsh and bitter. "Oh, yeah? You don't even drink."

"I will tonight," I snapped. "I want you to feel what I feel every time you don't come home. I want you to feel anxious and lonely, wondering where I am, what I'm doing, and if I'm coming back."

"If you leave, I'll walk out, too. I won't stay with the boys," Richard snarled. "You'll be abandoning your children."

His words hung in the air like a trap, but I wasn't falling for it. "You're bluffing," I said, grabbing the car keys off the counter. My hands trembled, but I kept moving.

Let him feel what I feel, the fear and the uncertainty.

I walked out the door and didn't look back.

Once in the car, I rolled the window down and let the cool night air wash over me. The hum of the engine and the wind against my face felt like freedom.

I pressed on the gas, heading for the interstate with no real direction in mind. It felt good to just go.

But reality hit fast. Would he really leave the boys? He wouldn't, would he? The questions tumbled through my mind, each one tightening the knot in my stomach. *But what if he does?*

Panic set in and I turned the car around.

I'd only been gone for thirty minutes. As I rounded the corner, I saw flashing blue-and-red lights reflecting off the buildings. Three police cars were parked outside our place.

I pulled into my parking space and stepped out of the car, my legs shaking. An officer approached me.

"Do you live here?" he asked, his voice calm but firm.

"Yes, sir," I said softly. "I live here." I glanced past him and saw officers moving through my living room, inspecting the house.

Richard was nowhere to be found.

"Your husband called us," the officer said. "He reported that you abandoned your children and that you're a terrible mother." His tone was stern. "Where have you been?"

I swallowed hard, my stomach in knots. "I just went for a drive. My husband was here with the boys when I left."

The officer's expression didn't soften. "That's not what he told us. He said you called him and told him you were leaving and walking out on your marriage and children."

Panic gripped me. I wanted to scream that it wasn't true, that Richard was lying.

Tell them you only have one car; this will prove you're telling the truth. But fear silenced me. And there was something else. I didn't want to admit that he wasn't my husband, just my boyfriend. I couldn't risk them thinking my situation was unstable. I couldn't risk them taking my boys.

"No, officer, that's not true," I pleaded. "I love my children."

I stepped closer, hands trembling. "Please, officer, don't take my children. Please. I would never hurt them. I'm a good mother. Please don't take them away."

Desperate to make them believe me, I wanted to tell them the truth. That Richard left us for days at a time. That he hit me and bruised my body. That he drank until he couldn't stand.

But I couldn't. I was too scared. *What if they think it's my fault? What if they think I'm unstable?*

The officer's gaze softened just slightly. "Are you going to stay home tonight, ma'am?"

"Yes, sir," I whispered. "I promise I'm not going anywhere."

He nodded, slipping his notepad back into his pocket. "All right, we're going to leave now, but we don't want to be called back here tonight."

"I understand," I said quickly. "You won't be called back, I swear."

As the officer left, I shut the door and leaned against it, gasping for air, my body shaking uncontrollably. *What just happened?* I pressed my hands against my face, trying to calm down, but my mind was spinning. *They almost took my boys away.*

I hadn't fully caught my breath when the front door opened again, pushing me into the wall.

Richard walked in, smug and cocky, a smirk plastered across his face. He shut the door slowly behind him and leaned against it like he had all the time in the world.

I stared at him, torn between fury and terror. My hands clenched into fists. *How can he do this to me? To the boys?*

I stepped forward, my voice quivering with rage. "Do you understand they were about to take the boys away?"

He walked to the armchair, flopped down, and leaned back with a lazy grin, arms draped over the armrests like a king on his throne.

"I told you not to disobey me," he said, his voice low and menacing. "I'll kill you and your family if you ever try to leave me."

CHAPTER 8

Sudden Changes

One afternoon, I was on the phone with my sister Jane and shared the news that Richard's tire company was transferring him to Tampa, Florida. "I'm excited about the move," I said, trying to sound more enthusiastic than anxious. The thought of finally living near one of my siblings gave me a tiny bit of optimism.

"I'm a little concerned about where to live, though," I admitted. I dreaded the thought of uprooting the boys again. I didn't want a repeat of the last move: nine months pregnant, exhausted, unprepared.

"You'll find a place," Jane reassured me.

But moving wasn't just about finding a place to live. We needed money for the first and last months' rent, deposits, and moving expenses. And I knew Richard didn't have much saved; he never did. He flew by the seat of his pants, never considering how chaotic and traumatic these sudden changes were for me and the boys.

"I'm worried about how much it's going to cost to get settled," I confided.

Jane paused for a moment. "Why don't you and the boys come now?" she offered. "Richard can finish up in Kentucky, and you can stay with me and my kids in the meantime."

"Really?"

"Of course. I have plenty of room. You can stay here until you find a place."

"Thank you so much. I really appreciate it."

Jane had recently gone through a divorce, and I knew she understood the toll of living in an unhappy home. Still, we never discussed my abuse. I suspected she had an idea of the emotional turmoil I was dealing with, but she had no clue about the physical abuse, or its severity.

For now, that didn't matter. The thought of being away from Richard, even for a short time, felt like a breath of fresh air. The boys and I would finally have a moment of peace.

To my surprise, Richard agreed to the arrangement without a fight. He probably saw this as an opportunity to drink as much as he wanted, whenever he wanted, without me there to nag him or confront him about it.

Still, I didn't care why he agreed. I just wanted some peace.

Jane picked us up at the airport and drove us to her house. It was a beautiful, older Florida house with big windows that let in the sunlight. There was plenty of room for all of us. As we pulled into her driveway, I exhaled. A weight lifted from my chest. I was finally free from Richard.

At least for now.

For the first few days, life felt almost normal. The boys played with their cousins, and Jane and I stayed up late, catching up over a glass of wine. I felt safe. I felt human.

Then Richard started calling. At first, it was once a day. Then, multiple times a day. Harassing me. Accusing me. Every conversation was the same: exhausting, degrading, relentless.

The phone would ring, and my stomach would immediately start hurting. I knew it was him. I'd quickly answer and tiptoe into the corner of the room, covering the mouthpiece with my hand so Jane wouldn't hear.

"Hello?" I'd whisper.

"What are you doing?" His voice sharp and suspicious.

"We're just hanging out at Jane's house, watching the kids play."

"Where have you been?" His tone grew darker. "Did you and your sister go out drinking last night?"

"No, Richard, please stop. We had a glass of wine last night."

"Oh, so now you're drinking. You're probably flirting with men and having sex with them, too. You're turning into a fucking whore."

I hung up, the nausea overwhelming. Every single call left me bone-tired.

"Was that Richard again?" Jane asked. "Why is he calling so much?"

Forcing a smile, I replied, "Oh, he's just asking about what to pack and where things are. You know men, they can't find anything by themselves."

One evening, about a week into our stay, we were all sitting around the kitchen table, enjoying dinner. The house was filled with laughter and the smell of home-cooked food. I was feeling relaxed. Richard had not called all day.

Then, the doorbell rang.

Ding dong. Ding dong. Ding dong.

We all jumped up.

"Who the hell is that?" Jane asked. The doorbell kept ringing over and over, frantic and insistent. "Who are you?" she yelled toward the front door. "Stop ringing the doorbell!"

Then I heard it. His voice.

"Candy! I know you're in there! Open the damn fucking door

now!"

The sound of his voice sent a jolt of fear through me. My heart raced so fast, I could hear it pounding in my ears.

"Oh, for the love of God, Richard," I called out. "Stop. Go away."

Jane grabbed my arm. "Don't you dare open that door," she whispered, her voice firm. Then she yelled, "Richard, go away and come back when you've calmed down. We are not opening this door so you might as well leave."

Her voice held steady and firm, and for a moment, I felt a flicker of hope. I could hear Richard breathing heavily, pacing on the porch. Then after a long silence, he stomped down the steps and disappeared.

Jane double-checked the door lock and turned to me, her face pale. "What's wrong with him?"

Trying to downplay the situation, I said, "He'll be fine, I promise. He just gets upset sometimes. I can calm him down."

Jane's eyes widened in disbelief. "This is nuts. I can't have this around my house."

Her words hit me hard. "Please, Jane, it'll be okay, I just need to talk to him. I'll make sure it doesn't happen again."

But she wasn't buying it. "I have kids here," she said, glancing toward the kitchen where the kids were playing, oblivious to the tension. "I can't risk this kind of drama."

The phone started ringing, the shrill sound cutting through the silence. I didn't have to guess who it was. Richard had found a pay phone.

Jane flinched. "Aren't you going to answer that?"

I shook my head. "No, I'm not ready to talk to him."

The phone rang again and again.

Jane said, "You have to leave."

My heart stopped. "No, Jane, please. Don't do this."

She crossed her arms. Her expression hardened. "You can't stay here," she said firmly. "I can't deal with this. It's too much."

"Jane, I don't have anywhere to go," I pleaded. "What am I supposed to do? What about my boys?"

Tears welled in my eyes as she shook her head. "I'm sorry. I really am. But you have to figure something out."

The following morning, I packed our things and closed the door behind us. I stood there for a moment, staring at the closed door that had once felt like a lifeline.

Jane barely said goodbye.

CHAPTER 9

The Blue House

A few years later, Richard was transferred to Titusville, Florida, to manage another tire store. Titusville was about a two-hour drive from Tampa. Not long after we moved, I met my next-door neighbor by chance. It was a sunny afternoon, and the boys were outside playing in the front yard. I'd just finished making an early dinner and stepped out to call them inside. To my surprise, they weren't alone. The neighbor's children were out, too, older than my boys but that didn't seem to matter. They were all laughing and chasing one another around the yard.

A woman wearing a floral apron stood by her mailbox, watching them with a warm smile. Her brown hair was pulled back into a bun, a few strands escaping in the breeze.

"Are these your boys?" she asked, waving as I approached.

I nodded, smiling shyly. "Yes, they are."

"They're sweet. It's nice to see them playing together."

I stood there awkwardly for a moment, unsure of what to say. "I'm Candy," I finally offered. "We just moved in."

"I'm Linda." She extended her hand. Her grip was firm and her smile genuine. "Welcome to the neighborhood. Let me know if you ever need anything. I'm right next door."

"Thank you," I said softly, holding back tears. *How long has it been since someone offered me kindness?*

For a moment, standing there in the sunlight, watching our kids play together, I almost forgot about the chaos inside my home.

"Would you like to come in?" Linda asked, wiping her hands on her apron.

"I would love to," I said, feeling a flutter of excitement.

We stepped inside, and I immediately smelled the warm, sugary scent of freshly baked cakes. Her kitchen was cozy but cluttered with mixing bowls, measuring cups, and cake pans.

"Don't mind my kitchen, please, it's such a mess. It's always a mess, I bake cakes all day long."

"Wow, you're a baker?" I asked, looking around at the stack of cake boxes.

"Yes, I make cakes for weddings, birthdays, really any kind of celebratory event." She handed me a photo album filled with pictures of her cakes.

"Your cakes are beautiful!" I flipped through the pages, impressed with her artistry.

I was about to ask her more about her business when I glanced down at my watch. My stomach dropped. Richard would be home any minute, and I knew he would be furious if he found me next door.

"Thank you so much for inviting me," I said quickly, handing the album back. "But I need to get home and get dinner on the table."

"Please, come back anytime," she said, her voice genuine, her kindness palpable.

Linda quickly became my first real friend. I was so grateful to finally have someone to talk to. Someone who didn't judge me, who didn't yell, who didn't hurt me.

Ben loved going to Linda's house, especially when she was baking. One afternoon, as we walked into her kitchen, Ben tugged at my hand. His eyes sparkled with excitement.

"Mom," he whispered, motioning for me to bend down. "Can I lick the bowl?"

I smiled. "You should ask Ms. Linda."

Linda chuckled, already knowing what he wanted. "I heard that." She held out a mixing bowl nearly as big as Ben. "Of course you can lick the bowl."

Ben's face lit up as he sat on the floor, the bowl between his legs, using his fingers to scrape every bit of the batter from the sides, licking it clean. He was one happy four-year-old.

I only visited with her while Richard was at work. I couldn't risk him knowing about our friendship. I concealed the truth about my own abuse. I was gripped by the fear that if I confided in her, Richard would harm her.

Each time I visited her, Linda shared more about her life. She was recently widowed and single-handedly raising a teenaged daughter and son. There was a quiet strength in her, a resilience I admired.

One afternoon as I sat at her kitchen table, watching her carefully decorate a wedding cake, I couldn't help but wonder about the love she'd shared with her husband.

What is it like to love someone so deeply? To feel safe and cherished?

"Please tell me more about your husband," I said softly, not wanting to intrude. "If it's too painful, I totally understand."

Linda glanced up, a wistful smile on her face. "I miss my husband every day, Candy. He would light up a room when he walked in. I loved him dearly."

I nodded, feeling a lump in my throat. "I'm sorry you lost your husband. May I ask, how did he die?"

She closed her eyes for a moment, collecting her thoughts, and placed another flower on the cake. "He passed away from a massive heart attack last year. The kids miss him so much. There isn't a day that goes by that I don't think about him."

Her voice held a quiet sadness, but also gratitude, as though the pain of losing him was worth the love they had shared.

I sat in silence for a moment. Her movements were precise, almost therapeutic. I wondered if I would ever experience a love like that. Would I ever know what it felt like to be truly loved, without fear or pain?

I wanted to know more about her life, her love, and the happiness she had once known.

But I would never get the chance. That evening, Richard handed me a letter. The owners of the house we rented wanted it back and we had to move.

* * *

Within a week, Richard found another house to rent in Titusville. It was a small house, just two bedrooms and one bathroom, in a quiet subdivision. The only distinguishing feature was the shaggy blue carpet that stretched from room to room. Richard loved that carpet. He bought a bright blue couch to match while I found some secondhand furniture to complete the house. It wasn't much but it made the space livable.

During the years we lived in what I call "the blue house," Richard's drinking worsened. He disappeared for days, sometimes a week at a time, on drunken binges. He drank at work and after work with his buddies. Where he was sleeping, I had no idea.

He hit me if my hair was out of place.

If I answered him in a tone he didn't like, he beat me.

And if he wasn't hitting me, he was tearing me down with his words.

Every night, he demanded that I take a bath with him. It had become a ritual I dreaded.

"Get in here, it's time for us to take a bath," he yelled from the bathroom. "Now run some bath water for us."

I stood in front of the mirror, staring at my reflection. The bruises. The exhaustion in my eyes. I didn't even recognize myself anymore.

I turned on the faucet, watching the water rise in the tub. Richard stepped in behind me, his gaze fixed on my body.

He sneered. "Look at those stretch marks on your stomach." He shook his head, disgusted. "No one would ever love someone with a stomach looking like that." His voice dripped with cruelty. "I'm the only one who would put up with that."

I bit my lip to keep from crying. "Richard, I'm trying to be a good wife. I love you and I'm really trying to make you happy."

"I love you, too, but I'm the only one who could ever love you."

"I'm trying," I whispered, my voice breaking.

"You're not trying hard enough. You're not worth much. I'm the only one who could love you. Don't forget that."

His words echoed in my mind. *You're not worth much.* And I believed him.

The next morning, I had the television on for background noise while cleaning the house. *The Phil Donahue Show* was on. I hadn't paid much attention to it before. The show was groundbreaking for its time, being the first talk show to incorporate live audience participation. Donahue would typically feature a single guest discussing a specific topic for the entire hour, with audience members encouraged to ask questions and share their thoughts.

Jason's laughter echoed through the house, a deep little-boy belly giggle that warmed my heart.

"Mommy, get me!" he squealed, dodging around the furniture.

I laughed and chased after him, my worries momentarily forgotten.

On the screen, Donahue's familiar voice cut through my thoughts.

"…these are the signs that you're being abused.…"

Jason darted around the bed, giggling, his chubby hands clutching a pillow.

"I'm going to get you," I teased, lunging toward him.

"…verbal abuse is the same as physical abuse; they are both harmful.…"

"Jason, bring Mommy that pillow, please."

He giggled and threw the pillow at me before running into my arms. His sweet scent filled my senses, and I kissed his neck, holding him close.

"… it's not okay for husbands to hit their wives.…"

But what if I did something to make him mad? Maybe it was my fault sometimes.

"… here are the three things you need to do if you are being abused. Number one: go to the police. Number two: run away. Number three: seek help from your church."

I hugged Jason. *Could this be me? Am I being abused?*

But the question was too heavy to face.

No. Don't think about this now. Maybe later.

CHAPTER 10

"Seek Help from Your Church"

*A*m *I being abused?*

This question lingered on my mind, planted there by the guest on *The Phil Donahue Show.*

No. That can't be me.

I'm not being abused. I just need to be better, a better wife, a better person. If I fix myself, everything will be okay. It has to be.

But the thoughts wouldn't stop.

If I call the police, what if they think I'm crazy? What if they take my boys? And what are they going to do to fix me?

Run away?

Where would I go? I have no family to turn to, no money to start over. Richard would hunt me down.

The church?

Maybe. I could try the church. I think I should try the church. They will help me be a better wife.

The boys and I started attending the local Baptist church regularly. We went to Wednesday afternoon services, and on Sundays, we were there for both morning and evening services.

Jason always asked, "Mom, do we go to turch today?" I loved hearing him ask me this question. It always put a smile on my face.

The boys loved everything about church. They each had their own Sunday school class, where they quickly met new friends. They came home eager to show off their drawings by displaying them on the refrigerator. Their joy was contagious, and for a while, I let myself believe we had found something good.

On those rare Sunday mornings when Richard came with us to church, I clung to a glimmer of hope.

Maybe this time will be different.

Maybe he won't drink anymore.

Maybe God is working on him.

If we could just embrace Christianity together, I believed everything would be okay.

One Sunday after service, I made an appointment to meet with the pastor. I was desperate for guidance. I needed answers, someone to tell me how to fix what felt broken.

The pastor was a tall man in his late sixties with a commanding presence. I sat down in his office, folding my hands tightly in my lap. I tried to gather the courage to speak. I'd never told anyone about the things Richard did.

My voice shaky, I finally began. "Pastor, things aren't very good at home. I don't know what I'm doing wrong, but I need advice on how to make my home life better."

He leaned forward. "What's happening at home, Candy?" His voice was steady and calm. "How can I help you?"

"My husband hurts me when he's been drinking, and even when he's not drinking, he yells at me and calls me names." I twisted a tissue between my fingers. "I don't understand the change in his behavior. What can I do, Pastor?"

"Can you tell me more?"

I hesitated but forced myself to continue. "In the beginning he was so kind to me. He would tell me how much he loved me, how pretty I was, how he couldn't live without me." I paused, swallowing hard. "But after we started living together, he began hitting me."

The pastor straightened in his chair, his expression shifting. "Excuse me?" He sat back, his posture stiff, and crossed his arms. His voice hardened. "You're living together? The two of you aren't married, but you have children together. This is part of the problem. You're living in sin. This is a violation of God's commandments and the law of the Church."

His arms spread wide, as if he were bearing the weight of the world or had just been nailed to the cross himself.

I flinched, startled by his sudden change. Composing myself, I tried to calm my nerves. "I'm sorry, Pastor, I don't want to be a sinner. I want to become a better person. I'm here to serve God."

"The only way God will help you is if you help yourself. First, you need to marry Richard, and second, you must repent."

"Yes, Pastor." Now sitting on the edge of my chair, I listened intently to his every word. "I'll marry Richard, repent my sins, serve God, and become a better person for Richard. I'll do whatever it takes."

His expression serious, he opened the Bible and pointed to Scripture. "Candy, the Bible teaches that a wife should be submissive to her husband. This is what God wants for you. If you become more submissive to Richard, it will help prevent him from getting angry. And if he doesn't get angry, he won't hurt you."

I sat there, stunned, listening to his words as he repeated them over and over again. "Candy, just don't make him mad, and he won't hit you."

He continued, "You also need to get more involved in the church. Start tithing ten percent of your income. Surrender your life to God.

Embrace salvation through Jesus Christ and undergo baptism. Then and only then will God create a better life for all of you."

I walked out of his office with a renewed sense of purpose. I had a plan. I was going to be more submissive to Richard, trust God's guidance, and make myself more lovable.

That very week, I began scraping together money to tithe, even though we barely had enough for groceries. I joined the choir, volunteered to teach Sunday school, and immersed myself in church activities.

While making dinner one evening, I rehearsed in my mind how I was going to tell Richard about the pastor's advice. As I set the table, a wave of tension moved through me. "Richard, the pastor at the church said that we should get married." I kept my voice calm but firm. "He said we're living in sin."

Richard glanced up from his chair, his expression surprisingly neutral. "When do you want to get married?"

"As soon as possible," I said. "I don't want to live in sin anymore."

"That's fine with me."

It's all going to be okay now, just like the pastor said.

Two weeks later, we stood together at a tiny ready-made chapel on Cocoa Beach, Florida. There was no fanfare. No diamond ring, no pretty dress, no flowers. Just the two of us, the officiant, and two strangers who served as our witnesses. The ceremony was short and simple.

In the weeks that followed, Richard seemed happy to be married. He treated me much better: less yelling, fewer insults, no beatings. The pastor was right. We just needed to get married and go to church.

I threw myself into church life, wanting to build new friendships with other women. Richard wouldn't let me have friends outside the church, but he seemed fine with me socializing inside those walls.

At first, I was hopeful. The women were friendly enough, but it didn't take long to see the cracks beneath the surface.

One Sunday after choir practice, a woman pulled me aside. Her voice dropped to a hushed, conspiratorial tone. "Candy, did you see the dress Mary had on today?"

I blinked, taken aback. "No, I haven't paid any attention. Why? What's wrong with her dress?"

She rolled her eyes dramatically. "It looks like she bought it at a thrift store. And did you hear her in the choir? She was so off-key! Should I talk to the choir director about this? What do you think?"

Oh, for the love of God and everything that's holy.

"I'm sure the choir director knows and will take care of it," I replied, stepping away.

We're here to serve God. Not judge each other's clothes or voices.

But it didn't stop. Week after week, I overheard the same chatter. It was endless. Gossip, cattiness, and judgment disguised as "concern."

I was frustrated, but I kept pushing forward. *I don't have time for these games. I'm on a mission, a mission to trust God's word and become a better person.*

* * *

Not long after we took our wedding vows, I woke up with a tightness in my stomach. A strange, uneasy feeling.

Ignore it. It's fine!

The past weeks had seemed almost too good to be true. Richard continued to be kind and loving. He even played with the boys after work, laughing and rolling around with them like a father who genuinely cared.

I wanted to believe this was our new reality.

But that gnawing feeling in my stomach wouldn't go away.

That night, after giving the boys their bath and tucking them in bed, I curled up on the end of the sofa, sitting in the dark, watching the cars pass by. Each set of headlights made my heart jump. *That's him. He's coming home now.*

But it wasn't. With every passing minute, my hope faded.

Why isn't God helping me?

Three nights later, I was in the kitchen putting the dishes in the dishwasher while the boys were playing quietly in their rooms, freshly bathed and ready for bed. I heard the familiar sound of a car pull into the driveway.

Finally. He's probably drunk.

The kitchen door slammed. *He's drunk.* Richard stumbled in. His clothes were rumpled and dirty, the same ones he'd been wearing when he left three days ago. He looked like a homeless man.

"Hey, bitch," he slurred as he grabbed my ass.

I flinched, spinning around with a glare. "I don't like you grabbing my ass."

His face twisted with rage. "Listen here, you slut, I'll grab you any place I want, any time I want."

Before I knew it, he shoved me hard. I stumbled backward, hitting the floor with a thud. Pain shot through my hip as I struggled to sit up.

Then he kicked me. "What are you making for dinner, bitch? I'm hungry. Get up off the fucking floor," he growled. He tangled his hand in my hair, yanking me upright with a vicious pull.

Leaning against the kitchen counter, I pleaded, "Richard, please go take a shower and I'll make you a plate of food."

"I want something good," he barked as he stomped off to shower.

I stood there in silence, trembling.

We never talked about where he'd been.

CHAPTER 11

"You Should Go To College"

One beautiful sunny day, the boys were outside riding their Hot Wheels bikes. I walked outside to check on them and noticed a young lady bending down to chat with them. She was pointing at their bikes.

As I approached, she stood up and smiled at me.

"Hi. I live in that house." She pointed to the house just two doors down from ours. "I just graduated from high school, and I'll be going to a local college starting in the fall." Her voice was full of excitement.

Our first conversation didn't amount to much more than that. From time to time, I saw her walking by. She always waved and called out. I waved back with a smile.

One day I invited her in. She stepped into the kitchen, her smile as bright as ever. "It's great to see you," she said. "It's been a while."

I poured her a glass of iced tea and sat down across from her. "How are your college classes coming?"

"Really good. I'm really enjoying college life."

"That's wonderful."

She smiled and leaned in a little. "Ms. Candy, you should go to college."

I was shocked. My mind screamed at me to move, to say something, but my body refused to cooperate. *Go to college? Me?*

I rose slowly, tension knotting in my stomach, and walked to the kitchen sink. I gripped the edge tightly, my back to her. *She doesn't know how stupid I am.*

"I'm so busy with the boys," I said.

She didn't give up. "Then just take one class. You can at least do that, right?"

Richard would have a fit!

"What have you always dreamed of being?"

No one had ever asked me that question. Not once.

I swallowed hard, my voice barely a whisper. "I've always wanted to be a nurse."

But my father said I'm too stupid to be a nurse.

Her face lit up with a smile, as if I'd just shared the most wonderful secret.

"Then go enroll. Take one class, any class."

Can I really do it? The doubt clung to me like a weight. But something about her enthusiasm made me feel lighter.

I stared at her hopeful eyes, feeling a shift in me. For the first time, the voice of doubt grew quieter.

Maybe I *could* do it.

She never came back to visit after that. I assumed college classes kept her busy.

* * *

It pains me to my core to say it, but I don't remember this angel's name.

I've thought about her often over the years, wondering why her name escapes me. Maybe it's because, at the time, I didn't believe in myself enough to fully grasp the importance of our conversation. But I clearly remember how I *felt* that day.

I felt the possibilities. Of hope. Of permission to dream. Because of her, I dared to believe in something better. That changed everything.

Later that night, I lay awake, replaying our conversation over and over in my mind. Could I really go to college?

I had thoughts, quiet secret thoughts, that a college education might free me from Richard. But hope is a stubborn thing, and part of me still believed he could change. If I became a nurse and brought in a steady income, maybe it would ease his stress. Maybe he wouldn't need to drink so much.

A few months earlier, Richard had finally gotten tired of me asking to use the car to run errands or take the boys to their activities, so he bought me a used car. It wasn't much, but it was mine.

One morning, I stood at the window and the thought crept into my mind: *I do have a car now. At least I could go to the college and check it out.*

The idea lingered for a few days, growing more insistent with each passing moment. Finally, I mustered the courage to do it.

I didn't tell Richard; I knew better than to bring it up.

I parked in the college lot, fingers clenched around the steering wheel until the color drained from my hands. I sat there staring at the building in front of me, my anxiety rising. I could practically hear my father sneering, *You're too old. You're too stupid. You won't fit in.*

With a quiet tremble in my voice, I whispered a prayer. *Please, God, help me do this.*

I stepped out of the car, nerves buzzing in my chest, and put one foot in front of the other. I found the admissions door and pushed it open.

A kind-looking woman sat behind the desk and greeted me with a warm smile.

I swallowed hard. "I would like to enroll in a class."

She nodded, pulling out some papers. "What is your major?"

Wow! I'm really at a college, telling this woman what my major is.

I straightened my posture. "I'd like to be a registered nurse, ma'am."

She gave me an encouraging smile, clearly sensing my nervousness. "That's wonderful. Let me explain how it works." She took her time walking me through the process, her voice calm and reassuring. "I suggest you start with an English class your first semester. Once you get comfortable, you can take two classes in the next semester."

I nodded, taking it all in as she continued.

"It's best to take all your prerequisites before applying to the nursing program. The program is intense. It's a four-year course of study compressed into two years, with no summer breaks. You'll attend classes year-round." She leaned in slightly. "We're offering it now because there's a nationwide shortage of registered nurses."

She handed me the college application. "Take this over to that desk and fill it out. When you're done, bring it back to me."

But then I hit the question on the form: *What is your major?*

I stared at the blank space, panic rising. I couldn't remember how to spell the word "nurse."

How in the hell am I going to become a nurse if I can't spell the word? My mind spiraled. *This is a sign. I'm too stupid to be here. I'll never make it.* I took a breath, closing my eyes for a moment. *Calm down. I've made it this far.*

Slowly I opened my eyes, picked up the pen, and returned to the question. I wrote the word "nurse" in the space.

When I handed the application back to the woman at the desk, she gave me a big smile. "You're all set."

Her kindness gave me a little more courage. There was one more thing I needed to know.

"Ma'am," I asked hesitantly. "Can I still go to college if I didn't graduate from high school?"

She didn't flinch or hesitate. "Absolutely, but you must have completed your high school diploma requirements before you can graduate from college. Here is an application to take the GED. This is the equivalent of a high school diploma. All you have to do is sign up and take the test."

Relief washed over me.

I was the first person on either side of the family to go to college.

Guess I'm not fucking stupid, Dad!

CHAPTER 12

My Name Is Candy

I hadn't told Richard that I had enrolled in college. The thought of it filled me with anxiety. But a couple of days after I signed up for the English class, he came home in a good mood. His rare good moods never lasted long, so I decided to take the chance and tell him.

I stood at the sink, washing dishes, trying to keep my voice steady. "Richard, I need to tell you something."

He glanced up from his dinner plate. "What?"

My hands trembled beneath the suds. "I've enrolled in an English class at the community college."

There. It was out.

I braced myself for his reaction. I half expected him to explode, to throw a fit, grab his dinner plate and smash it on the floor.

Instead, he shrugged. "Okay, that's fine."

I blinked, confused. "I'll be attending classes on Tuesdays and Thursdays."

"Okay, that's fine," he repeated, going back to eating his dinner.

I stood there, stunned. Why wasn't he angry? Why wasn't he yelling, calling me names, or forbidding me to go?

Maybe he didn't really understand what I was doing. Maybe he thought it was just a passing whim and I'd fail.

After all, he thought I was stupid, too.

* * *

"Boys, you need to hurry up and eat your breakfast because Mom is going to school just like you guys."

"You're going to school with us?" Ben asked.

"No, honey, I'm going to a different school than you go to. I'm going to college."

"Wow." Jason grinned, his face lighting up. "Mom's going to school!"

"Yes, I am," I said proudly. "Mom's going to learn, too."

I watched their smiles, and something inside of me shifted. I felt hope, not just for myself, but for them, too.

They deserved to see a different version of me.

A mom who believed in herself.

A mom who didn't just survive, but thrived.

I arrived forty-five minutes early for my English class.

As I walked across the campus, a sense of liberation washed over me, something I'd never felt before. This was freedom. The freedom to learn, explore, and grow. The campus wasn't extravagant, no ivy-covered buildings or grand architecture, but to me, it was perfect.

I couldn't contain my excitement. *Candy, you're a real college student!*

For the first time in my life, I felt important.

Slow down, take this all in.

I stopped walking and took a deep breath. Spinning in a full circle, I let my eyes drink in the details around me. The manicured lawns, the freshly painted buildings, the students rushing with arms full of books, deep in conversations about classes and assignments. It all felt surreal.

An inner voice rose up, stronger that the doubts I'd carried for so long.

I can do this.

I am smart.

I'm good enough.

By the time I walked into the classroom, I felt something new: confidence.

I scanned the room, looking for the right seat. I wanted to be near the front, not too close, but close enough to stay focused. Since I was early, I had my pick of options. *Second row, third seat. Perfect.*

My English teacher was a nondescript, middle-aged woman with a stern presence. She wasn't what you'd call warm or encouraging; in fact, her demeanor felt downright discouraging. From the start, it seemed like she had a radar for vulnerability and channeled her frustration directly at me.

On the first day of class, she asked everyone to stand up and state their name and major.

I dreaded this moment. Even on a good day, I struggle to remember names, and I knew I wouldn't remember anyone's here. My nerves were too distracting.

As one student after another stood and introduced themselves, I could feel my anxiety rising. When it was finally my turn, my heart was pounding so hard I was sure the entire room could hear it.

"Hello, my name is Candy, and my major is nursing."

The words felt monumental as they left my mouth. I looked at the professor, hoping for some small acknowledgment, maybe even a smile. Instead, she glared at me, her expression unreadable.

She handed out an outline of what she expected us to accomplish over the next few weeks. I scribbled down every word she said, afraid I'd miss something important.

"I expect your first essay to be completed and turned in by the end of the class next Thursday."

I marked it in my calendar to submit the assignment by the following Tuesday. I wanted to finish early.

As the semester progressed, I couldn't shake the feeling that no matter how hard I worked, she'd already decided I didn't belong. I couldn't understand why. I paid attention in class, turned in my assignments early, and always gave my best effort.

But when I raised my hand to ask a question, her answers were curt and dismissive, as though I was bothering her. When I compared her feedback on my essays to my peers, hers were noticeably harsher toward me.

Even one of the students noticed what I'd been feeling for weeks.

"Why is she being so hateful to you?" she asked after class one day.

I shook my head, baffled. "I don't understand, either. I'm going to speak to her."

After class, I stayed behind after the other students had gone. "Professor, can I speak with you, please?"

She glanced up from her desk with a bored expression. "Yes, what is this about?"

I steadied my voice. "I'm trying hard to do well in your class. This is my first prerequisite for the nursing program, and I want to succeed, but it seems like I'm doing something wrong."

Her expression didn't soften. Instead, she folded her arms across her chest. "I don't know what you're talking about. Everything is fine, just keep doing what you're doing."

I pressed on. "I really want to get an A in your class."

"Make sure your final essay is thorough and well-researched."

"Okay, I will do my very best. Thank you for your time."

I walked out of her classroom more determined than ever.

You will not break me!

* * *

The fact that I didn't have a high school diploma weighed on me, so I found a local place offering the GED test and scheduled my appointment. But there was one problem: I hadn't picked up a textbook since I dropped out of high school.

I decided to go to the library. Surely they'd have books to prepare for the GED. But I'd never been to a public library before and didn't have the first clue how to even look for a GED review book. Because of my dyslexia, books had never been my friend. Trying to decode the jumbled words on the page always turned reading into a frustrating task.

As I pulled open the heavy door, I was immediately overwhelmed by the vast rows of books.

Breathe, just breathe, Candy.

How in the hell am I going to find a GED book?

Unsure where to even begin, I wandered aimlessly, pretending like I knew what I was doing. I watched people go to a large file cabinet, look through white three-by-five cards to find one they wanted, write information from the file card on a piece of paper, then walk to one of the rows of books and pull a book from the shelf.

Okay, I can do that.

I made my way to the cabinet, pulled open the drawer that started with the letter G, and began to look for any card that had GED on it. Not one card had GED on it. Embarrassed but determined, I had no other choice: I had to ask for help.

I approached the librarian, a stern-looking woman with glasses perched on her nose. Leaning in, I whispered, "Ma'am, I need to find a book to study for the GED test. Could you help me?"

To my surprise, her face softened. "Of course I can help you. Let's step over here." She walked to the file cabinet with practiced ease and found a card. "Here you go." She pointed to the title: General Education Development.

"Follow me," she said pleasantly. "Here is where you can find all the books for the GED test."

"Can I check out any of these books?"

"Absolutely. When you decide which books you would like to check out, come back to my desk and I'll help you."

I was surprised by how helpful she was. She didn't look at me like I was bothering her, but instead she had a genuine interest in helping me.

With the GED prep book in my hands, I stood a little taller.

* * *

On the day of the test, my nerves were at an all-time high. I had studied for a solid week, poring over every page of that GED prep book, determined to pass.

I sat down at the test table, trying to slow my breathing. I opened the test, reminding myself that I could do this.

I passed it on the first try. I was thrilled, but that joy was quickly swallowed by shame. Instead of celebrating, I tucked the accomplishment away in my mind. I never told my sons. I didn't want anyone to know.

Instead, the next morning, I woke to the sound of Richard's voice cutting through the house like a knife.

"Where's my ironed shirt for work? Why don't I have an ironed shirt for work, bitch?" he yelled.

"I'm sorry, I haven't had a chance to do the laundry," I stammered, thrusting a freshly ironed shirt his way. "Here, here's an ironed shirt." But it wasn't enough to calm him down.

"What the fuck? This school is taking up too much of your time. Get the damn laundry done today." He stormed out, slamming the door behind him.

My mind was a blur of exhaustion, GED test, my relentless English professor, taking care of the boys, housework. The last thing I wanted to think about was Richard's damn shirt!

CHAPTER 13

"Go to The Police"

I had one year to complete my prerequisites for the nursing program, so during my second semester, I decided to be brave and push myself harder. I enrolled in two classes: psychology and biology.

Richard had been missing for a couple of days, which wasn't unusual. His drinking binges often kept him away a couple times a month. I never knew when he would return, but I always knew what to expect when he did. I would be his target, his punching bag. The routine was as predictable as it was terrifying.

This time, though, he'd been calling throughout the day. Short, sharp phone calls, just to make sure I was home. It wasn't out of concern. It was to remind me that no matter where he was, I wasn't free from him.

By the time night fell, the house was still. The boys had finally fallen asleep. I sat in the quiet, feeling the familiar tension creeping up in my stomach, bracing myself for when Richard would inevitably walk through the door. But he hadn't shown up yet.

To keep my mind busy, and to push back the fear, I opened my biology textbook and spread my notes across the dining room table. I immersed myself in the material, focusing on terms and diagrams, letting the steady rhythm of studying calm my nerves.

The phone rang again, startling me.

"Bitch, what the fuck are you doing?" Richard's voice was slurred and angry, dripping with drunken venom.

My hands shook as I gripped the receiver. "Richard, I can't talk right now. Please just leave me alone."

"What the fuck are you talking about? I'm your fucking husband and you will talk to me anytime I say so, you fucking whore!" His words were barely coherent.

"Richard, I'm going to hang up now."

His voice exploded through the line. "I'm going to come home and beat the living hell out of you."

My hand clenched tighter around the phone. "If you come home wanting to beat me, I will call the police. Do you understand? I will call the police."

Silence. I could feel his shock through the line. I had never threatened to call the police before.

"You're not going to call the police," he finally sneered. "And if you do, I'll tell them you're just mad because I've been drinking. They'll believe me, not you."

"Richard, I'm hanging up now." Click.

I sat there for a moment, breathing deeply, my heart racing. I had never defied him like that. I knew it would make him angrier, but I also knew that I had to stand my ground. Every day as I attended classes, I grew stronger, more independent. But when I came home, it was like being dragged back into a dark prison.

The phone rang again. And again. And again. I refused to answer. Each time it rang, I held my breath, willing it to stop. He called six more times, each time hanging up and calling back within seconds. I still didn't answer. Eventually, the phone fell silent.

Finally!

I went back to my studies. Suddenly, there was banging at the front door. The doorbell rang over and over. I knew it was Richard.

"Let me in, bitch!" he yelled, pounding his fist against the door. "I don't have my house key. Open the fucking door, you cunt!"

I sat unmoving at the dining room table. I prayed he would just give up, maybe pass out on the porch, or leave and find somewhere else to sleep off his drunkenness. I stayed put.

Without warning, there was a loud crash and the sound of glass shattering. I spun around just in time to see him forcing his way through the kitchen window, glass flying everywhere. The window, directly over the kitchen sink, was too small for him to fit through easily. But that didn't stop him. His body twisted and shoved through the frame, his face red with fury, veins bulging from his neck. He looked like a real-life version of the Incredible Hulk, all rage and destruction.

"You fucking bitch!" he roared. "Don't you ever not answer my calls! I will always find a way to get in this house, bitch."

Startled, I jumped up from the dining room table, knocking my chair over with a loud crash. My heart pounded in my chest as I backed away.

"Richard, I'm calling the police. Do you hear me? I'm calling the police right now."

He lunged forward, still screaming obscenities, but I didn't wait to see what he would do next. I grabbed the phone, my hands shaking uncontrollably, and dialed the police.

"My husband has just broken through the window and he's going to hurt me," I screamed, my words tumbling out in a panicked rush.

"What's your address, ma'am?" the operator asked calmly. "What's your name?"

I struggled to steady my voice. "Candy." Barely able to speak, I gave my address.

"An officer will arrive in the next few minutes."

I hung up the phone. Richard still stood in the kitchen, panting from the effort of climbing through the window, his fists clenched at his sides.

"You called the cops?" he growled, stepping toward me.

"Yes," I said, my voice shaking but firm. "They're on their way."

Before the police arrived, Richard unleashed his fury. He stormed through the kitchen, dining room, and living room, breaking everything in sight: shattering glass, smashing picture frames, flinging dishes to the floor.

Then he turned his rage on me.

"You fucking whore!" he screamed as he grabbed a handful of my hair and yanked me to the floor. I hit the shaggy blue carpet with a thud, the impact knocking the air out of my lungs.

"Who do you fucking think you're messing with?" he snarled, his face twisted with rage as he dragged me across the room by my hair.

"Richard, stop, stop, stop!" I screamed, tears streaming down my face as I struggled to get free.

He ignored me, kicking me hard in the ribs. "You think you're going to get away with treating me like this? You're a fucking cunt, and you will obey me, bitch." Another kick landed on my side, and I curled into a ball, trying to protect myself from the blows.

"I can kill you, you know that? I will fucking kill you."

"Please stop, please stop, Richard. You're hurting me. The police are on their way."

But that only made him angrier. He pounded his fists into me, careful not to leave any marks where they could be seen. He knew exactly what he was doing. He always did.

"If you cooperate with the police in any way, I promise you I will beat you even worse than I have," he hissed, breath hot against my face. "I might even kill you. Do you understand me?"

I nodded, choking back tears.

The doorbell rang, "This is the police. Open the door."

Richard glared at me, his face red and dripping with sweat, twisted into a snarl as he glared down at me. He wiped his face with a towel he grabbed from the kitchen and ran his fingers through his hair to smooth it down. In a matter of seconds, he transformed from a violent monster into a calm, collected man.

"Remember what I said, bitch," he muttered under his breath before turning toward the door.

When he opened it, his entire demeanor shifted. A broad smile spread across his face, and his speech, which had been slurred from the alcohol, was suddenly crisp and controlled.

"Hi, officers," he said, cheerfully, extending his hand. "Come on in."

It was chilling. Just moments earlier, he'd been smashing everything in the house and kicking me while I begged for mercy. Now, he was acting like he was welcoming old friends over for coffee.

One officer stepped inside and immediately took Richard aside to speak with him while the other officer approached me.

"So, what happened here?" the officer asked.

I stumbled over my words, desperate to explain what had just happened. "Sir, this man broke in through the kitchen window, started breaking everything he could get his hands on, yelling at me, threatening me, calling me names. Then he started hitting me." I spoke as fast as I could, trying to get everything out before Richard could twist the story.

The officer glanced around the room, taking in the broken glass on the floor and the overturned furniture, but he didn't seem concerned. His posture was stiff, and he refused to make eye contact with me. It was like I could read his thoughts. *Here's another crazy, dramatic woman wasting my time.*

"Officer, there are two small children here," I said, pointed toward the closed bedroom doors. "He broke in through the window. See the broken glass everywhere?" I struggled to make him understand the danger we were in.

He nodded slowly but still didn't seem alarmed.

"Sir, he hit me," I said with a shaky voice. I wanted to show him the bruises forming beneath my clothes, but I was terrified. Terrified of what Richard would do to me once the police left.

The officer raised an eyebrow. "What did you do to make him hit you?"

The question sliced through me like a blade. "What?"

"What did you do to make him mad?" he repeated, as if it were a perfectly reasonable question.

"I didn't do anything to make him mad. He's been drinking, and I was just sitting here doing my homework."

The officer shrugged. "Ma'am, I don't see anything wrong with him drinking. All guys like to have some beers after work. If you wouldn't make him mad, he wouldn't hit you."

I felt sick. No one was going to protect me. Not the police. Not anyone. And Richard knew it.

I could hear him laughing softly from across the room, chatting with the other officer like nothing had happened. His manipulation was in full swing, and it was working.

Richard and his officer buddy strolled toward me, both smiling like old friends.

"Okay, Richard, when I need some tires, I'll definitely come see you, man," the officer said, slapping his back.

"No problem, I'll give you a good deal," Richard replied, his voice smooth and confident, unlike a man who had just shattered glass and threatened to kill his wife.

As they walked toward the front door, the officer draped his arm around Richard's shoulder. "I'll see you later, buddy."

I stood there in stunned silence, my mind reeling.

"See? I told you, bitch," Richard said with a smirk as he passed me. He didn't even glance back.

He walked straight to the bedroom and kicked off his shoes. With the same casual ease he'd shown the officers, he crawled into bed and pulled the blanket over himself as if nothing had happened.

The silence in the house was deafening.

As I stood there, the truth hit me like a punch in the gut. Richard wasn't just my abuser. He had allies. He had people who would protect him, excuse him, and dismiss my suffering.

And that smirk on his face told me everything I needed to know.

He believed he was untouchable.

CHAPTER 14

The Envelope

In early March, 1976, while completing my prerequisites, I applied for entry into the nursing program. I was told there were over one hundred seventy-five applicants competing for only sixty-five spots. The odds weren't in my favor, but failure simply wasn't an option.

It felt like I was walking a tightrope with no safety net; one misstep and everything could come crashing down. The constant anxiety of unpaid rent, overdue utility bills, and the looming threat of the lights and water being shut off weighed heavily on me. Richard's daily drinking binges only added to the stress. But through it all, I kept telling myself, *Keep moving forward. There has to be solid ground just around the next corner.*

Over the next several weeks, I anxiously waited for the mailman to arrive every day to learn if I'd been accepted into the nursing program. I would stand by the window, watching for his truck, my heart pounding every time I saw him pull up to the mailbox. Each time I opened the mailbox and saw only bills and junk mail, my heart sank.

Every day, I waited. And every day, my hope flickered just a little more.

In mid-April, I saw the familiar white truck turn the corner onto my street. My heart quickened as I whispered, *Please let it be today,*

God. I watched as he pulled up to my house, slipped the mail into the box, and drove away. Once he was out of sight, I walked quickly to the mailbox, barely able to breathe. There it was, a letter from Brevard Community College addressed to me.

This is it.

I held the envelope in my hands, scared to open it, scared of what it might say. It felt heavier than it should, as if the weight of my future was inside. I stood there for what felt like an eternity, just staring.

Open the letter, Candy.

My fingers shook as I ripped it open, my eyes scanning the page for one word. One word that would determine everything. And then I saw it.

"Accepted."

Tears filled my eyes, blurring the text.

In concurrence with the Associate Degree Nursing Admissions Committee, I wish to inform you that you have been accepted as a student in the Associate Degree Nursing Program of Brevard Community College for the term beginning August 1976.

I pressed the letter close to my heart and a wave of emotions came over me. Relief. Joy. Pure excitement.

I had done it.

I had been validated!

* * *

One afternoon not long after my nursing school acceptance, Richard stumbled through the door and collapsed into a chair at the kitchen table, a beer already in hand.

"I got fired today," he said nonchalantly.

Panic hit me instantly. "What do you mean you got fired?"

"Don't worry, I'll find another job." He shrugged.

"Richard, we haven't paid the rent in two months, the lights are going to be turned off, what are we supposed to do?"

He jumped up, eyes cold and empty. "Listen here, you fucking cunt," he snarled, closing the distance between us in two quick steps. He grabbed my hair and yanked me off balance, then threw me to the floor. "I said I'll find another job. What is your fucking problem?"

I lay there, stunned. He stepped over me without a glance and stormed to the bedroom, muttering to himself as he yanked open drawers. He ripped his work shirt off and threw it on the bed before grabbing a fresh one.

"I'm leaving." He shoved his arms into the sleeves. "I don't know if I'll be back."

He started tossing clothes into the bag.

I struggled to sit up. "What do you mean you don't know if you'll be back?" This wasn't like his usual drinking binges where he wouldn't show up for a few days. He was deliberately and intentionally packing a bag and leaving us.

"You can't just go like this," I pleaded, my voice breaking. "I'll be better. After I graduate, I'll get a good job, and I can help with the bills. I can take some of the pressure off you. Please, just stay."

He barely glanced at me. His expression hardened. "I said I'm leaving." He zipped the bag and slung it over his shoulder.

"Please, Richard, I need you to stay." My voice trembled with fear. "How am I going to do this alone? How am I going to feed the boys?"

He shoved past me toward the door. "Get out of my fucking way, bitch."

"Please don't leave me," I cried, chasing after him, but he didn't look back.

The door slammed shut, the sound reverberating through the empty space he left behind. I stood there, staring at the door.

He was gone.

My mind spun with panic, the weight of everything crashing down on me. I slowly sank to the floor, wrapping my arms around my knees and rocking my body back and forth, as if movement might somehow quiet the storm inside me.

How am I going to go to school now?

Why do I feel this way? He hurts me.

But I couldn't escape the truth. I didn't know how to survive outside of his prison. For so long, even with the violence and chaos, Richard had been my constant. And now, that constant was gone, leaving me with two boys to care for, no money, and no idea how to move forward.

Eventually, I pulled myself off the floor and walked to the bedroom, my body heavy with exhaustion. I sat on the bed, staring at the rumpled sheets where he had tossed his clothes.

I didn't sleep much. As the sun rose, the first light creeping through the window, I felt a fleeting moment of peace, until fear took over again. The knot in my stomach tightened, twisting painfully. I clutched my belly, curling into myself. The ache wasn't just physical, it was the weight of abandonment, codependency, and years of living in fear crashing down all at once.

One step at a time. I've survived this long. I'll figure it out.

But in that moment, I wasn't sure I believed it.

* * *

I'd been stashing a little money here and there since I first started taking college classes. If I had a few dollars left after buying groceries, I'd slip them into an envelope carefully hidden in a shoe in my closet. Occasionally when Richard was passed-out drunk, I'd take money from his pockets.

It wasn't much, just a few dollars at a time, but I added to it whenever I could.

I'm not exactly sure why I did this. Maybe deep down, I knew there would come a day when I'd need it. In a world where I had no control over what happened next, the envelope became a small source of power, a quiet reminder that I wasn't completely helpless.

When Richard left, that little stash became my lifeline. It wasn't enough to change my circumstances entirely, but it was enough to keep the lights on a little longer, to buy food for the boys, to get through one more day.

* * *

My sister Sue was the one person in my family I felt I could call, even though our relationship had its limits. We talked often, but our conversations stayed on the surface. We shared updates about our kids and our everyday struggles of keeping up appearances. But when it came to the deeper wounds, our abusive marriages, we only hinted at the truth. I knew Sue was being abused, and she knew I was, too. But neither of us dared to dig too deep into the other's pain.

Even so, for months I'd gently encouraged her to go back to school and finish the Associate of Arts degree she had started years earlier. She'd dropped out of college early in her marriage, a choice that seemed to reflect the belief we both shared at the time: that our worth came from taking care of our husbands, not from pursuing our own goals.

At first, she resisted, but I kept pushing, gently reminding her she deserved more. After a few months, something shifted. She agreed to take one class per semester while working full-time. It wasn't much, but it was a start. I could see a flicker of pride in her.

Now, Richard gone, my abandonment and codependency clawing at me, I found myself needing her in a way I hadn't before. Still feeling like the life had been drained out of me, I picked up the phone and dialed her number.

"Richard left me and the boys, Sue," I said in a weak, shaky voice. My words hung in the air, heavy with pain and uncertainty. "I've got to move and get settled before school starts."

I waited, hoping for some sign of sympathy. For someone to say, *I'm sorry, Candy. Are you okay?* But Sue's response was practical, distant, lacking the warmth I so desperately craved.

"Yeah, well, you need to find an apartment, right? Where are you going to go?"

A sharp ache of disappointment settled in my stomach. Still, I reminded myself that at least she was talking to me. I knew Sue had her own struggles, her own pain kept locked away.

"I'm not sure," I replied. "I'm going to start looking today." I paused and then blurted out, "We could rent an apartment and share the expenses if you wanted."

Though she didn't agree right away, not long after our conversation, Sue called back. She had decided it was time to leave her abuser.

I needed to get a job before my first semester of nursing school. But there was a major problem. The old clunker Richard had bought for me had broken down, and there was no money to repair it. Sue didn't own a car.

Out of desperation and with no one else to turn to, I called my older sister, Jane. I explained our situation: no transportation, no money for a car. To my surprise, she offered to loan us her Suzuki motorcycle.

There had to be a motive behind this sudden generosity because it wasn't in her nature. Maybe guilt. Whatever her reason, I didn't ask. I didn't care. Sue and I needed that motorcycle.

Jane brought it to us in Titusville and gave me a quick lesson in how to drive it. I'd never even been on a motorcycle before, but I was determined to figure it out. After a few wobbly turns around the parking lot, I started to feel more confident. The roar of the engine wasn't as intimidating as it had been just a few minutes before.

Okay. I've got this.

I loved Sue deeply, often excusing her behavior because I so desperately wanted to hold on to the idea of family. We celebrated the small victories together, like Sue acing a test or me figuring out, at the last possible moment, how to pay the rent. Those moments, however fleeting, reminded us of the bond we shared and gave us something to cling to.

But there were difficult moments, too, especially when old habits and unresolved wounds surfaced. Balancing the weight of our responsibilities alongside our personal struggles often led to tension and misunderstandings. Along with going to school, I was working two jobs—delivering newspapers at dawn and working at a pizza restaurant at night—while Sue worked at a T-shirt shop in the mall.

Sue was eight years younger than me, just ten years old when I left our mother's house. By then Dad had already moved out, Jane had left, and our brother Asser had gone to live with Dad. That left Sue alone to endure our mother's erratic mood swings and her drinking.

"You know you left me alone with our crazy mother," she would say, her words cutting deep with both accusation and pain.

"Yes, I know," I replied quietly, unwilling to stir the waters. I wanted to scream, *I lived with both of them for eighteen years!* But it was easier to agree, to let her version of the past stand unchallenged. Peace came at a price, even if it meant silencing my own experience.

* * *

I had completed all my prerequisites, except one physical education class that I could easily take alongside my nursing program studies. I had saved enough money to cover my nursing classes, but not enough money to buy the required textbooks. It was a harsh reality; I simply couldn't afford both.

During my prerequisite courses, I managed by purchasing one book at a time, stretching every dollar I had. But the nursing program was much different. The books were not optional or something I could buy one at a time. I had to buy all the books for that semester all at one time, for both clinicals and academic classes. The cost was staggering, over five hundred dollars. To put it in perspective, each college credit hour cost thirty dollars, and I was taking twelve hours per semester. The books alone cost more than my tuition.

As the first day of nursing school loomed, the weight of this reality pressed down on me. I prayed for a miracle, something, anything, to help me bridge the gap.

On the first day of class, I overheard several of my classmates grumbling about the hefty cost and weight of their medical books. In the seventies, there were no computers or internet; we relied solely on typewriters and textbooks, which meant lugging around at least four massive books at a time.

As I stood there listening to their complaints, I couldn't help but feel a pang of envy. Those books, so casually dismissed by my peers as a burden, were a treasure to me. Unlike them, I had no books at all. They looked like precious gold, just out of reach.

Ten days into classes and clinicals, my miracle still hadn't shown up. Worries danced around in my head. *I'm getting behind in my studies! I can't afford to do this! I'm going to fail! I've got to get the money for books!*

The thought pounded in my head as I walked into class and took my usual place: second row, third seat.

"Can we share your book?" I asked a classmate sitting next to me, trying to sound casual.

"Sure, but where are your books, Candy?" she asked, sliding her book toward me.

"Oh, the bookstore said they're looking for a used book for me to buy. They said they're expecting a former student to turn one in any day."

This was a complete lie. I was too embarrassed to admit the truth, that I didn't have enough money to buy even a used book. I couldn't bear the thought of anyone knowing.

"Candy, did they find you some books?" one of my other classmates asked. "If not, go see the lady who's in the bookstore today. She helped me."

Inside I was mortified. Asking for help felt like admitting failure. I'd spent years trying to shake the shame from middle and high school, when I'd been labeled a slow learner. In nursing school, my dyslexia and ADHD were still unrecognized and I thought my struggles were all my fault.

Still the reality was clear: I needed to ask for help, or I was going to fail.

That afternoon, I waited until all my classmates had left the campus. I didn't want anyone to see me walk into the financial aid office. The last thing I needed was for them to know how desperate I was.

Steeling myself, I opened the door and walked in. Behind the counter a woman stood shuffling papers, her expression a mixture of professionalism and impatience.

She barely looked up as I explained, "I'm in the nursing program right now, and I'm in need of assistance to purchase my textbooks. Unfortunately, the cost of these books is beyond my means. I was hoping there may be a program that could help me."

"Do you mean you need money for books?"

Isn't that what I just said?

"Yes, ma'am," I replied, my voice faltering. "I need money for my books. Are there any organizations that can help me?" My cheeks burned with embarrassment. Asking for money was the last thing I wanted to do, but I had no choice.

"You mean you've been in classes for ten days and don't have books?" she said, her tone sharp. "Why on earth did you enter the program knowing you didn't have money for books?" owHowiiefnmk

Her words stung, and for a moment, I couldn't decide whether I wanted to cry or snap back at her.

"At this time, unfortunately, there is no funding left to help you with purchasing your books," she said flatly. "It's all been allocated. Perhaps you should drop out now, save some money for books, and reapply to the nursing program for next year."

The thought made my stomach churn. I had to get money for my books today.

"Ma'am," I said, trying to steady my voice. "I really need money for books, and it does say financial aid on the door. I understood when you told me there are no organizations that can help me this late in the process, but I'm going to go over to that chair and have a seat."

She raised her eyebrow as I continued. "And I'm going to wait until someone can help me. I can't afford to wait another year to get my textbooks, to succeed in my nursing classes. I'm determined to find a solution today, and hopefully you can help me."

Without another word, I picked up my purse and turned to find a chair, adrenaline leaving me shaky and lightheaded.

Just get to that damn chair, Candy. You're okay.

I lowered myself into the seat, clutching my purse like a lifeline. I wrapped my arms tightly around it as if it could shield me. I laced my fingers together, willing them to stop trembling, desperate to hold myself together. A mix of fear and pride washed over me, fear of the unknown, but pride for standing up for myself and what I needed. For once, I hadn't backed down, and that small victory gave me a flicker of hope amidst the uncertainty.

I will stay here all night if that's what it takes. If I can handle being beaten by Richard, I can handle this!

An hour passed, and I hadn't budged. Eventually, I heard the sharp click of her heels on the hardwood floor as she walked toward me. Her expression was softer now, almost kind. She took a seat next to me and handed me some papers.

She said, her voice sympathetic, "I just called this organization. It's part of the American Legion. They said they may be able to help you. Give this woman a call. She's waiting to hear from you."

"Ma'am, I can't thank you enough for your help!" I said, my voice trembling with relief. "You have no idea how much this means to me!"

"You're welcome," she replied with a faint smile. "You are one determined young lady. Good luck."

I called the organization as soon as I could and that same day I was awarded a grant for books. As I hung up the phone, I couldn't contain myself. I began to jump up and down with excitement, tears streaming down my face. I didn't know where my tenacity and courage came from, maybe years of struggle had hardened me, but I was tired of the endless obstacles life kept throwing in my path. This was the last hurdle I needed to overcome, and I had done it.

I felt unstoppable.

CHAPTER 15

The Mechanism of Action

We were scheduled to have our first biweekly clinical rotation meeting soon after nursing school started. Each student received their patient's name and diagnosis on the Friday before. It was the responsibility of the student to go to the hospital and read through the patient's chart and present their plan of care to the group the following Monday.

That Monday morning, I was ready. I'd spent hours poring over my patient's chart at the hospital on Friday, reviewing every detail and crafting a thorough plan of care. I spent hours on my presentation, wanting it to be perfect.

The students crowded into the meeting room and took their places at the table, waiting anxiously. Finally the door opened and an imposing middle-aged woman with light gray hair stepped inside. She was dressed in a perfectly starched white nursing uniform and had glasses perched on her nose. Her presence commanded the room as her heels clicked against the floor, the unmistakable sound of old school, hard-sole nursing shoes. The kind that seemed to announce authority with every step, leaving no doubt she meant business.

"Good morning." Her tone was sharp and commanding. "It's nice to see all of you here. My name is Mrs. Cooke, and I will be your senior clinical instructor for this nursing program." She sounded like a military sergeant—disciplined, no nonsense, and utterly assured in her authority.

We all repeated in unison, "Good morning, Mrs. Cooke."

"You will be divided into groups, four students to one instructor," she continued. "But, before we begin, introduce yourself. Share your name along with your hobbies and interests outside of nursing."

I listened as the other students shared about their lives: tennis groups, book clubs, biking with their families, parties, and more. Their worlds seemed so normal, a far cry from mine.

Hell, my only hobby is keeping me and the boys fed and alive!

They really have a real life. They have no idea the challenges I face at home.

When it was my turn, the words came tumbling out before I could stop them. No hesitation, no second-guessing, just pure, unfiltered honesty. "My name is Candy and I'm so tired."

The room erupted in laughter. Everyone except Mrs. Cooke and me. My face felt like it was on fire with embarrassment as I sat frozen, wishing I could crawl under the table and disappear.

"All right students, that's enough," Mrs. Cooke said sharply, her tone cutting through the laughter like a blade. "Let's get to work. You will abide by the following. Number one, you will wear a crisp, clean, white uniform when you're on the hospital premises. Number two, you will wear white stockings with absolutely no tears. Except, of course, for the one gentleman in our class." She gave a pointed glance at the lone male student, who shifted uncomfortably in his chair. "Number three, you will wear freshly polished white shoes, with no scuff marks. Number four, your nursing cap is to be worn *only* while in the hospital. It is strictly forbidden to wear it outside of this building. Again, this does not apply to the gentleman."

She paused, her gaze sweeping the room like a hawk surveying its prey. "Does anyone have any questions?"

The room fell silent. No one dared raised their hand.

From that moment on Mrs. Cooke had me under a microscope. She watched me like a hawk, and I swear she had eyes in the back of her head. She would appear out of nowhere, around corners, at the nurses' station, or in the middle of a hallway. The only warning I ever got was the sound of her heels, *click, click, click.*

Whenever I heard those heels, I braced myself, knowing she was about to test me or scold me.

"Candy, what is the mechanism of action for acetaminophen? Come on, I need the answer now," she barked one day, snapping her fingers for emphasis.

What? How does Tylenol act in the body? Is she serious?

Mrs. Cooke scared the bejesus out of me. Her relentless questioning, her snapping fingers, her constant scrutiny terrified me. For the next two years, during every clinical rotation, she tested my knowledge, my stamina, and my patience. I was convinced she just plain hated me from that first day in clinicals.

At my graduation pinning ceremony, I finally learned the truth.

After the ceremony, I watched Mrs. Cooke scan the crowd, her sharp eyes darting back and forth with unmistakable purpose. She was on a mission. I'd seen that determined look many times before, usually in the hospital when she was searching for me.

Oh, no, what have I done now?

She moved swiftly through the sea of people, her steps deliberate as ever. When she reached me, she paused only for a moment before opening her arms wide and pulling me into a hug.

I froze, completely puzzled. *Was this real?*

Then she stepped back, gently placed her hands on my face, and looked me directly in the eyes.

"Candy," she began, her voice soft but steady. "As you know I've been doing this for a long time. From the time of our first meeting, I saw something in you, a spark, a hunger, and I knew you had something great to give to the field of nursing."

Stunned, I could only stare at her, unable to find any words.

"I knew you were struggling," she said, her voice softer than I had ever heard it, filled with deep sincerity. "I didn't know what you were facing at home, but I could see the weight you carried. I was so worried you might become disheartened and quit the program, but you have so much to give to this profession." She paused, her eyes searching mine. "That's why I adopted the strategy of keeping you on edge these past two years. I wanted to make sure you stayed strong, even when it felt impossible. If I coddled you, you would have crumbled."

Her words hit me like a wave and tears welled in my eyes as I realized just how much her tough love had shaped me. In that moment, all the challenges and fears faded, replaced by a deep sense of gratitude.

I pulled her into my arms and hugged her. "Thank you for believing in me when I needed it most." My voice was thick with emotion. "I will never forget you, Mrs. Cooke."

She smiled. I saw warmth in her eyes. "And I'll never forget you, Candy."

* * *

One afternoon during an especially tough stretch of the semester, feeling trapped and out of control, I impulsively asked my neighbor for her car keys and took off for a ride. With no destination in mind, I drove aimlessly, my thoughts swirling. I was angry, sad, overwhelmed, and scared. The exhaustion of juggling school, exams, clinicals, and life had pushed me to my breaking point. I felt like a prisoner of my circumstances, with no control over anything.

At the red light, I turned on the blinker to make a right-hand turn. Suddenly, I couldn't move. I stopped the car and stared at the blinking light, something clicking in my mind. *Oh my God, I can make this decision. I can independently decide whether or not to make this turn.*

It hit me like a bolt of lightning: *This is my decision. My choice. My control.* For the first time in my life, I felt the weight of that realization. This small, seemingly insignificant moment of control felt monumental. It was a turning point, one that shifted my mindset and gave me the strength to take ownership of my life.

* * *

At the end of our first year, we were given a one-half black stripe to place on the right wing of our nursing cap, a proud symbol of completing our first year of nursing school. It was about then that the phone rang unexpectedly.

"Hello, beautiful, it's Richard. How are you?"

My heart sank. "How did you get this number?" I asked sharply, gripping the receiver.

"It's not important how I got this number," he replied, his tone casual, almost disarming. "I'm so glad to hear your voice."

I wasn't sure how Richard had tracked me down, but in a small town like Titusville everyone pretty much knew everyone else's business.

"What do you want?" I asked, my voice firm but strained.

"I don't want anything," he said. "I just wanted to let you know I've stopped drinking and I've been going to AA meetings for a couple months now."

I paused, unsure how to respond. "I'm happy for you."

There was a moment of silence before he added, "I'm going to let you go, but I'd like to call you from time to time."

I didn't reply. I hung up the phone and quickly sat down on the edge of the sofa to keep from falling on the floor.

I couldn't breathe. My chest felt tight, and my heart was pounding so hard it felt like it might break through my ribcage. I pressed my hands to my chest, willing myself to calm down.

Breathe, Candy, take a breath, you need to breathe.

I remembered how, in the beginning, he held me so tight and told me how beautiful I was and that he couldn't live without me.

How I used to feel safe with him.

Wait a minute—I never felt totally safe with him.

How we danced the first night we met and how intoxicating it all felt.

Maybe we have a chance. I want this to be real. Once I finish school, I'll be making money, and this will help keep him from drinking for good.

The happy moments kept surfacing, giving me a strange, fleeting sense of comfort.

Candy, stop thinking like this. He hit you, he hurt you, he left you. STOP!

* * *

Richard continued calling me a couple times a week. He didn't have a lot to say and would talk mostly about his work at the new tire store. He wasn't too happy about not being the manager anymore, but he was happy he was making some decent money.

"I'm going to AA meetings every day," he said during one call. "I committed to ninety days of meetings."

"That sounds like a good thing," I said, keeping my tone neutral.

"Yeah, I have an AA sponsor and he says this is the way to stay sober."

"What's an AA sponsor?" I asked, more out of politeness than curiosity.

"He's someone who helps support me and makes me accountable. He also helps me with the twelve-step program. This will help me stay sober."

I didn't bother asking what the twelve-step program was because I really didn't give a shit. I had too many other things to worry about.

Out of nowhere, he said, "I have a surprise for you. Can you meet me in an hour?"

"What? What kind of a surprise?"

"Just meet me in an hour in the mall parking lot. You'll like it, I promise."

I hesitated, then said, "Okay, the boys are in school right now, so I'll be there."

Setting my study notes aside, I grabbed the keys to the motorcycle and headed out.

As I pulled into the parking lot, I saw Richard sitting in a gray car that had clearly seen better days.

"Here's your surprise! I bought you a car," he said, stepping out of the car with a proud smile.

I stared at the car, unsure how to feel. "Okay. Well, thank you."

"It's not much, but at least you won't have to ride that motorcycle in the rain anymore."

"I really appreciate your help." I took the keys from him.

Richard had not raised his voice or his hand to me since we reconnected. While he was being supportive and his monetary gifts were helping me achieve my goal of finishing school, I couldn't help but notice how little he asked about the boys. It concerned me but I didn't dwell on it too much. My focus was on finishing school.

Of course, I knew Sue would ask me where I got this gray monster of a car, and I'd have to tell her.

The boys quickly came up with a name for the car: The Gray Ghost. Every time we drove over a bump, the trunk would fly open, and when we hit another bump, it would magically close again.

Ben sighed in frustration. "Mom, this is embarrassing. I think you need to tie it closed with a rope."

"I think it's funny," Jason squealed.

"All right, I'll find some rope and tie it closed when we get home," I said, smiling at their reaction.

I did my best to tie the trunk down with rope, but after a few bumps, the rope would inevitably break, and the whole cycle would start over.

* * *

Toward the end of my third semester, Sue had moved out of the apartment. She'd been seeing someone, and while I was happy for her, it was hard to watch her go. We'd shared so many good times together, and now it felt like my support system had vanished.

This also left me with paying one hundred percent of the living expenses and the reality hit hard.

It's impossible for you to continue like this. You're going to have to make some extremely difficult decisions and do it NOW!

Two choices loomed in front of me.

Quit school, get a full-time job, and give up my dream. Or find another way to care for the boys, keep a roof over our heads, and power through the last damn ninety days of school.

I was so angry, angrier than I'd been in a long time. I was pissed off! Why was I the one shouldering all this responsibility? *By myself!* It took two people to bring a child into this world, yet here I was carrying both boys all alone.

Scott, you've been skating along, doing your thing child-free for nine years now! You've paid ONE child support payment and have nothing to do with your son! It's time for you to put on your big-boy pants!

Fueled with anger, I sat up, wiped my face, and found Scott's phone number. Straightening my spine to give me confidence, I dialed his number. To my surprise, he answered.

"Scott, this is Candy. I need to talk to you about our son."

"What is this about?" he replied cautiously.

"I'm in my last semester of nursing school."

"Wow, I just finished nursing school," he said casually. His words felt like a slap in the face, igniting my anger even more. I was sure he wasn't struggling anything like I was. No juggling kids, no sleepless nights, no constant financial worries.

I forced myself to stay calm. "I'm exhausted. I'm trying to care for our son along with his brother, working, going to school full-time, keeping up with the daily expenses. I'm not going to make it if I don't get some help. Could you please take Ben for the next three months so I can finish school?"

Dead silence.

I wasn't hanging up. I gripped the phone tighter, determined to hold him accountable. I could hear his heavy breathing on the other end of the line, and for a moment, I thought he might hang up.

"I need to talk it over with my girlfriend," he finally said, his voice calm, almost nonchalant. "Can you hold on a minute?"

What the fuck! You must talk it over with your girlfriend? This is YOUR son, that you haven't seen in nine years! And no one in your damn family has had anything to do with their first-born grandchild, either!

"Okay, I'll wait," I replied, keeping my voice steady despite the rage boiling inside me.

Please, please, say yes!

Minutes passed, each second stretching endlessly, until he finally came back on the line.

"Yes, we can take care of him for three months while you finish school."

Relief and sadness hit me all at once. "Thank you so much. I really appreciate your help." My voice broke slightly. "I need you to make his flight arrangements because I don't have the money. He'll need to fly to Michigan within the next couple of weeks for you to get him registered before school starts up there."

I hung up the phone and burst into tears.

Even though I was proud of myself for standing up to Scott, the reality of what I'd just done crushed me. I had no choice but to send Ben away, but the decision was almost unbearable.

Where to send Jason for three months was more complicated. I certainly couldn't send him to stay with his so-called rehabilitated alcoholic father. My alcoholic mother was too unstable and even if she were in a better place, her selfishness made her unwilling to help. My siblings were out of the question as well. That left only one person who was somewhat stable: my father.

Living in Michigan with a mail-order bride from Mexico, he seemed to have mellowed under her influence. We didn't talk much, and when we did, he never asked about my life or my struggles in nursing school. Still, I wondered, would Jason be safe there? I hadn't been safe when I lived with my father. But his wife seemed kind and since marrying her, he seemed more in control of his temper.

You have no other choice. Make the call.

"Hi, Dad, it's Candy."

"Hi, hold on while I get May on the phone."

He would never speak to me unless his wife was listening, and I never understood this behavior.

"Hi, Candy," she said in her Spanish accent.

"Now we can talk," Dad said. "What's going on, Candy?"

"I'm going into my last semester, and it's been hard. I'm exhausted! Trying to keep up with my studies, taking care of the boys, financially it's been hard, too." My voice trembled. "I'm wondering if it would be possible for Jason to come and stay with you guys for three months while I finish school? This is so hard for me to ask, but I'm not going to finish if I can't get some help. Scott has agreed to take Ben for the next three months."

Dad hesitated. "Um, well, May and I will need to talk this over and get back to you with our answer. We'll need to check on schools and everything. This is short notice, you know."

May stayed silent, the pause on the other end of the line feeling heavier than it should.

"Okay, I really appreciate you at least considering this," I replied, swallowing the lump in my throat. I quickly ended the call, unable to linger in the awkwardness any longer.

I sat staring at the phone. *I don't have a backup plan. What am I going to do if they say no?*

* * *

My father did eventually agree to watch Ben until I finished school, and a week later, I took both boys to the airport. Because they were children, I was allowed to walk them onto the plane, help them get to their assigned seats, and make sure their seat belts were fastened.

The day I put my boys on that plane to Michigan was the day I truly understood what it meant to have a broken heart. Kneeling in front of Jason, I took his face in my hands, staring into his eyes as if I could pour all my love into him in that moment.

"I love you so much and I will see you soon. You're going to have a great time."

His eyes filled with tears. Then, without a word, he threw his arms around me in a hug so tight it felt like he was trying to hold us together.

"I love you, Mom."

"I love you, too, my son." My voice cracked as I held him close, willing myself not to cry.

As I stepped back and looked at Ben, I saw his quiet strength. He avoided eye contact, keeping his emotions buried deep. I hugged him tightly, too, whispering how much I loved him and promising we'd talk every day. He stared back at me as if to say, "I'll be okay, Mom."

I walked off the plane and turned to wave one last time, the sight of their faces burned into my heart.

Each step felt like my shoes were glued to the floor, heavy and unyielding. I could barely breathe. Every fiber of my being screamed I was the worst mother in the world, abandoning my children like this.

As I walked off the jet bridge into the terminal, the familiar hum of the airport noise faded into a dull roar in my ears. My vision blurred, and the room started to spin. I stumbled into the nearest seat, gripping the armrests as if they were the only things holding me together.

CHAPTER 16

I'm Going to Kill You

Several students had dropped out of the program, unable to withstand the unrelenting pressure. Some struggled with poor grades, others couldn't keep up with the intense pace of the coursework, and a few were forced to leave due to personal or family matters. By the beginning of the final semester, fewer than half of the original students remained.

Somehow Richard always sensed my vulnerability, circling back into my life at the worst times, leaving me constantly battling to protect my peace. He continued calling on a weekly basis, carefully weaving himself back into my life with a mix of kindness and contrition. He'd been giving me money so I didn't have to work as much, which was a relief. He seemed sympathetic, saying all the right things. I was vulnerable, desperate to be loved.

"You are such a wonderful, beautiful woman. I'm so proud of you and what you've accomplished," he told me one day, his flattery making me momentarily forget his past transgressions. "I just wanted to tell you I've almost completed my AA commitment of ninety days and ninety meetings. I'm so sorry for what I have done in the past. I didn't mean to hurt you; it was the alcohol, not me."

His words hung in the air, teetering between sincerity and manipulation.

"I'm glad to hear your meetings are going well," I said. "But I can't talk, I've got to finish studying for my final."

"I'll call you later then. But please think about letting me come back? I promise everything will be different this time."

"I'll think about it," I replied, shutting down the call but not the internal conflict.

As I sat with my notes, his words lingered. *Maybe he's serious this time.*

But another, sharper voice quickly cut in: *He hurt you! You need to study!* I forced my focus back onto my books.

I'd been sitting on the damn living room sofa for hours, scribbling furiously on my yellow legal pad, writing the same content over and over, committing it to memory for my final exam. My hand ached, but I didn't stop; I couldn't stop.

Suddenly, a noise broke my concentration. Annoyed, I pushed my books and yellow pad to the side and walked over to the large living room window. It was a beautiful sunny day, the kind of day that begged for joy and freedom. I watched as children played in the street, giggling and chasing each other. Their laughter was like a gut punch.

My boys used to play like this. The thought came unbidden, sharp and painful. *I'm so angry!* But I forced myself to return to studying.

The next morning, walking into the classroom for the final exam, I slid into my usual seat, feeling nothing, not fear, not determination, just a dull numbness. The clinical instructor began handing out the test pamphlets. I was angry at everything: at the program, at Richard, at myself.

I just want this to be done! I thought, staring at the test in front of me. *Whatever grade I get, I've done my best. I have nothing left to give.*

I worked my way through the questions mechanically, my mind flickering between focus and exhaustion. Finally, I finished. I walked to the instructor's desk and placed my test on top of the growing pile. Without a word, I left the room, stepping into the hallway to wait for my grade.

Snippets of conversation floated behind me as students debated answers.

"What did you put for question number five?"

"Oh, that was easy, I chose B."

"I wasn't sure because it could have been A, so I chose A."

I rolled my eyes, gritting my teeth. *Oh, for the love of everything holy, here we fucking go again!*

After a few hours, the clinical instructor made her final walk to the corkboard outside the classroom and posted the grades.

My heart was pounding as I rushed to the board, pushing through the crowd of anxious students. My eyes darted frantically, scanning the list for my name. Then...I saw it!

I got a B!

The relief hit me like a wave, followed by an overwhelming rush of joy. I turned and headed toward the big glass doors at the front of the building. Pushing them open, I stepped outside, feeling the weight of months of self-doubt lift from my shoulders. I smiled, a huge, uncontrollable smile. I reached the Gray Ghost, climbed inside, and let out a scream that echoed through the parking lot.

"Holy shit! I got a B on the final! I've graduated from nursing school!"

Against all odds, against the voices in my head that told me for years *you're too stupid to be a nurse*, against limited financial and emotional support, I had done it. Through sheer determination, countless prayers, and a reservoir of hope I didn't know I had, I broke through the barriers and defied every expectation.

I proudly wore my cap and gown for my graduation—the first time I had ever had a graduation ceremony. My father wasn't there but my sons were and so were Aunt Gen and Uncle Willis.

I was the first in my family to obtain a college degree.

* * *

Coming down off the high of my graduation ceremonies, I knew it was time to buckle down and study for the Florida State Boards examination. The nursing board examination is a standardized test graduate nurses must pass to obtain their registered nurse's licensure to practice.

Richard had promised not to cause problems at my graduation, so I had let him come, and he had kept his promise. Since then, he'd been coming around more often, begging me to give him another chance.

"Look, I found a house for us to rent," he blurted out one afternoon, his voice filled with excitement.

"Richard, I'm not sure how long I'll be here. Once I take my boards, I hope to move to Tampa."

"I know," he said. "But you still have to wait a few months to take your boards before we leave for Tampa, right? So, I found us a house to rent until you take the boards. The lease is up here at the apartment."

"I know, but—"

"No, no buts," he interrupted. "I've changed. You've seen how I've changed. I'm a different man. I'm not drinking. I'm going to my AA meetings. After your boards we'll move to Tampa. I've already been looking for jobs there. It's going to be different now. A new beginning for us, now that you've finished school. Look at me, just look at me, see how different I am."

I looked at him, searching for the man he was promising to be. "Yes, I do see how different you are. I'm scared. I can't be hurt again."

His eyes softened as he stepped closer, his voice pleading. "I give you my word, I will never hit you again. I never wanted to hurt you. It was the alcohol. It wasn't me."

Maybe this time will be different, I told myself. *He's not drinking. I'll be working and helping financially.*

My heart desperately wanted to believe it. I wanted my marriage to work. I wanted to feel loved. I hoped Richard would love me the way he had in the beginning. *This time, I won't be a burden,* my heart reasoned. *I can contribute financially, and maybe that will ease his stress.*

But my head screamed: *Don't do it!*

Despite the warning signs, my heart won. A few weeks later, we moved into a small house in Titusville. It was a modest but charming two-bedroom, one-bath home in a quiet older neighborhood with mostly older couples without children.

Richard continued to work at the same tire store as he had while I was in college. The boys, who had returned home in time for my graduation, were out of school for the summer and the house was constantly buzzing with their energy. Meanwhile I spent hours every day studying for my boards.

I never knew when or if Richard would disappear, leaving me

alone to manage everything. Afraid of not having enough food to feed the boys, I planted a small vegetable garden along the fence in the backyard.

The boys and I also picked tomatoes, green beans, and potatoes at local farms. We spent days canning jars of food, lining them up neatly in the hall closet for storage. It gave me a small sense of security, knowing we had food no matter what happened.

Not long after moving into the rental house, my stomach began hurting. I couldn't shake the nagging feeling that Richard wouldn't come home from work one night and would be out drinking. He hadn't touched alcohol since we moved in, but my fear clung to me, making it hard to concentrate on studying for my exam.

One evening while making dinner for the boys, I looked up at the clock. It was six o'clock, and Richard still wasn't home.

"Boys, it's time for dinner," I called and they came running.

"Mom, aren't you having any dinner?" Ben asked, his concern clear in his voice as he watched me set the table.

"No, I'm not really hungry right now. You guys go ahead and eat. I'm going to keep studying for my test."

The truth was, even if I wanted to eat, I couldn't. The pain and nausea, a constant reminder of my fear and anxiety, made food impossible to swallow and keep down.

After the boys were settled, I tried to focus on my studying, but it was no use. My thoughts were consumed by the growing realization that Richard might not be coming home. Feelings of abandonment and fear pressed down on me like a weight I couldn't shake.

Not again, please, God, not again!

He never came home that night, or the following night. On the third night I sat at the dining room table, studying. Richard's absence brought a conflicted mix of relief and anxiety. Part of me was glad for the quiet, but the fear of what his disappearance could mean gnawed at me.

The boys were in their beds fast asleep, giving me a sense of stillness as I read through the pages of my study guide. My eyes started to become heavy, so I decided to call it a night and get ready for bed.

After finishing my normal nightly routine, I climbed into bed, giving a sigh as I laid my head on my pillow. The quiet in the house seemed eerie now, and the ache in my stomach refused to subside.

A loud screeching of tires just outside my bedroom window jolted me awake. Startled, I got out of bed and peered through the curtains, but the darkness concealed the source of the noise.

Please don't let it be him.

Climbing back into bed, I lay there staring at the ceiling, my senses on high alert. Then a car door slammed loudly, breaking the stillness, followed by the heavy, uneven sound of footsteps approaching the door.

I knew there was no mistaking it. Richard was home.

I heard him fumbling with the door, his frustration building as he struggled to fit the key into the lock.

Just pretend you're asleep. Willing my body to stay still. *He'll leave you alone.*

The front door flew open so hard it slammed against the wall, reverberating through the house. His footsteps were loud and deliberate, each one closer than the last. I could hear his labored breathing as he approached the bedroom.

Lying still, I cracked my left eye open slightly, enough to see him standing over me, his face contorted with absolute rage, his jaw clenched, his chest heaving with heavy, rapid breaths. In an instant, his right arm shot up behind his head, his hand balled into a tight fist, and with all his force, he brought it down, punching me squarely in the stomach.

"You fucking cunt!" he screamed. "You're a worthless piece of shit."

The impact knocked the air out of me. My body doubled over as I tried to sit up, gasping for breath. Before I could recover, his fist connected with me again, this time harder, more deliberate.

"You're nothing but a fucking cunt!"

"Richard, stop, please stop!" I screamed, my voice raw with fear and pain. Another punch landed squarely on my back, sending a shock wave through my body.

He leaned in closer, his voice now cold and menacing. "You better not ever try to leave me. I will fucking find you and kill you and your fucking family! I'm the only one who could love your ugly ass."

Tears streamed down my face as I begged, "Richard, stop hitting me, please."

After delivering one final blow, he turned and stumbled out of the bedroom. His body swayed as he staggered down the hallway, hitting the walls on either side. The sound of his footsteps grew distant until I heard the thud of his body collapsing onto the sofa. The house fell silent except for his heavy snores as he passed out in a drunken stupor.

Intense fury came over me. Anger and disgust I couldn't control overwhelmed me. Holding my stomach, I got out of bed, walked to the living room, and stood over him, my body trembling.

I hate you! You're a disgusting piece of garbage!

The words screamed inside my head, echoing louder with each passing second.

The only way to get rid of you permanently is to kill you!

The thought was sudden and absolute. My legs carried me to the kitchen almost involuntarily, and I began digging through the cabinets, searching for something, anything, that I could use to end this nightmare once and for all.

Then I saw the iron skillet.

I know this will kill him!

I picked up the skillet, its weight heavy in my hands, and walked to the sofa. Standing over him, I stared down at this vile, disgusting piece of garbage who had made my life a living hell. My chest heaved with every breath, my body shaking with fear, pain, and rage. Raising the skillet over my right shoulder, I held it high, the muscles in my arm straining under its weight. My mind raced with the primal urge for revenge.

Kill him! Kill him! Go ahead, kill him now!

I contemplated exactly where to strike his head. My mind raced through everything I'd learned in anatomy class, pinpointing the spot on his head that would kill him instantly. I had to make sure that when I hit him, it would be final. He wouldn't have the chance to get back up and come after me.

The voice in my head grew louder, more insistent.

Just swing the damn skillet and kill him. Do it! Do it now! Swing the skillet now!

Then out of nowhere, another voice, a calm, quiet woman, interrupted my thoughts. It startled me, cutting through the noise in my head.

Who's going to care for the boys?

There is no one who will care for them.

You will go to prison.

You don't have one family member who would take them and raise them.

The police won't help you. The pastor won't help you. The church won't help you.

Those words echoed in my mind, their finality wrapping around me like chains I couldn't break. My grip on the skillet faltered, my resolve crumbling under the weight of helplessness. Shaking, I placed it back in the cabinet, my actions mechanical and detached. The air felt thick, oppressive, as I walked back to the bed, the same bed where I lay as his rage left its mark on my body and soul. I got in the bed, staring into the darkness, my mind racing. Sleep never came, only the suffocating realization that I was trapped, not just by Richard's cruelty but by a system and a world that turned its back. Fear, pain, and hopelessness seeped into every corner of my being, whispering that freedom was a dream far beyond my reach.

The next morning, he was so hungover that his apologies came slurred and unsteady. "I'm so sorry," he said in a soft tone, clutching his head. "This will never happen again."

His words had a familiar ring, a hollow promise I'd heard too many times before. "Please don't leave me," he pleaded. "If you leave me, I will find you."

But this time, he added something new, a fresh weapon in his manipulative arsenal. "I will kill myself if you leave me. I will do it."

His words hit me like a punch to the chest. As a registered nurse, I knew the weight of those words. Threats of suicide couldn't be ignored; they had to be reported. If I left and he followed through, if someone found him dead, it would be my fault. I was afraid I could lose my nursing license, my career, everything I had worked so hard for. The irony of his manipulation wasn't lost on me. This new tactic, as cruel as it was calculated, left me trapped in yet another way.

CHAPTER 17

The Blue Convertible

Shortly after graduation, I applied for a job at a hospital in Tampa that specialized in the care of women and newborns. This area of medicine intrigued me deeply. To my delight, they agreed to hire me as a graduate nurse, contingent upon providing proof of having taken the boards. Once I provided that proof—even before I knew if I had passed—I was allowed to start working.

I was thrilled about my new nursing job, and the move to Tampa represented a fresh start for us, offering stability and reduced stress. I would be working and contributing to our finances, easing the pressure on Richard and, I hoped, diminishing his urge to drink.

On May 20, 1978, I worked my first shift, three p.m. to eleven-thirty p.m. I was assigned to the Neonatal Intensive Care Unit, also known as NICU, a highly specialized area where sick or premature babies were closely monitored by a specialized team of physicians, nurses, and ancillary staff. Some babies only stayed a few days while others stayed for months. Tragically, some never went home with their parents. This was, and is, a highly stressful environment for parents and the entire medical team.

For the first several weeks, I was paired with a preceptor (an instructor) named Angel, who truly lived up to her name. As a highly skilled registered nurse, she was the one every parent trusted to care for their precious infant.

Angel guided me through every treatment, procedure, and protocol, and taught me how to provide comfort to anxious parents. She was my lifeline during this critical time, and I hung on her every word.

After a long shift, I said, "Angel, after work tonight, let's go to the restaurant next door, I want to buy you breakfast."

"Oh, thank you, but I can't."

"Why not? Do you have to rush home for something?"

"No, I just can't go."

"Oh, come on, please? You've help me so much and I love spending time with you."

After a few moments of hesitation, Angel walked over to me. With her right hand, she touched her own forearm, then gently touched mine.

"What is this supposed to mean?" I asked. "I don't understand."

Her voice was soft, almost a whisper. "Because your skin color is different than mine."

I stared at her, stunned. "What? Are you ashamed to be seen with me?"

"No, of course not," she said, her voice still low. "But some people in the restaurant don't want to see a black woman and a white woman sitting together."

"Are you kidding me?" I said, my voice rising. "What the hell! I don't care what they think! Let them think anything they want to. I'm taking you to breakfast and that's all there is to it."

We went to breakfast that night and had a great time together. For two hours, we joked, reminisced, and bonded like lifelong friends. Months later, I had the incredible honor of being invited to Angel's wedding, a beautiful and joyous celebration of love.

Angel was there for me during some of the most challenging moments I faced in the NICU. When one of my first babies passed away, and I found myself comforting heartbroken parents, Angel knew exactly what to do. She quietly came over and wrapped me in a comforting hug and gently said, "You did your best; we can't save them all."

I have never forgotten Angel, her kindness, her wisdom, and her unwavering support.

She truly was my Angel.

* * *

I had just received my first paycheck from the hospital. For working 39.10 hours, my check after taxes was one hundred and sixty-nine dollars and thirty-four cents. I was rich!

I thought, anyway.

With my newfound fortune, I decided it was time for me to give myself a graduation present: a new car.

When I arrived at the dealership, I was greeted by a friendly salesman. "Hi, my name is Josh, can I help you find a car?"

"Yes, I'm looking for a blue convertible Mustang and it has to be brand new," I replied, my voice brimming with excitement.

Josh's face lit up. "I'll show you what I've got in stock. How about this beauty?"

It was exactly what I was looking for, a brand-new, light-blue, convertible Mustang.

"I want that car!" I exclaimed, unable to contain my excitement.

"This is the price tag on the car," Josh said with a grin. "Will you be financing it?"

"Yes," I replied quickly. "But I don't have any credit established. I just graduated from nursing school and I'm working at the hospital now."

He nodded reassuringly. "Oh, that shouldn't be a problem, since you're a nurse."

For the first time in my life, I felt a sense of importance. Unlike my college years, where I often had to beg or struggle to prove my worth, having a nursing degree seemed to open doors for me. I wasn't seen as a risk, I was seen as someone reliable, someone valuable. It was an empowering feeling.

"Have a seat and we'll start the paperwork so you can get out of here with your new car," Josh continued. "It may take a couple of days to process the financial paperwork, but I don't see a problem, since you're not high risk. Did you happen to bring a pay stub with you?"

"Yes, here it is." I handed it over.

"Great. I'll get working on this and give you a call tomorrow."

As I walked out of the dealership, it hit me. *WOW, I'm getting a new car!*

At the time, I had no idea you could negotiate the price when buying a car, but honestly, it didn't matter. I was so proud of myself for taking this step.

Once I was approved and all the documents were signed, it was time to tell Richard. I knew it wouldn't be an easy conversation, but I was determined not to let anything dampen my excitement.

That evening, Richard came home in a surprisingly decent mood, so I decided it was as good a time as any to break the news.

"Richard, I bought myself a graduation present," I said. He hadn't bought me anything for my graduation and this was my subtle way of reminding him. I waited anxiously for his response, maybe an acknowledgment of the milestone that I had reached.

Instead, he replied, "Oh, that's good."

I stared at him, waiting for more. Nothing. That was it, no congratulations, no questions about what I bought, no excitement. Just those three dismissive words.

"That's it?" I asked, my voice tight with frustration. "You don't want to know what I got?"

Richard sighed and finally looked up from whatever he was fiddling with. "Okay, what did you get?"

"I bought a brand-new convertible Mustang," I said, my excitement bubbling over.

His eyebrows shot up. "A Mustang? How much did that cost?"

"It doesn't matter how much it cost, Richard," I snapped. "I've been working hard, and I deserve it. It's my money, and I wanted to buy it."

Richard shrugged. "Okay, if that's what you want."

His response annoyed me, but I decided I wasn't going to let it bother me. I worked hard and deserved to celebrate my new car, whether Richard cared or not. This was my moment, and I wasn't about to let him take that away from me.

* * *

It had been seven weeks since I'd taken the boards. The house was quiet, too quiet. The boys were outside riding their bikes and Richard was at work. I was alone with my thoughts, wondering when I would get my results.

The phone rang, breaking the silence. It was Diane, a classmate from nursing school.

"Candy, have you gotten your results yet? I got mine in the mail. I passed!"

"No, I haven't gotten mine. You got yours today?" I asked, my heart skipping a beat.

"Yes, so you should get yours either today or tomorrow. Listen, if the envelope is thin you passed, but if it's thick that means they're sending another application to retake the test."

"Oh, okay, my mail hasn't come yet," I said, my anxiety spiking. "I'll be watching for it. Thanks for letting me know."

After I hung up, I glanced at the clock. It was three o'clock. The mailman would be coming any minute. I moved to the living room window, wringing my hands, waiting.

Finally, the familiar sound of his truck echoed down the street.

There he is.

Please have my test results! Please, please, I silently begged.

I watched as he made his way up the street, stopping at every mailbox with what felt like excruciating slowness. Then, as if to torment me further, he seemed to take forever as he paused to make a U-turn to come down my side of the street. Of course, mine was the last mailbox on that side.

Why am I the last one on the street to get mail? For the love of everything holy! This is torture!

The moment he drove away, I rushed to the mailbox. My heart was pounding as I reached inside and pulled out the envelope.

It was thick. My breath caught in my throat. I ran back into the house and stood in the living room, frantically opening it.

I had passed every section of the test except the psychology exam—missing the passing grade by just two points. My stomach sank as I read the results.

God, why? Why didn't you let me pass? Why has this been so hard?

Now I had to wait forty-five days to retake the entire exam all over again, plus find a testing site that would offer it. My thoughts spiraled.

Am I going to lose my job? I just bought a car! What's going to happen?

When Richard got home that evening, I mustered up the courage to tell him the news.

"I didn't pass my boards," I said.

"You can take it again, right?" he said casually. "You'll pass it next time. Don't worry about it."

What the hell, Richard? His nonchalant attitude stung more than I expected.

"I can take it again," I snapped, trying to hold back tears. "But I have to wait forty-five days and then find a place that offers it. I'm heartbroken, Richard."

"Don't worry, you'll pass it next time," Richard said, planting a quick peck on the top of my head as he walked out of the kitchen.

I clenched my fists, frustration and fear rising to the surface. "I'm worried about my job. What if they let me go until I pass the exam? I won't be able to contribute to the household finances, either. I'm not even a real registered nurse until I pass that damn exam."

He paused for a moment, leaning on the doorway. "It will be fine. Even if they let you go, we'll make it work."

Yeah, until you get pissed off about not having my income and go out drinking, come home, and beat the crap out of me! I didn't say it aloud, but the words burned in my throat.

CHAPTER 18

Playing Dead

The next morning, I woke up with a sick feeling in the pit of my stomach. After getting the boys off to school, I sat down on the sofa with my cup of tea. *What am I going to say to my nursing supervisor? Will she let me keep my job until I can take the test again? I'm so embarrassed! All my coworkers are going to be asking me about my board results.*

I decided to go to work early so I would have plenty of time to speak with my supervisor. When I arrived, I stood outside Mrs. Allen's office for a moment, mustering the courage. Finally, leaning my head inside her office, I said, "Hello, Mrs. Allen, may I speak with you, please? I got my board results back."

"Sure, Candy, please come in," she said, looking up from her paperwork and gesturing for me to have a seat.

I sat down in the first chair I saw, afraid my legs were about to give out on me. The heat rose in my cheeks. "Mrs. Allen, I'm afraid I have some bad news," I said nervously. "I didn't pass. I passed all the sections except for one, psychology. I missed passing by just two points. I'm so upset about this. What's going to happen now? Can I continue to work?" I struggled to hold back my tears.

Mrs. Allen lowered her head and took a deep breath, her disappointment unspoken.

She's going to fire me! I just know it!

After what felt like an eternity, she finally raised her head and said, "I'm so sorry, Candy. But I have the authority per hospital policy to keep you working as a graduate nurse until you retake and pass your boards. You must pass the boards this time. If you do not pass, I will have no other choice but to let you go. During this time, you will remain at your current hourly wage, as a graduate nurse. If you pass next time your hourly rate will increase, reflecting your registered nurse status. Do you understand?"

I wanted to stand up and scream with excitement, but instead I politely said, "Yes, ma'am, I totally understand. Thank you so much for your support. I will pass next time; I just know it."

Leaving her office, I walked to the clock-in machine, took my timecard out, and clocked in.

Thank you, thank you, God, I still have a job!

Walking into the NICU, I immediately spotted Angel. "Angel, I didn't pass my boards," I said in a soft voice so no one else could hear. "But I just spoke to Mrs. Allen, and she said I can stay on as a graduate nurse. But I have to pass the next time. I'm so embarrassed."

Angel stopped what she was doing and met my gaze. "Why are you embarrassed? Half the nurses in here didn't pass the first time. Don't worry about it, you'll pass next time."

"Really, do you think half didn't pass?" I replied, surprised. "I'll bet you passed the first time!"

"Well, yes, I did pass the first time, but you know I'm different," she said with a deep belly laugh. Her laugh was contagious, and in that moment, it felt like everything was going to be okay.

* * *

Not long after moving to Tampa, after Richard had gotten a job managing a tire store, we were invited to one of his work parties. It was a casual outdoor barbeque about an hour's drive from Tampa. Since the boys were at a sleepover at a friend's house, Richard and I decided to go the day before for a little getaway and to spend the night in a motel.

On the way, we stopped at a small, cozy restaurant for dinner. Out of nowhere, Richard said, "I'm going to have a drink with my dinner."

I was shocked. "Richard, you said you weren't going to drink anymore. Why are you doing this?"

"I'm just going to have one drink. There's nothing wrong with that."

But one drink turned into two drinks. On the way to the motel, he abruptly pulled into a liquor store and came back with a bottle in hand. My heart sank.

When we arrived at the motel, the parking lot held just a few scattered cars parked under dim, flickering street lights. The check-in was quick and I noticed how bare and dated the place looked. Once inside our room, my uneasy feeling deepened. The furniture was old and battered. The air was heavy and stale, as if the room hadn't been properly cleaned or aired out in ages. Everything felt off, amplifying the tension already building.

I went into the bathroom to do my nightly routine. On the other side of the door, I could hear Richard sitting on the bed, TV blaring, drinking from the bottle he bought, muttering at first, then yelling at the screen. His voice grew louder and more agitated. The sound of his anger echoed in the tiny, confined space. My stomach churned.

"What are you doing in that bathroom so long?" he yelled, startling me.

"I'm getting ready to go to bed."

"Bitch, get out of there," he snapped. "We're supposed to be spending time together."

I gripped the bathroom sink, my heart pounding. *I'm locked in a small hotel room with this drunk. Please let him pass out!*

"Bitch, I told you to get out here," he yelled, his voice rising to a roar. My chest tightened as I heard his heavy footsteps stomping across the thin carpet, each step coming closer to the bathroom.

I have no place to hide!

Panicked, I opened the bathroom door, forcing myself to face him, hoping to calm him down. "Richard, I'm right here. See, I'm right here," I said with a soft voice.

But it was too late. His rage had already consumed him. Without warning, he reached out and grabbed a fistful of my hair. I yelped in pain as he dragged me out of the bathroom. With one violent motion, he hurled me against the wall. My body crumpled on impact, landing hard on my right hip. My legs folded awkwardly beneath me as I instinctively covered my head with my arms, bracing for what might come next.

"Richard, stop! Please stop!" I cried. "I'm right here. I want to spend some time with you, too." My desperate plea hung in the air while his anger raged on.

"You fucking cunt! You don't want to spend any time with me, you're too busy with your fucking nursing job!" he yelled, his voice thunderous with venom. Each word was punctuated by the sickening thud of his foot slamming into my body.

"Richard, please stop, you're hurting me!" I screamed, my voice crackling under the weight of panic and pain. I tried to get up off the floor, but my legs buckled beneath me. I dropped back down and began crawling on my hands and knees, desperate to get away.

His kicks came relentlessly, first with his right foot, then his left. Over and over again, they landed on my ribs, my back, my legs. *Crawl, keep crawling,* I told myself, biting back the tears. *Get between the beds. There's less space between the beds and he won't be able to kick as hard.*

I can't survive much more.

I have to survive. I'm not going to die on this disgusting carpet.

The filthy, coarse fibers of the carpet scratched against my palms and knees as I dragged myself forward, the smell of stale beer and mustiness stinging my nose. My body ached, my mind screamed for it to end.

Maybe he'll stop kicking me. Maybe this is the last one. Then another kick landed, sending a jolt of agony through my side. *It'll stop after this kick.* I kept my hands pressed tightly over my head, my arms shielding my temples and eyes, praying the blows wouldn't break me completely.

"You fucking cunt! No one could love your ugly ass. You're so fucking ugly. I think I'm going to kill you tonight. How about that? How would you like to die tonight? You'll never see your fucking kids again," he snarled, followed by a cold snicker. "Yeah, I think it's a good idea if I kill you!"

"Richard, please stop, please stop!" I screamed.

Can't anyone at this motel hear me screaming?

He yanked me up by my hair to a standing position, the pain searing through me. Before I could even process the agony, his right fist slammed into my ribcage with a force that echoed through my body. The crack was undeniable, my ribs giving way under the assault. Gasping for air, I collapsed onto the floor between the double beds, each breath jagged and excruciating.

"Richard, you broke my ribs! I can't breathe. Stop!" I managed to scream through the torment.

His response was hateful words and threats, each one cutting as deeply as his fists. "You fucking whore! You fucking cunt! I want to kill you! You worthless piece of shit! You're so fucking ugly and you're stupid, you're fucking stupid!"

My mind raced through the haze of pain and fear, survival instinct taking over as I curled back into a fetal position between the beds.

I need to play dead, NOW! He'll kill me! Play dead! If he thinks I'm dead the beating will stop.

He was in a full rage, continuing to kick me. "Are you fucking dead yet? Bitch, are you dead?"

Play dead! Don't move!

The kicking suddenly stopped, leaving an eerie, deafening silence. My body screamed with pain, but I didn't dare move. Fear rooted me to the floor as I strained to hear anything, his breathing, footsteps, or even the rustle of fabric. Nothing. Minutes felt like hours as I lay there, motionless, my chest searing with sharp stabbing pain every time I tried to draw even the shallowest breath. Slowly, I cracked my eyes open, scanning the room as best I could without lifting my head. Every nerve in my body was on high alert. Was he gone? Would he come back? I fought to stay calm, forcing my mind to answer the simplest question.

Am I alive?

Easing myself up to a sitting position, clutching my right side, I looked around the room with cautious eyes. Richard lay sprawled on his back on one of the beds, mouth wide open. He had passed out.

Relief mixed with rage coursed through me. My body ached with every small movement.

How could you do this to me?

The urge to call the police surged, but fear was quick to smother it. I couldn't call the police. I remembered what happened the last time. Richard told them I was crazy and threatened to take my children away.

You have to get off this floor.

Something about lying there felt like surrender, and I couldn't bear it. Slowly, I reached for the edge of the mattress, gripping it with one hand while holding my side with the other. My breath came in shallow gasps as I dragged myself upright. Every inch of movement was agony, but I made it. Bent over, I hobbled toward the bathroom. Once inside, I flicked on the light and turned toward the mirror. The sight before me was horrifying. My entire body, from my neck down to my legs, was mottled with black-and-blue bruises, each one a testament to the brutality I had endured. Twisting slightly to see my right side sent a lightning bolt of pain through my chest.

You need to lie down before you pass out.

The room spun slightly; my vision began to darken. I gripped the sink for balance, my legs threatening to give out. Summoning what little strength I had, I shuffled back to the bed. Lowering myself carefully to the mattress, I perched on the edge, trying to control the waves of pain that radiated through my chest and side. I closed my eyes for a moment, desperate for relief, and Mrs. Cooke's calm voice from my training surfaced in my mind. *Support the injured ribs to minimize movement and decrease pain.*

Taking a slow agonizing breath, I shifted my right side onto the bed first, keeping my injured ribs as still as possible. Slowly, I inched my feet up onto the mattress, grimacing with pain. Every move was calculated, every adjustment unbearable.

Damn, I wish I had one of those stretchable elastic wraps she talked about, something to stabilize my ribs and apply gentle pressure.

I could almost hear her explaining how compression could reduce strain on the chest and make breathing easier. I let the thought linger for a moment, as I finally lay still, cradling my ribs and praying for the pain to subside.

You piece of garbage, Richard! My thoughts seethed with anger. *Why didn't anyone knock on the door? They had to have heard me screaming. Walls this thin couldn't have hidden it. Were they afraid? Indifferent? Or had they just decided it wasn't their problem?*

The bitterness of that realization stung almost as much as the physical pain. I shifted slightly, wincing as fire shot through my ribs.

The next morning Richard woke up with his usual hangover and predictable routine of half-hearted apologies and feeble excuses for what he'd done.

Sitting on the edge of the bed, cradling his head in his hands, he muttered, "I'm sorry about last night. I just got drunk. I know I shouldn't drink. I don't see any bruises on your face, though." His voice had the hollow tone of someone who believed they could excuse their actions with the right words.

"Richard, you broke my ribs!" I shot back. "The bruises may not be on my face but look what you did to me!" I pulled up my shirt just enough to expose the dark, mottled bruises covering my torso, a physical map of his violence. Even as the words left my mouth, I knew I had to tread carefully. I knew I could only push him so far before his remorse turned to rage again.

He glanced at my bruises briefly, then turned his gaze back to the floor. "I'm going to call AA and get back in the program. I need to get a sponsor in Tampa, just like I had in Titusville. I really didn't mean to hurt you, but you made me mad when you were spending so much time in the bathroom. If you wouldn't make me mad, I wouldn't hit you."

His words felt like a slap in the face, shifting the blame onto me, as if my actions had caused his violence. Biting my lip, I knew better than to respond. Saying too much or showing too much emotion could ignite his temper all over again.

It was a survival skill, honed from years of living in fear.

I need to figure out how to get out of this mess!

As if oblivious to the weight of his actions, or perhaps choosing to ignore it entirely, Richard broke his silence. "We can still go to the company picnic, right?"

I stared at him for a moment, dumbfounded by the audacity of his question. Did he really think a picnic could gloss over the bruises, the pain, the broken ribs?

"Okay, Richard," I replied, my voice flat and lifeless. I turned away from him, focusing on the monumental task of getting dressed, each movement a fresh wave of agony.

Somehow I'd get through today. I always did.

* * *

Over time, I learned how to navigate life with Richard, especially in the aftermath of a beating. I came to recognize a grim pattern. I had about forty-eight hours of relative safety after the physical violence. During this window, his rage would subside into a kind of guilt-ridden remorse. He still lashed out verbally, with sarcasm, demeaning comments, and endless put-downs, but those forty-eight hours brought a temporary reprieve from the terror of his fists. In those moments, I felt the faintest glimmer of control, a fleeting illusion that I could somehow manage him. But once that fragile period ended, the fear returned full force, hanging over me like a storm cloud. I lived in constant fear.

At the time, I believed the verbal abuse wasn't as damaging as the beatings. What I didn't understand was his words left scars far deeper than his fists ever could. His relentless cruelty, calling me worthless, stupid, and unlovable, shaped how I saw myself. Over the years, those words became my own inner voice, whispering doubt and self-hatred. I spent so much time chasing validation from others, desperate for someone to tell me I mattered. But the more I searched outside myself, the more elusive that worthiness became. No one's approval could ever fill the void his abuse had carved inside of me.

CHAPTER 19

Quiet Determination

Working at the hospital gave me a glimpse of something different, a side of society I had never experienced. Growing up in isolation, later trapped in Richard's prison, focused on college and survival, I had been shielded from what the real world could offer. Here, I saw fragments of a life I never imagined for myself.

I witnessed tender moments that seemed pulled from another universe. Mothers and fathers cradled their newborns with pure love, singing softly or gently rocking them in their arms. I saw fathers beaming with pride as they held their babies, soothing them with whispered words or changing a diaper with careful hands. There was a gentleness I had never known, a softness I craved without even realizing it.

Even coworkers seemed to exist in a world foreign to me. They joked and laughed, sharing stories about their families, their weekends, and their lives. Their conversations were open, inviting, and warm. Watching them was like peering into a world I had been locked out of. It was a sharp contrast to the cold, controlling, and violent life I knew.

I began to understand what was missing. *I want that. I want to be loved and happy!*

* * *

The time had come to travel back to Orlando to take the nursing boards again. For the last sixty days, I'd practically never been without my damn yellow legal pad, relentlessly studying every concept, every detail, determined to conquer the test that had previously defeated me. This time, though, I had a new tool in my arsenal. Angel had suggested hypnosis sessions to help quiet the relentless noise in my head and sharpen my focus. I was skeptical at first, but the sessions worked wonders. I felt calm, centered, and more prepared than ever.

Although my nerves were still present, the crushing anxiety from the first attempt had been replaced with a quiet determination. I could do this. *I would do this.*

Walking into the testing site, I handed my registration papers to the lady at the entrance desk. She handed me the first test portion and the list of the rules and regulations. I scanned the familiar space, the memory of my first attempt still vivid. Almost instinctively, I made my way to the same seat I had chosen before: first row, farthest seat from the entrance door. Sitting down, I smoothed the edges of the papers in front of me, taking slow, steady breaths to keep the anxiety from rising.

I didn't pay attention to other test-takers this time. I wasn't distracted by the rustling of papers, the creak of chairs, or the shuffling of feet. For the next two days, nothing and no one was going to rattle me. I was laser focused.

After the proctor announced the rules and regulations, the room fell silent, and I heard the words I'd been waiting for.

"You may open your first test now. You will have ninety minutes to complete this portion."

Here we go. Focus and concentrate.

Opening the test booklet was different this time. I felt different. I reminded myself to read each question slowly and to take my time, to ignore everything else in the room.

I completed each test well within the time limit. After finishing each section, I raised my hand, and a proctor promptly came over and took my test. Then I sat and waited for the timer to ring, signaling the end of the time limit for that portion of the exam. Then, a proctor handed me the next exam, and I started the process again.

On the second day of testing, I completed the last portion of the exam, handed my booklet to a proctor, and promptly exited the building, pushing the heavy glass door open and walking into the fresh air. Under the beautiful blue sky, I felt at peace. I had a good feeling that I'd passed.

Start the timer: six to eight weeks.

* * *

"The unit is really busy tonight," I said as I monitored the intravenous drip of my assigned neonate, whose vitals had been touch-and-go since the start of my shift.

"And I heard we've got a mother in labor and delivery right now," Angel replied, adjusting her patient's equipment. "She's in active labor and four weeks early. Neonatologist said she'll deliver tonight."

I let out a sigh, already feeling the weight of the night ahead. "It's going to be a crazy night."

"Candy, Candy, where are you?" a voice called out from across the unit. "You have a phone call."

"Put them on hold and I'll be right there," I yelled back, my focus still on stabilizing my patient.

Once satisfied that everything was set, I headed to the phone. "Hello, this is Candy, how can I help you?" I kept one eye on my baby's monitor.

The voice on the other end sent a chill down my spine. "Bitch, you better come to the parking lot right now or I'm going to destroy your car!"

Panic coursed through me. *Shit! It's Richard and he's drunk! Crap! Crap!*

Cupping my hand around the receiver to muffle my voice, I said, "Richard, I can't talk right now. I'm caring for a baby that's really sick. Where are you?"

"I don't give a fuck what you're doing," he screamed, his voice full of rage. "You better come to the parking lot *now*! I'm on the fucking pay phone outside of the hospital." His voice dropped into a menacing tone. "Do you hear your fucking kids crying right now?" Then, a loud cracking punctured his words. "I broke the turn signal off your car!"

The boys were screaming in the background. My mind raced. *Think! Think! He's destroying my new car! The boys are terrified!*

"Richard, please calm down," I begged, my voice a whisper as I tried not to draw attention. "Stop this, please. I can't leave the unit right now. Please, the boys are scared."

"Candy, do you want me to reposition your baby? She seems restless?" one of the nurses asked, her voice soft and filled with concern.

I shook my head. "No, thank you, she's been unstable, and I don't want her moved right now." I tried to sound composed even as my insides churned.

Richard's voice snarled through the phone, louder and more venomous. "Fuck yeah, they're upset, all you do is spend time at this fucking hospital." He gave a cruel laugh. "Listen, I'm breaking the mirror now." A loud crash followed. His laughter rang in my ears.

"Hold on, Richard," I said, forcing an even tone as panic clawed at my chest. "I'm going to see if I can find someone to watch my baby so I can come to the parking lot."

With trembling hands, I placed the call on hold and hung up the receiver. I turned to Angel. "Angel, I need to go to the parking lot to pick something up. Can you watch my baby for me?"

She frowned, glancing at her own monitor. "What? Now? I can't watch her. I've got my own problems keeping my baby stable. Go ask the charge nurse."

Desperation rising, I pivoted to the charge nurse. "Allie, I'm so sorry, but I need to run down to the parking lot and pick something up. Could you please keep an eye on my baby for five minutes?"

Allie hesitated, looking uncertain, but finally nodded. "Okay, but hurry up. We have a new admission arriving at any time and he's only thirty-six weeks."

"I promise I'll hurry right back," I assured her, grabbing the phone, still shaking. "Richard, are you still there?"

"Yeah, I'm here," he growled. "Are you coming, cunt?"

"I'm on my way now." I swallowed the fury and fear rising in my throat. I hung up and ran to the elevator.

This has got to end! I have to find a way to get away from him!

When the elevator doors opened, I rushed into the parking lot, my eyes immediately locking onto my Mustang. The sound of the boys crying hit me like a gut punch.

"Richard, what is wrong with you? Why are you here?" I asked, teetering between anger and desperation.

"Wrong with *me*?" he sneered, staggering closer. "You're asking what is wrong with me, bitch? You leave your children at home alone for days." He laughed. "Watch me break this mirror off!" he shouted, smiling as he yanked at the side mirror with brutal force.

"Boys, I'll be home soon, it's okay," I said, trying to comfort them while holding back tears of my own. "STOP IT NOW, Richard! I've got to get back to the NICU. Please take the boys home and put them to bed. I will be home as soon as I finish my shift."

Richard turned toward me, his face twisted with anger. "You better come straight home, BITCH!" he yelled before speeding off, tires screeching.

I stared after him, saying a desperate prayer. *God, please help the boys get home safe.* Watching that piece of drunken garbage drive off with *my* boys in his back seat, after damaging *my* car—the helplessness weighed down on me like a stone.

Alone in the elevator as I headed back to the NICU, I leaned against the cold metal wall, my head cradled in my hands. My mind spun, a whirlwind of fear, anger, and hopelessness.

I've got to get away from him! The thought pounded in my head like a drumbeat. *But I don't know how. I wish I knew someone who would understand. Who could possibly understand this mess? I don't understand it myself.*

The ding of the elevator snapped me back to reality.

I took a shaky breath, trying to steady the rising panic clawing at my chest. *Don't think about this now, you've got to get back to your baby!*

There was no time to fall apart. I had a job to do. That tiny life depended on me.

* * *

I arrived home about midnight, my body aching with exhaustion. Richard's car wasn't in the driveway, and the house was eerily quiet. I quickly ran to the boy's room. Pushing the door open gently, I found them both sleeping soundly. A wave of relief washed over me. At least they were safe.

The next morning, while making breakfast, I watched the boys as they sat at the table, eating their oatmeal.

"Boys, I need to talk to you," I said, setting down the spoon and leaning against the counter. "I have to work tonight and I'm not sure if your dad will be home." I tried to mask my worry. "So, I need for you guys to come straight home after school and call me when you get here. I want to know you got home okay." I glanced at their small, innocent faces, wishing they didn't have to carry this burden. "I'll have your dinner ready in the refrigerator. You'll just need to take it out and put it in the microwave to warm up."

Ben agreed immediately. "Okay, Mom." Jason followed with a quick nod of his head.

"That's my boys." I smiled faintly, ruffling their hair. A moment later, I called after them as they ran to the school bus, their backpacks bouncing on their shoulders: "I love you! Have a good day at school!"

I stood there for a moment, watching the bus drive off, and said quietly to myself, *Just get through tonight's shift. Then figure out what to do.*

I sat on the sofa, absently watching a mindless program on the television, but my mind was far from relaxed. Thoughts of escape churned in my head. *How am I going to get out of this marriage?*

He's threatened to kill me, kill himself, take the boys away, kill my family, how in the hell am I going to get out?

Suddenly I heard his car pulling into the driveway and that jolted me out of my thoughts. *Oh shit! He's home!*

Richard walked in the front door and stood just inside the doorway, disheveled and unsteady. His clothes were wrinkled and stained, his hair matted, and the stench of alcohol, sweat, and something sour hit me from across the room. He looked horrific.

"I'm so sorry, Candy," he mumbled, his voice cracking. Then shockingly, he started crying.

I sat there unmoved. *Well, this is another new one! What's his angle this time?* "Richard, I can't do this anymore."

"I know. I'm so sorry. I didn't mean to break your car." As the tears streamed down his face, he looked small, something I'd never seen in him before.

He's vulnerable right now. He's never vulnerable. It's time to tell him I want a divorce! Tell him now!

"Richard," I began, the words coming out sharper than I intended, but I didn't care. "You were driving drunk with the boys screaming in the back seat! What is wrong with you? NO! Don't answer that! You're a damn drunk is what you are!" My voice rose, filled with years of suppressed rage and frustration. "I can't, no, *won't* put up with your disgusting behavior anymore. It never changes. You start drinking, beat the hell out of me, scare the boys to death, and then go missing for days. I'm done, I want a divorce!"

"I know," he said quietly. To my shock, he nodded slowly. "Everything you're saying is right. I'm sorry." He paused, his gaze flickering to the floor. "I'm just going to get a few things and leave. Is that okay with you?"

I blinked, stunned by his response. *What has he done? He's never acted like this before. He hasn't raised his voice.*

Something else must be going on.

"Yes, that's fine," I said cautiously, my voice steady despite the turmoil inside me. I watched him walk to the primary bedroom, his shoulders hunched, his movements slow.

A few minutes later, he reappeared with a small bag. He hesitated at the front door, his hand resting on the doorknob. "I really do love you." The door shut.

Is this real? Is it over?

CHAPTER 20

A Woman in Uniform

It was a quiet Saturday afternoon. The boys were outside playing, their laughter drifting through the open windows. I sat alone, cradling a cup of tea in my hands, the warmth of the mug grounding me in the moment. My thoughts were anything but calm, drifting back to the conversation we had about their dad.

I had told them he wouldn't be living with us anymore, bracing myself for tears or protests. Instead, their calmness surprised me. It was almost as though they'd seen it coming. I'd reassured them over and over, "No matter what, I'm here. I'll never leave you." But even as I spoke, I couldn't help but feel the weight of my guilt pressing down on me.

The past two weeks without Richard had been difficult. It wasn't just his absence, it was the flood of emotions that came with it: abandonment, fear, and an overwhelming sense of isolation. Some days, I could barely breathe under the weight of it all. I felt paralyzed.

The years of control, manipulation, and emotional wounds had hollowed me out, leaving behind a fragile shell. Abusers don't just harm with their hands, they unravel your sense of self, piece by piece, until you don't even know who you are or what you want. Though Richard was absent, his voice echoed in my mind, sowing seeds of doubt and fear. *You're nothing without me.*

As I took a sip of my tea, my thoughts began to shift.

Was it really that bad?

Could I have been a better wife?

Memories from the early days of our relationship surfaced: the time we went out for pizza, laughing about our shared dreams, solving the world's problems, and sharing our first kiss. I felt so special then.

But now, the pain was overwhelming. My stomach churned with anxiety, and I just wanted it all to stop.

* * *

"Candy, your son is on the phone, and he sounds upset," one of my coworkers said one Sunday evening.

Racing to the phone, I picked up the receiver. "What's wrong?"

"Mom, Jason is hurt!" Ben yelled, his voice filled with panic.

"Honey, calm down and tell me what's going on."

"We were out in the woods across the street, and Jason cut his foot on something and it's really bleeding a lot!"

"Where is he now?" I asked, trying to keep my voice steady despite the surge of worry rising inside me.

"He's right here, I carried him on my back all the way home!"

"Wow, that is so brave of you," I said, my heart swelling with both pride and worry. "Now listen carefully. Go get a towel, wrap some ice in the towel, and wrap it around his foot. Have him lay down on the sofa and put his leg on a pillow to elevate his foot. Hold pressure on it. Can you do that for me?"

"Mom, it's really bad and it's bleeding a lot!" Ben cried.

"I'm leaving the hospital right now. I'll be home as quickly as I can. Just stay calm and do as I said. I promise he'll be okay. You did a great job of getting him home and calling me right away."

"Hurry, Mom."

I hung up the phone and immediately found my supervisor. "I have a medical emergency at home," I said, trying to hold back the tears.

"Go ahead, don't worry. I'll assign your baby to another nurse," my supervisor said with a reassuring smile.

As I walked briskly to my car, I heard the roar of a crowd, cheering in the distance.

Damn, it's Sunday!

The hospital was located right next door to the Tampa Bay Stadium, where the Buccaneers played football. During football season, or any big event, the traffic was always a nightmare.

Jumping in my car, I groaned as I saw several streets blocked off and traffic crawling at a snail's pace.

Then, out of the corner of my eye, I spotted an officer directing cars. A spark of hope ignited as I rolled down my window and waved, ready to plead for help.

"Officer, please, I have a medical emergency at home, and I need to get through this traffic." My voice trembled with urgency. "Would you please help me?"

"What's the problem, ma'am?" he asked, walking toward my car, his tone steady and professional.

"Sir, my son has been injured at home and I need to get there quickly. Can you help me get through this traffic?" I noticed his eyes glancing at my medical scrubs, the required uniform for the NICU. My uniform must have caught his attention, lending a sense of credibility to my words.

"Give me a second." He reached for his radio.

The next thing I knew, cars were moving aside, parting like the Red Sea, clearing a path for me to get through. I didn't waste a second. Pressing the accelerator, I exceeded the speed limit all the way home.

That moment stayed with me, not just because of the urgency, but because I felt seen and respected by someone whose job it was to protect and help.

I pulled into the driveway with tires screeching and ran into the house. Ben was sitting on the sofa next to Jason, holding his foot just like I had instructed him to do. I quickly assessed the injury; his foot was cut from his toes to his heel with subcutaneous fat protruding out of the wound. My nursing skills kicked in, bringing a sense of calm. The cut was deep enough to require sutures, but thankfully it wasn't life-threatening.

"Mom, am I going to be okay?" Jason asked.

"You're going to be fine but we have to go to the hospital so you can get some stitches."

Jason was terrified of needles. He cried and screamed so much we had to hold him down while the physician sutured his foot.

"Please, Doc, give him a little sedative, this is breaking my heart," I pleaded.

The nurse quickly prepared the sedative, and within minutes, Jason's cries softened.

Ten days later, when his sutures needed to be taken out, I asked my supervisor if I could take a suture removal kit home and do it myself and she graciously obliged.

I arrived home that night at my usual time, midnight, grabbed a flashlight, and snuck into Jason's room. Fortunately, he was sleeping on his stomach, making it much easier to remove his sutures without disturbing him. As I gently snipped and pulled each tiny stitch, my eyes began to well up with tears. The weight of everything he had endured pressed on me.

"I'm so sorry you've had to go through all of this. I'm sorry, I'm so sorry." My thoughts spilled over in a silent prayer. "You shouldn't have to see the beatings, hear yelling, endure your father being drunk and hateful. Please, God, help me to do better. I love you, my son." I leaned in and placed a gentle kiss on his forehead, letting my lips linger for a moment, as if I could will my love into him, shield him from the pain that had already settled too deep in his young heart.

He never stirred. Not a flinch, not a sigh.

Then I walked into Ben's room. He was sound asleep, his chest rising and falling in the soft rhythm of childhood dreams. I sat on the side of his bed, watching him, taking in the peacefulness that sleep allowed him.

"I'm so sorry, I'm so, so sorry." The words swelled in my chest, something I could never say out loud. "You're far too young for this. You shouldn't have to carry this weight. Your own father has forgotten you, and now I've subjected you to this horrible drunk."

Tears slipped down my cheeks as I brushed his hair back, tracing the curve of his cheek with my fingers. "I love you, my son. Please, God, help me do better." I kissed his forehead softly, hoping he could feel the depth of my love.

Silently, I rose and walked into my bedroom. I sat on the edge of the bed, dropping my face into my hands.

"How in the hell am I supposed to do all this alone?"

* * *

I was in the kitchen making dinner for the boys, stirring a pot of spaghetti on the stove while the garlic bread warmed in the oven, trying to focus on the simple rhythm of cooking, stirring, tasting, setting the plates, grounding myself, but the weight of my worries pressed down on me.

"You're going to be fine," I whispered to myself. "You've got your education, you've taken the boards again, it's all going to work out."

I reached for the colander and drained the pasta, steam rising around me.

"Calm your nerves so you can eat with the boys. You're strong, you can do this on your own," I continued to tell myself, when suddenly I heard his voice.

His voice.

No, it can't be him! He's been gone for over a month!

"Candy, where are you?" he called out.

"Richard, what are you doing here?"

"I live here, remember?" His demeanor was stern. He was holding the duffle bag he'd left with.

"But I told you I want a divorce. I can't live like this anymore."

"I'm not leaving, and we're not getting divorced."

"But I—" I tried to respond.

He bulldozed over me. "I'm moving back in. We're staying together. I haven't been drinking since I left." His voice sounded steady, almost rehearsed. "I've been going to AA meetings, and I have a sponsor, too. So let's try again, please. What do you say?"

How many times am I going to hear this story?

In that moment, anger surged through me, not just for myself, but for the boys, for everything they'd suffered. The fear, unpredictability, the way their childhood had been shaped by his rage. But instead of paralyzing me, that anger fueled something else: determination.

I was done living in fear. Done allowing him to dictate our lives. I wanted more for my boys, a life beyond abuse, beyond the constant tension of waiting for the next explosion. I was determined to have a different life even though I was uncertain of the road ahead.

But I also knew the danger of saying no.

If I refused to let him move back in, he would become enraged. I was always his first target. His words might be calm now, but I knew how quickly that could change. I had lived this nightmare for too long, learned the delicate balance to survive. Today, I wasn't sure where that balance stood, as I watched the way his fingers twitched at his side and his jaw tightened ever so slightly. A warning. A signal I knew all too well.

I let out a slow, measured sigh. "Okay, Richard."

I knew it wouldn't be long before he would go on another drinking binge. I started planning. I needed to save as much money as I could, look for an apartment that was secluded and hard for him to find. Check on what school district the boys' school would be in. My list was in my mind, never written down for fear of him finding it.

One night, I brought up a bill he hadn't paid. He whirled around, his eyes dark with anger. "I said don't worry about it, bitch. I'll take care of it." And then he was gone, slamming the door behind him.

I wasn't surprised when Richard didn't come home that night. The next morning, I put my plan in motion. I got the boys off to school. Then I called the management company of a townhouse I'd found to let them know I was ready to move in.

Next, I called the moving folks and told them I was ready to move. I started frantically packing the kitchen, the boys' room, and lastly my belongings. The move went smoothly. The boys were excited to help.

I had a sense of pride in having accomplished the move on my own, a small victory in our new life. But along with that pride was a lingering heavy fear and anxiety. I had never allowed myself to get attached to any place I lived, because deep down, I always felt it would be taken away from me at any moment. This fear wasn't just about Richard or his abuse, it was something deeper, something that had been ingrained in me long before. A fear of instability, of losing everything just when I started to believe I was safe.

I never had a conversation with the boys about the move. I was so focused on escaping my horrific marriage, getting them enrolled in a new school, and simply keeping the three of us alive that I overlooked their feelings. In my mind, it was just another box to check: find a safe place, get them into school, keep moving. I convinced myself that as long as I could keep afloat, the rest would fall into place.

To my relief, they seemed to settle in quickly. Having each other helped. Being together at the same school gave them a sense of security. But looking back, I wonder how much they were holding inside, how much they had learned to bury, just like I had.

I picked up a part-time nursing job to help with the expenses, working at an OB/GYN practice in the mornings from nine to noon, then heading straight to the hospital to work my three to eleven-thirty shift in the NICU. The two jobs barely covered our expenses with little left over for any extras. Every dollar was accounted for, every paycheck stretched to its limits.

We quickly settled into a daily routine. Every morning, I started the day at six, preparing breakfast for the boys and packing their lunches. By seven-thirty, they were off to school, and I had a short window of time to prep their dinner and store it in the fridge, so they had something ready when they got home from school.

On the days when I was too tired to cook, they went to a small restaurant next to our complex for dinner. I made sure they knew how to order their meals and taught them the etiquette of tipping. They enjoyed the independence and found it fun. I was so proud of them!

The boys had a close bond during this time and seemed to be happy. They did everything together. If you saw one, the other would not be far away.

I had secured medical insurance for the boys and myself through the hospital. I made the decision to have a tubal ligation; it was a choice I didn't need to think twice about. I'd been prescribed birth control pills by my gynecologist and I was concerned of potential side effects from taking them for so long. Birth control pills in the seventies and eighties had several possible side effects, including blood clots, high blood pressure, liver problems, and pelvic inflammatory disease.

More than that, though, I knew in my heart I never wanted to have another child I would have to fight to protect. I was not sexually active; I just didn't want even the remote possibility of having to save another child from harm.

I had accumulated some vacation time, so I only took a couple days off for the procedure and all went well without complications.

While I recovered from surgery, the board exam results weighed heavily on my mind. It had been weeks since I'd retaken the exam and I knew the results could arrive any day. The waiting was agonizing.

Sitting on the sofa, I happened to look out the living room window just in time to see the mail truck drive toward the exit of the complex. *Could this be the day?*

I grabbed my key. My hand shook as I unlocked the mailbox, and there it was, the only piece of mail in my box that day. I immediately checked to see if the envelope was thick or thin.

I opened it so fast I ripped the envelope in half. I saw the words that I had been waiting so long to see. "Passed." Pressing the paper against my chest, I looked up and said, "Thank you, God. No one can ever take this away from me."

CHAPTER 21

Breakfast and a Bullet

I had successfully hidden from Richard for about six months, giving us a brief period of peace with the hope of rebuilding our lives.

I finally had a day off from both jobs. Standing in the kitchen, preparing a nice dinner for me and the boys, I heard a knock on the front door.

There were no peepholes in my door so I cracked it open just enough to see, and my breath caught in my throat. All the anxiety and fear that I'd worked so hard to push away came rushing back. My heart began to race.

"Richard." A jolt of terror shot through me. *He's here to kill me!* My breath hitched. My hands curled into fists at my sides, but my legs wouldn't move.

"I'm not going to hurt you," he said, his voice softer than I remembered.

I stared at him, my mouth open, but no words would come out.

He took a small step toward me. "Candy, I'm here only to apologize. I'm not here to hurt you. I'm so sorry. I'm really sorry about how things ended. I've been going to AA and I have a sponsor now. I just wanted to tell you this. I'm going to leave now," he said with tears welling up in his eyes.

He then turned and walked away.

Shutting the door, I twisted the lock with shaking fingers, pressing my back against the door. A wave of dizziness hit me hard. Grabbing the nearest chair, I collapsed into it, my head dropping between my knees as I struggled to breathe. My pulse pounded in my ears.

What the hell just happened? He found us. Will this ever end?

* * *

Even though Richard knew where we lived, he surprised me by keeping his distance. I braced myself for the worst: relentless visits, intimidation, and demands, but instead he lingered on the periphery. He'd call a couple times per week, always with updates on his recovery, as if I were supposed to applaud his efforts. Every so often, an envelope with cash would appear under my doormat. No note. No explanation. Just money.

He hadn't paid or offered to pay one penny toward supporting his child, yet he made sure I knew he was helping me. He gloated about it, speaking as though he was doing me some grand favor, as if his handouts erased the past. But I knew his money came with strings attached and a price to pay.

I hadn't filed for divorce yet, not because I was hesitant, but because I simply didn't have the financial means to do so. Even when Richard gave me some money, unexpected bills piled up, draining what little savings I had. It seemed like I could never catch up.

As the weeks passed, the exhaustion from working long hours and caring for the boys left me vulnerable and his manipulations were wearing me down. One evening the boys and I were having an argument over them getting their homework done. Jason was crying while Ben stomped up the stairs and slammed the bedroom door. I slumped down on the sofa, exhausted and defeated, wondering if I could continue to do this on my own.

Whether I liked it or not, I could feel myself slipping back.

Maybe he has changed. He hasn't been drinking—that I know of, at least. He's giving me money. Maybe I should try?

* * *

I'd agreed to let Richard come over for breakfast with me and the boys. It was a beautiful summer day but my stomach was warning me that the day would not go well. Even so, I could not have imagined that within minutes of opening the door, Richard would follow me to my bedroom, heave a heavy dresser and mirror to the floor, and beat me within millimeters of death.

My sons witnessed all of this.

Richard wasn't finished. He ordered me to obey him.

Yet some primal instinct roared inside me, and I defied him. I told him I'd never obey him.

He pulled out a hidden, sawed-off shotgun, and leveled it at my face.

Paralyzed, I stared into the jagged barrel.

He pulled the trigger.

The ringing in my ears was deafening as the bullet brushed by my left ear. Instinctively, I pressed my hand over my ear, as if I could silence the high-pitched whine.

Am I dead? Am I deaf?

Panic surged through me. I frantically patted down my body,

feeling for blood on my clothes. *No blood. I must be alive.* A sharp acrid stench filled my nose. Gunpowder. It clung thick in the air.

My heart slammed against my ribs as my mind snapped to my boys. *Oh, God, the boys.* I turned so fast I nearly lost my balance. They were still standing just inside their bedroom door, their wrinkled pajamas hanging loosely on their small frames. Their faces were pale, eyes wide with disbelief, terror freezing them in place.

"Mom, are you okay?" they asked, their voices trembling.

Trying to stay positive, I forced a smile. "Yes, I'm okay, boys. Everything will be okay."

"Yeah, she's okay," Richard said, laughing. His eyes gleamed like he had just conquered a monumental task. "I told you I would kill you. Guess now you know I mean what I say." He kept laughing. "Go finish getting dressed and make us some breakfast. And I want you to quit your jobs and stay at home. I'll take care of everything."

"Okay, Richard." The words left my lips, weak and hollow, my voice quivering with fear. My body felt disconnected from my mind, moving on autopilot as I turned toward the bathroom to finish getting dressed. Devastated, terrified, and beaten.

A closet separated the bedroom from the bathroom. As I walked past it, something inside me made me stop. Compelled, I opened the door and pushed the clothes aside. My hand skimmed over the wall, searching for the bullet hole—proof that what just happened was real.

Did he really try to kill me? The thought sent a shiver down my spine.

What if he'd killed Ben or Jason?

I stumbled into the bathroom, gripping the sink. My knees knocked together, nausea rolling in waves. I looked up at my reflection, my face pale, my eyes wide with shock.

I'm going to vomit.

Everything inside of me shut down. My body, my emotions, my fear, they all collapsed.

I was in survival mode.

* * *

It was either quit or be killed. I was forced to walk away from the profession I had worked so hard to obtain. There was no other choice. Nursing was more than just a job—it was my passion, my escape, my identity. It was if he was stealing the last piece of myself that I had left.

When Richard shot at me, I was focused only on surviving. It wasn't until later that I realized he wasn't drunk. It was the first time I can recall that he'd been physically violent without being drunk.

I hated him so much I wanted him to die. I wished I'd killed him with the iron skillet when I had the chance.

* * *

Richard's behavior became increasingly suspicious. He never explicitly mentioned leaving his job at the tire store, but large rolls of cash in his pockets, secretive phone calls, and late-night outings spoke volumes. I could only assume he was involved in illicit activities, possibly dealing drugs.

Although his alcohol-fueled rages had ceased, the verbal abuse persisted. He continued to belittle me, issuing demands and hurling insults at every opportunity.

About a month after shooting at me, Richard bought a house in Carrollwood, just north of Tampa. It was a spacious tri-level home in a very nice neighborhood.

On the outside, the house looked pretty with its cream-colored paint and brick accents, but inside was a different story. Richard refused to let me buy new furniture unless it was absolutely necessary, leaving the house looking empty and cold. On the other hand, he would occasionally buy furniture, but only antiques, saying if we needed money right away, we could always sell them for quick cash. The lack of warmth and the bare rooms exacerbated my anxiety and insecurity, leaving me feeling more vulnerable than ever.

Richard struck up a friendship with a local antique dealer, Sarah. One day, he came in the house carrying a rocking chair, proudly saying this was "his" rocking chair, and he had purchased it from Sarah. He didn't understand the meaning of a true, close friendship. To him, all relationships were transactional, built on what he could get in return. His so-called friends were there to serve a purpose, to build him up and give him what he wanted and what he could take from them.

Every single damn day, he smoked marijuana from sunup to sundown. He would sit in that fucking antique rocking chair with a smug look on his face, like he was the king of his castle, managing a drug ring. With the phone on the floor by his side, he'd rock back and forth for hours upon hours, waiting for it to ring.

CHAPTER 22

Jets and Jail

I convinced Richard to enroll the children in a private Catholic school so that they could get the best education possible. The boys settled into their new school and seemed to enjoy it. Every afternoon when I picked them up, they would talk about their day, the new friends they made, and what they learned. Some days they would describe how the nuns handled their classmates when they got into trouble for even the smallest things. A snarky remark from a classmate would lead to the nun marching the offender to the principal's office within seconds.

It was surprising to hear how strict the school could be, but I felt this was exactly what they needed.

To help further their stability, I wanted to decorate their bedrooms to feel like a real home for them. One day during our drive home from school, I told them about my idea.

"Boys, I want to decorate your bedrooms, maybe put some wallpaper on the walls, and get some new bedding. What do you guys think? What colors would you like to have in your rooms?"

"I don't know," Jason replied.

"What's your favorite color?" I asked.

"I don't know, maybe blue?"

"Ben, what's your favorite color?"

"Mom, I really don't care. Do whatever."

I glanced in the rearview mirror and caught the look of disgust on his face. Lately, this attitude had been surfacing more and more. A knot tightened in my stomach. *Is he starting to act like Richard?*

"All right, I'll go to the wallpaper store and pick up some samples so you can take a look at them and decide what you'd like."

"Whatever. Mom, I just want to get home. I'm hungry," Ben said, slumping back into his seat.

* * *

Due to Richard's new "career," he had more money, but that didn't mean I had access to it. Every dollar I needed still came with a price. If I asked for money for groceries, school supplies, or home projects for the boys, I had to carefully time my requests, gauge mood, choose my words wisely. Anything could set him off. If I asked at the wrong moment, I would pay for it, not in bruises anymore, but in words that cut just as deep. His accusations weren't just words, they were weapons, meant to break me down and keep me in my place.

"You whore! Why can't you do anything right?"

"You look like a slut in those clothes. Go change, you know I don't like you looking like that."

"I saw that man looking at you and you looked back at him. What the fuck are you doing? You're wishing he would fuck you, aren't you? Bitch, last night I shot a man right in the face because he disobeyed my orders. Do you want to die?"

His jealousy was all-consuming, suffocating. It didn't matter where we were or who was around, if another man so much as glanced in my direction, it became proof of my supposed behavior.

Being under Richard's total control, stripped of the independence and nursing degree I had fought so hard to achieve, was a constant ache. He had taken away my ability to make choices for myself, to work, to have purpose, to be free. Every sacrifice I'd made to build a career, every long night spent studying, every challenge I had overcome to earn that degree, it all felt like it had been for nothing. I was trapped, not just in a marriage but in a life that wasn't mine anymore.

For the next year and a half, I kept myself busy with home projects. I started with the boys' rooms, carefully picking out their favorite choices that reflected their pre-teen and teen personalities. At Sarah's antique store, I found two oak antique beds and two dressers, which made Richard very happy in case he had to sell their beds for cash. I bought two new twin mattresses and wallpapered one wall in each room, choosing designs that matched their personalities and the colors they liked. To complete their rooms, I hung curtains to match their wallpaper and new bedding, creating an inviting, cozy retreat.

Next, I moved on to the kitchen, hanging wallpaper that had a cream-colored background with bright red strawberries to brighten the space. I even found an old kitchen table and chairs that I spent hours sanding and refinishing.

* * *

Several times a month Richard would leave for a few days or a week for what he claimed was a business trip.

One afternoon, while rocking in his chair, he informed me that he was driving my car to North Carolina that weekend.

I frowned. "Why do you have to take my car? Why not take your car?"

"I need to drop some things off in North Carolina and your car will be a better choice to drive."

Something about his tone, so dismissive, made my stomach tighten. "How long will you be gone?"

"A few days. I'm not sure how long."

I wanted to push back, but I knew better. Arguing with him was pointless, and questioning him could send him into one of his rages. So I simply said, "Okay."

It was a quiet morning in May, 1982. I had just gotten home from dropping the boys off at school. I had put a load of laundry in the washer and started to clean the kitchen when the phone rang.

It was a recording: "You have a collect call from the Charlotte County Jail. Will you accept the charges?"

I'd never received a collect call from a jail before. Sharp pains stabbed in my stomach as I hesitated. A hundred thoughts ran through my mind. "Um, yes, I will accept the charges."

The phone line clicked, then I heard his voice.

"Hi, honey. I wanted you to know I got arrested last night for dealing drugs. But don't worry, everything is going to be fine," he said, his tone almost cheerful, as if he were telling me about a minor inconvenience.

I stood there in shock, my mind spinning, trying to process what I'd just heard Richard say. *Arrested?* I couldn't move, couldn't speak.

"Are you there?" Richard asked.

"Yeah, I'm here," I finally managed, my mouth and brain remembering how to function. "What am I supposed to do now?"

"They'll only allow me to talk for a couple more minutes, so listen, there's some cash in the closet downstairs, in one of my coat pockets. Go find that cash, buy a plane ticket, and fly up here today. Make sure you bring that cash with you."

I blinked, gripping the phone tighter. "Richard, what's going to happen? Where's my car?"

"Everything's going to be okay, don't worry. Your car, well, they took it."

"Who's they?"

"The police impounded the car when they arrested me, but don't worry, I'll get it back when I get released on bail," he assured me, as if this was just a minor hiccup. "They're telling me I have to get off the phone now, but I'll see you later today."

Click. The line went dead.

I stood there for a minute, still gripping the receiver, my mind whirling. Then as if on autopilot, I rushed downstairs to find the money he was talking about. Digging through the pockets of his coats, my hands shook as I finally pulled out a thick wad of cash, several hundred-dollar bills and some fifties and twenties all stacked together. I tried to count it, but between the shaking of my hands and the pounding of my heart, I couldn't focus. The numbers blurred; my thoughts scrambled.

Grabbing the phone, I dialed my younger sister.

"Sue, can you pick up the boys from school and let them stay with you for a bit?" My voice sounded foreign to me, tight and rushed.

"Sure, I'll pick them up. What's going on?"

"I don't have time to explain everything right now. Richard's been arrested, and I need to fly to North Carolina."

There was a brief pause, but she didn't press for details. "Okay, I'll pick them up."

Packing a few things in my tote bag, I drove to the airport and purchased a roundtrip same-day ticket for a flight that would be taking off in an hour.

After landing in North Carolina, I followed the signs to the car rental area and rented the cheapest car I could find. The jail was in a rural area, a little over an hour's drive, mostly along two-lane winding roads. The farther I drove, the more isolated everything felt, the landscaping of the city shifting into vast stretches of farmland.

When I finally arrived at the jail, I stepped inside the building, my eyes scanning for the first person I could find to ask about Richard's whereabouts.

"Excuse me, do you have a minute to help me? My husband called me this morning and told me he was arrested and to come to this address."

"Come over here and I'll look him up." The officer asked Richard's name, then typed something in the computer, then glanced back at me. "Oh, yeah, he's here. Follow me. I'll take you to the detective that arrested him. You can talk to him."

As I followed the officer down a long, cold, dingy gray hallway with worn tile floors, I could hear distant voices echoing off the walls. The hollow sound of the place sent chills down my spine.

The officer stopped at a door and leaned his head inside a room. "Excuse me, y'all. O'Leary, there's a lady here looking for that guy Richard you arrested last night."

"Yeah, Richard's sitting right here," a voice responded. "Let her come in."

I stepped into the cramped, messy office. Richard was lounging in a chair, one arm casually draped across another chair next to the detective's desk, as if he were at a social gathering rather than jail.

"Yeah, Bill, this is my wife, Candy," Richard said, without

bothering to stand, his tone nonchalant. I expected to see handcuffs on his wrists, but there were none.

The detective stood and extended his hand. "Hi, I'm Detective O'Leary."

I shook his hand, but my mind was spinning, trying to make sense of all the madness, while the two of them sat there laughing and joking about what had happened.

What is so fucking funny about all of this?

"Richard, what is going on? Where is my car?" My voice shook as I forced the words out.

"I told you I got arrested last night," he said, as if that explained everything.

A whirlwind of emotions slammed into me: fury, terror, disbelief. *You threatened me and my family. You trapped me in this prison of control, stripping me of every ounce of independence. Now I have no car, no money, no self-worth. You've left me nothing.*

"I understand that part," I said, my voice rising. Now I was furious. "What's going to happen now? Why did you want me to fly up here? What am I supposed to do?"

Detective O'Leary leaned forward, his tone neutral, almost indifferent as he explained the process. "He's being charged with selling cocaine. The grand jury will meet, then there will be a trial. If he's found guilty, then there's the sentencing with possible prison time." It was as if he was speaking a foreign language.

I turned to Richard, searching his face for some kind of explanation, something that would make this nightmare less terrifying. But he just sat there, calm, unbothered, like this was just another day.

I swallowed hard, the weight of it all crashing over me. "What the hell am I doing here?"

"I wanted you to bring some cash for bail, but it looks like there won't be any bail right now. And when it's set, it's going to be a lot of money. What I want you to do is go to Sarah's antique store and ask her if she would put up some of her property for my bail."

Are you serious right now? This is insane. Now you want me to beg Sarah to put up her property to get you out of jail? I have other things to worry about than asking Sarah to put up her property for your fucking bail!

"I'm flying back tonight," I said, my voice sharp, laced with confusion and disbelief.

Before Richard could respond, Detective O'Leary stood up. "Richard, it's time for me to put you back in your cell."

"Yep, guess it's time for me to go back with the real criminals, right, Bill?" Richard laughed as he spoke, like this was some kind of joke. *What? He's made friends with this detective?*

Walking out of the jail, I shoved the door open so hard it slammed against the wall behind it. The sound hardly registered as I stumbled to the rental car, my legs weak beneath me. Reaching for the door handle, I froze, my hand trembling against the metal. A wave of panic crashed over me, my heart pounding too fast, sharp pains in my stomach.

"I can't breathe," I gasped to no one, clutching my stomach as I bent over, letting my head hang down so I wouldn't pass out. *I only have the cash in my purse, mortgage payment is due, boys' school tuition is coming up, we need food, my car is gone.*

I don't remember driving back to the airport. The next thing I knew, I was on the plane, sitting in the window seat, tucked away in the back row, leaning my head against the cold glass. My mind was still garbled, arguing with myself.

You're too ugly.

But I'll be free.

You can't make decisions; you don't know how.

But I'll be free.

He never asked about the boys, never once wondered how we were going to survive.

But I'll be free.

He didn't care.

But I'll be free.

He didn't tell me what to do.

But I'll be free.

He'd threatened my life and forced me into complete dependence on him, trapped in a cycle of control, where every decision, every action, had to revolve around keeping him appeased. As I gazed out the window at the scattered clouds, soft, weightless, untouched by the chaos below, a strange mixture of relief and fear washed over me.

I would have to make decisions on my own.

His words echoed in my head. *You can't make it on your own. You're too stupid and ugly to be on your own.*

I'll be free now.

This would be the last time I ever saw Richard. But I was far from being free of him.

CHAPTER 23

A Sense of Purpose

It was after ten when I finally walked in the house, exhausted from the long day of travel and unexpected events. I dropped my bag by the door and went upstairs to check on the boys. Sue had brought them home shortly after giving them dinner. They were sound asleep in their beds. Relieved they were safe, I sat down on one of the steps leading to the main floor, bearing my head in my hands as I rocked back and forth.

What am I going to do now? I have no lifeline. God, my stomach hurts. I haven't eaten or drunk anything all day, not even a sip of water. Just the thought of food made me nauseous. *I can't eat, I'll throw up. I should at least drink some tea. I need to walk to the kitchen and make some tea right now. My throat is so dry.*

As I slowly pulled myself up from the step and walked to the kitchen, my thoughts completely took over, swirling in a relentless storm of doubt and fear. *Are we going to be homeless? I'm worthless.*

The words echoed, heavy and inescapable. I had lost all confidence in myself, in my ability to make even the smallest decisions. *Richard, I need you to help me make decisions. I can't do this without you.* My hands moved on autopilot, pouring the hot water over my tea bag. *Stop thinking this way. I'm free.* But I didn't feel free.

The silence of the kitchen wrapped around me as I sat at the table. My fingers traced the grain of the wood tabletop that I had spent hours sanding and staining. *At least for the next few hours before daylight, I need to rest. I need to rest my mind now.*

The following days blurred together, each one bleeding into the next as I moved through the motions, packing lunches, taking the boys to school, folding laundry, making dinners. It was all done mindlessly, trying to ignore the reality of things to come.

It had been a few weeks since Richard's arrest without a single word from him. Strangely, the boys hadn't asked where he was, and I wasn't ready to explain. How could I? The words felt too heavy, too final. So I avoided the conversation, hoping to buy more time or perhaps wishing it would all go away.

While driving home after taking the boys to school one morning, the reality of my critical situation started to set in, harder than it had before. *I've got to go back to work now.* The thought sent a wave of panic through me. *I'm scared. I'm so scared of everything right now. I need money. The mortgage needs to be paid in a week.* There was no more time to avoid it. This was survival.

I picked up a *Tampa Tribune* newspaper on the way home and started looking through the classified ads for nursing jobs. My eyes landed on an advertisement for a nursing agency that seemed to call out to me. *Make your own nursing hours and work whenever you want. Call now for details.* The word "flexibility" caught my attention. I picked up the phone and dialed the number.

"Would you mind explaining how this works?" I asked.

"Of course. Once you've filled out our application and we have confirmed you have an active nursing license, you'll be placed on our call list. When a hospital or any healthcare-related facility calls and has a need for a registered nurse for that day or the coming weeks, I'll call you to see if you're available to work for such-and-such facility for a specific shift. Their needs for an RN may be for a day, a week, or a month. You'll be paid daily, so after you complete your shift, you can come by the office and pick up your check either on the same day or the next day. You just tell us when and how much you want to work. We have plenty of work for RNs."

Her calm explanation gave me a sense of relief, a glimmer of hope.

"This sounds like it would really work for me, especially since I have two boys. Can I come by tomorrow and get the application process started?"

For the first time in what seemed like a lifetime, I felt a small sense of control.

Until the phone rang.

"Candice, this is Sister Phyllis from the Sacred Heart School. You have two children enrolled with us, correct? I must inform you that the tuition has not been paid to date, therefore making the tuition ten days late. Are you prepared to make a payment today? If you cannot make a payment today, you must come and pick up your children. The children will not be able to return until the full balance is paid."

"Unfortunately, I'm not able to make a payment today, Sister. I'll come and pick them up now," I replied, humiliated.

"They'll be in the office waiting for you."

Grabbing my keys, I hurried to the car, my hands shaking as I started the engine. The reality of what was happening settled deep in my gut like a heavy stone.

I had tried, God knows I tried, to keep things stable for them, to shield them from the chaos that continued to unravel around us. But now it was crumbling, and I couldn't stop it. The guilt was stifling.

The boys were losing the one place where they felt safe, where they had some sense of normalcy. And it was my fault.

Tears stung my eyes as I gripped the steering wheel. I forced myself to pull it together. Falling apart was not an option.

They didn't say much on the drive home. In the days leading up to this moment, it was as if they already knew something was wrong, and like me, were too afraid to face reality. They hadn't asked questions because they didn't want to hear the answers, and I didn't offer them answers. I was hiding behind my own denial. I was hanging onto the hope that somehow everything would magically work itself out, but deep down I knew time had run out. I could no longer hide the truth from them.

Later that evening, I made the boys dinner and called out for them to come to the kitchen.

"Mom, you're not eating again?" Jason asked.

"No, not tonight."

It had been weeks since I was able to keep any food down. My body felt hollow, weak, as if it were slowly giving up on me. I hadn't stepped on a scale, but I didn't need to. Every time I caught a glimpse of myself in the mirror, I saw my ribs jutting out like sharp edges beneath my skin, my clothes hanging from my frame like they no longer belonged to me.

I took a deep breath, steadying myself as I turned to face them. "Listen, boys, I need to talk to you about something. I really need for you guys to listen to me."

The boys were now fourteen and eleven, old enough to understand words like "arrest" and "prison." But how do you tell your children that their world is shifting?

"The reason why I had to pick you guys up from school today is the tuition hasn't been paid." I hesitated, the words catching in my throat. "And I won't have the money to pay the tuition anymore. You'll have to go back to public school."

"We can't go back to Sacred Heart?" Jason asked, his voice small and uncertain.

"I'm sorry, but no."

His face fell. "What about my friends? I'll never see them again."

I swallowed the lump rising in my throat, trying to hold myself together and sound positive. "I'm so sorry, but you'll make new friends at your new school."

Ben just sat there taking it all in, not asking any questions.

"Guys," I went on, my voice trembling. "Your father won't be coming home." I let the silence hang for a moment. "He was arrested a few weeks ago in North Carolina."

What mother has to tell their children their father is going to prison?

I watched their faces, searching for signs of anger, confusion, heartbreak, anything. They both just stared at me, confirming my suspicions that they already knew something had happened.

"I'm so sorry I have to tell you this," I said, my voice barely above a whisper. "But I want you to know we'll be okay. I promise." I needed them to hold onto something even if it was just my words. "I won't have a lot of money after I pay all the bills. So, this is what I'm asking of you guys: if you want fun money for things like movies, you'll have to earn it doing odd jobs in the neighborhood, like mowing lawns."

I braced myself for their reaction, expecting frustration and disappointment, but instead, Ben said, "Mom, it's okay, we've been making extra money already at the golf course."

"Yeah, we've been going to the golf course on our mini-motorcycles almost every day," Jason chimed in.

I blinked. "What? So how are you making money at the golf course?"

"A lot of the golfers hit their balls into the water," Jason said, laughing. "We dive in all the ponds, find the golf balls, and resell them to other golfers."

I stared at them, both amused and stunned. "And they actually buy these golf balls from you?"

"Some of them are rich and they give us extra money for the balls if they're in good condition," Ben said.

I exhaled, shaking my head. "I had no idea this is what you've been doing."

My boys had already learned how to hustle and take care of themselves. But as proud as I was of their resourcefulness, nagging questions crept into my mind. Did they learn this from Richard? Or was it because of my poor parenting, or the long hours I had to work, leaving them to fend for themselves? Feelings of guilt started to take over.

I didn't know how I should feel: proud or worried?

* * *

I'd been working for the nursing agency for about a month. The pay was good, but no matter how many hours I worked, sometimes sixty hours per week, not including drive time, it never was enough. Some of the hospitals were fifty miles away and the cost of gas added up. Between that and the never-ending household bills, it always felt like I was drowning.

Still there was something about being in the hospital that gave me a brief escape from the challenges waiting for me at home. The constant movement, the focused intensity of the patient care, it quieted the relentless fear of the unknown that gnawed at me day and night. For those hours, I wasn't drowning in worry about the mortgage or how I would keep the boys afloat. My nervous stomach settled just enough for me to eat at least one meal a day, and for the first time in weeks, actually keep it down.

More than anything, nursing gave me a sense of purpose again. No matter how shattered I felt in my personal life, I still knew who I was in the hospital. I'd never doubted my ability to be a knowledgeable, compassionate nurse, an advocate for my patients, unwavering in my commitment to their dignity and well-being. In a world where everything felt like it was slipping through my fingers, that certainty was something I could hold onto.

Whether it was a postoperative open-heart patient, or a post-stroke patient struggling to regain control, I was determined to get them out of that damn bed. Lying in a hospital bed complaining was not acceptable. "No pity parties," I would say. "That bed is not your friend. It will kill you."

If my patient was on a ventilator (breathing machine) and unable to speak, I became their advocate, conveying concerns and the plan of care to their families, so that no one felt lost or forgotten. If they were facing a terminally ill diagnosis, I met them with dignity and compassion, making sure their final days contained not just medical care but humanity.

When I stood beside a grieving wife who had just lost her husband unexpectedly or sat with parents paralyzed by fear as their child clung to life, I heard them, I felt them. Their pain, their terror, their helplessness, it was all too familiar. I carried their burdens with them, even if it was just for a moment, because I knew what it meant to suffer in silence. In so many ways their struggles mirrored my own. And maybe by helping them, I was finding my own way through.

I didn't build any close relationships with my coworkers. It was easier that way. Keeping my distance meant avoiding the inevitable questions, the ones I couldn't answer honestly. If I shared even half of the chaos that was going on in my personal life they wouldn't believe me, they would judge me or—worse—they would question whether I was competent to care for patients.

I enrolled the boys in public school and drove them to school their first day. Ben walked to his class without saying a word. He had always kept his emotions locked inside. Jason, on the other hand, was struggling.

"Mom, I don't want to go in there," he told me.

I crouched slightly, meeting his eyes. "I understand you're scared, but you have to go to school."

Tears spilled down his cheeks. My heart ached for him. So much had changed for him, and it was all weighing on his small shoulders. He'd always been a very sensitive child, and this was all so much for him to take in.

I gently reached down, cupping his face in my hands. My thumbs brushed against his soft cheeks. His eyes were wide with uncertainty. "Please listen," I said softly. "You are my son," putting the emphasis on *my*, "and you are strong," putting the emphasis on *you* "and we are going to get through all this mess together. I'm never going to leave you. I will always be here for you, always." I watched his bottom lip start to quiver. "Now proudly walk into your class and I'll see you when you get home from school."

Watching his little self turn and walk into his classroom, I wanted to scream. *This isn't fair. He shouldn't have to be this brave.* The anger burned through me, anger at Richard for putting us through one nightmare after another for years.

Pressing my hand over my mouth so no one could see me sobbing, I quickly walked out of the school to my car, resting my head on the steering wheel.

For the love of God and everything that's holy, how am I supposed to do this? I have no lifeline. I need something to help me stop this pain. I need some relief from this mental anguish.

This pain is unbearable. I'm suffocating. I need something, anything, to numb this pain, even if it's for a little while.

Find the nearest liquor store.

After being raised by alcoholics and living with an alcoholic, I didn't have the desire to drink alcohol, but in this moment, I was willing to try anything to escape.

I walked into the liquor store and bought a bottle of Bacardi rum.

I started having one Bacardi and Coke every night, which turned into two every night. For those few hours I could calm my fears.

* * *

Out of the blue, Ben came to me, his eyes bright with excitement. "Mom, I have some money saved up and I want to do something fun together."

This took me by surprise, since he had been a bit curt and talking back lately.

"Do you have anything in mind that you'd like to do?"

"Not really, maybe dinner?"

"I just heard about this place where they serve dinner while you watch a theater play. The production is called *On Golden Pond*. Would you like to do something like that?"

I wasn't familiar with the play, though a few years later there was a movie by the same name. It was about a cantankerous man, his wife, and their daughter attempting to repair the family's dysfunctional relationship.

"That sounds good," Ben said.

"I'll check on tickets for us. This is so nice of you, Ben."

I called the theater the next day and made reservations for the three of us for the upcoming weekend. I bought the boys new outfits to wear for our date night, khaki pants and plaid shirts. They looked so handsome.

We arrived at the theater in plenty of time before they started to serve dinner. We were so excited; this was our first time seeing a live production.

A gentleman escorted us to our seats and even pulled out my chair for me, making me feel very special. The boys sat on either side of me, wide-eyed, with big smiles on their faces. They pointed out the red velvet drapes on the stage and the beautiful chandeliers hanging from the ceiling. *This is magical.*

Our preordered dinner choices were served just before the play began. The lights started to dim. Both boys looked at me with such joy. Then the red velvet curtains opened.

None of us could take our eyes off the stage, captivated by the actors bringing the story to life. During the final act, I leaned back in my chair and looked at both of my boys. Their bodies were relaxed, faces shining with happiness, their eyes never leaving the stage. This filled me with joy. I hadn't seen them this happy in a very long time.

I wish this magic would never end. I don't want this night to end.

At the end of the production the audience rose to their feet, clapping as each actor took their bows. The three of us stood and clapped until our hands turned red.

"Mom, I loved this," Jason said, his eyes filled with happiness.

"I loved this, too," I replied.

I looked at Ben, my eyes filling with tears. "Thank you for giving us such a wonderful gift tonight. I love you."

* * *

About three months after Richard was arrested, I received a letter from him, filled with crap about how much he loved me, along with the news that he'd been sentenced to five years in prison. How ironic, I thought, that the man who had imprisoned me and my boys in fear and isolation, broke my bones, shot at me, and bruised my body for years, was now confined to his own prison. I wished his sentence were longer, more like the thirteen years of hell he'd put me and the boys through. He'd have three meals a day and a bed to sleep in, more than what the boys and I could count on.

I loathe you.

One thing I hadn't considered when Richard was arrested was that he owed money to other drug dealers in the area, and they would want their money. Soon a couple dealers began calling and even stopping by the house, asking where Richard was or how to reach him. I would simply say that he'd been arrested and was going to prison.

Surprisingly, they didn't demand their money from me. Instead they offered their support, saying things like "If you need anything, just let me know" and "Richard always took care of us, so I want to be there for you," and even "If anyone threatens you, I will protect you."

Given my vulnerable state of mind—emotionally drained, fearful, and isolated from the world by Richard for so long—I lacked the mental clarity and tools to make good judgments. I started to believe they might actually be concerned for me and my boys.

Not long after the Thanksgiving holiday in 1982, a man by the name of Paul started calling and coming by the house. Before Richard was arrested, I'd seen him quite a few times when he would come by and pick up packages from Richard. He was always polite and cordial toward me.

One afternoon Paul called and said he was down on his luck and had just gotten out of some legal problems with the police and wanted to come by to talk.

Cautiously I asked, "What's this about? If you're looking for money, I don't have any to give you."

"Oh no, I'm not looking for any money. I promise. You were always pleasant to me. I'm turning my life around and just want to talk to a friendly person."

"You can come by in an hour, but I won't have much time, the boys will be coming home from school soon."

Forty minutes later, Paul was sitting in my family room with a glass of water in his hand.

"It's been rough the last few months," he said. "I'm ready to turn my life around and get out of this damn drug business. I don't want any part of it anymore."

"I hear you. I've had a hard time since Richard was arrested. Just trying to keep up with the boys, the house, money, working long hours. It's been difficult."

"Has anyone been giving you any trouble?"

"A few guys have called and stopped by. No one has threatened me yet, but I'm always on edge. I'm frightened some night they'll break in, demanding their money, and hurt me and the boys. I don't know what I would do if anything like that happened."

"Maybe we can help each other?"

"What do you mean?"

"I need a place to stay until I get on my feet. It sounds like you need protection. I'm working at a restaurant as a cook now, and they pay me a decent salary. I just need a place to stay until I can save up enough money for my own place. What if I move in for a couple months, pay you minimal rent weekly, in return I protect you and your boys. How does that sound?"

"Let me think about this. What's a good number to get in touch with you?" I asked, grabbing a pen and piece of paper.

Taking the paper from my hand, he wrote down his number at the restaurant. "I'm there every day, so call me anytime. Thanks for letting me stop by." He closed my front door on his way out.

This might be a good idea. I could put the money he'll pay me toward the mortgage.

A few days later I called Paul and said, "Okay, let's do this. I think this arrangement will be helpful for the both of us."

"Me, too. I'll see you this afternoon when I get off from work."

Paul moved in that night and paid me the first week's rent. Everything seemed to be working out fine and the boys liked him.

Six weeks after Paul moved in, his behavior took a drastic turn. He started acting erratic, constantly on edge, unable to sit still for more than a few minutes at a time. He became paranoid, suspicious of everything and everybody. Despite my training, I'd never seen the symptoms of an adult using cocaine. I'd only seen neonates who were born suffering from their mothers' addiction. I didn't connect the dots. Every time I brought up the rent he owed, Paul had a new excuse. First it was the restaurant had to reissue his paycheck, then the manager wasn't there to give him his check. The excuses piled up, one after another, while he continued living in my home without paying a dime. He ate my food, used my electricity, ran up the water bill, and promised the money would come soon.

The longer this went on the angrier I became until one day I confronted him.

"Paul, you owe me nine hundred dollars in back rent. I was counting on that money for my mortgage payment, but you keep making excuses for not paying me. I can't afford to do this anymore. I think it's time you either pay me the money you owe me or move out."

Without hesitation Paul fired back, "Fine, I'll move out today, but you know I can cause a lot of problems for you! I know people!" he shouted as he gathered his few belongings and stormed out the door. "I'll get your fucking money to you next week."

I was proud of myself for standing my ground. Still, I wondered what he was talking about. What people?

A few weeks passed and I didn't hear a word from Paul.

My stomach had still been bothering me a lot lately. I was even having trouble eating my lunch at the hospital. It had been four days since I'd eaten any solid food. My only intake was iced tea or water.

You have got to eat something tonight.

I can't eat. I'll get sick.

If you don't eat something tonight, you will die, and there is no one who will raise your boys.

Walking to the pantry, I picked up the jar of smooth peanut butter and grabbed the grape jelly out of the refrigerator and placed them both on the counter. I stood there for a moment, staring at the jars, trying to gather the strength.

I have to do this.

I pulled out one slice of bread and cut it in half, making a quarter of a sandwich. I was malnourished and dehydrated and had been for weeks. My mouth was always so dry that any type of solid food was difficult to swallow. If I did take a bite the food would get stuck in the back of my throat. Then I would gag, causing me to vomit.

I have to keep this down.

I picked up my glass of iced tea and took a sip, chasing it with a small bite of the sandwich. I chewed quickly and swallowed, willing it to stay down. I repeated this process, bite after cautious bite, until only the core of the sandwich remained.

The phone rang and my body jerked. Every unexpected sound made me jump, my nerves were so on edge. Even the smallest noise felt like someone shouting in my ear with a bull horn. I was constantly bracing for something terrible to happen.

"This is Ralph. You don't know me, but I'm looking for Paul. I heard he was staying at your place."

"How did you get this number?" I asked.

"I got your number from a friend of Paul's. He knows your husband."

"He was here, but he moved out a couple weeks ago," I replied with a sharp tone.

"I need to get in touch with him right away. Could you please take down my number and call me if you hear from him?"

"Sure, and if you happen to find him, please let me know. He owes me a lot of money."

"I'll let you know. Don't lose my number," Ralph said.

Hanging up the phone, I folded the piece of paper with his number and placed it in the kitchen drawer.

I wonder why he's trying so hard to find Paul.

CHAPTER 24

Unmasking Deceit

It was late January, and I finally had a day off from the hospital. I was standing in front of my closet, looking for an outfit to wear to run a few errands.

The phone rang. I quickly pulled a sweater over my head and picked up the phone.

"Candy, this is Ralph, do you remember me? We spoke last week."

"Yes, I remember you," I answered reluctantly.

"I have some news, it's about Paul, and I could use your help. Can you meet me today or tomorrow?"

"Can you tell me what this is about?"

"I'd really like to speak in person, you know, face-to-face. We'll meet at a public place, so you won't have to worry. How about if we plan on meeting at The People's Lounge around eight tomorrow? Will that work?"

"That should be fine unless I have an emergency with one of my patients. Then I wouldn't be able to make it. What is this about?"

"Okay, great, I'll see you tomorrow. I'll tell you everything tomorrow." He hung up.

Should I meet this guy? Maybe he'll have some information

about Paul, and I'll be able to get the nine hundred dollars. That would really help pay the mortgage.

Finishing my shift the next day on time, I quickly changed out of my scrubs before leaving the hospital and heading to our meeting place, which turned out to be inside a hotel. I couldn't help but wonder why he would want to meet at a hotel bar. My mind raced between fear and curiosity, hoping I would finally get the money Paul owed me.

The bar was dark and dingy with loud music playing. I spotted a man standing up at a table, waving his hand for my attention. He looked to be in his mid-forties, with brown, graying hair and a thick body. I immediately noticed there was another man in his mid-forties sitting with him.

Why are there two of them?

How does he recognize me?

I don't recognize either one of them.

Fearful, I reluctantly approached the table.

"Hi, Candy, I'm Ralph and this is my buddy, Pete. We've known each other for years, right, Pete? Here, take a seat." He stood and pulled out a chair. "How was the hospital today?"

"It was good, just a long day."

"Thanks for meeting me. I have a couple things I want to talk to you about."

"Did you find Paul?"

"Yeah, I found him, and I need your help." He leaned forward, folding his hands together on the table.

"What? I'm confused."

"You see, Paul was supposed to connect me with this guy, someone who would help me get some cocaine, but the deal with the guy fell through," he explained, his voice tense. "I really need some quick cash. My child is sick and needs a procedure, and my wife and I don't have the money or medical insurance. I thought if I could do this deal, just one time, I could make some money for my kid. Paul told me your husband was a dealer."

"Your child is sick? I'm so sorry to hear that," I said, not wanting to make him feel uncomfortable by asking what kind of procedure. Instead, I lightly touched his forearm to offer comfort. "My soon-to-be-ex husband is in prison in North Carolina."

"Do you know of anyone I could get the cocaine from? Did he ever talk about anyone he got stuff from?" he asked, his voice desperate.

"I was not involved with his dealings. I do know the wife of one of his guys. We've met a few times for lunch," I said, thinking about his child.

"Could you ask that guy's wife to get it for me?"

"She's not involved with her husband's dealings, either. What about Paul, did you find him?"

"Yeah, I found him, but don't count on getting any of your money back. He doesn't have any money and never will. He just talks a big game."

"Damn you, Paul," I whispered.

"Listen, I know you were counting on that money from Paul."

"Yes," I interrupted him, "I was counting on that money, and I'm sick and tired of people taking from me and hurting me."

"Let's help one another here. I'll have plenty of money after this deal is done to pay for my kid's procedure and to give you the nine hundred Paul owes you—if you help me find some cocaine."

"I'll have to check with Lilly," I replied nervously.

"Who's Lilly?"

"She's the wife of the guy Richard got some drugs from."

"Okay, when can you talk to Lilly?"

"I'll call her tomorrow and let you know." My hand trembled as I picked up my purse to leave.

"I'll be waiting to hear from you," I heard him say as I rushed out of the bar.

Driving home, I began to wonder.

Should I call Lilly? But his poor child needs help. I'll get back my money. I'm so tired of being taken advantage of. I'll be able to pay the mortgage this month. His poor child.

* * *

As a domestic violence victim, I had not learned the tools to tell if someone is trustworthy. Navigating this process felt like walking through a maze wearing a blindfold. Since I have endured the cruelty of another's control and developed a heightened awareness of suffering, I have a deep desire to shield others from experiencing the same agony, making it difficult for me to determine the difference between good and evil. I didn't want anyone, even strangers, to feel the kind of torment I've known, leaving me unable to determine whether their intentions are genuine or if there is something darker. This is the very same thought process the majority of domestic violence victims experience, which makes them vulnerable to exploitation and manipulation.

The next day after work I called Lilly and briefly explained what Ralph had told me. She said she would speak to her husband, Jacob, and have him call me. About an hour later, Jacob called. He explained he would help, but it might take a couple of weeks to get the drugs and he would let me know the cost once he had them in his possession. I relayed Jacob's message to Ralph, who sounded desperate to get the deal done.

A couple weeks later, Jacob called to let me know he had the cocaine and I called Ralph to let him know the cost and to tell him that I could pick the drugs up whenever he was ready. We decided the next morning would be the best since I had the day off.

That morning, I made breakfast for the boys, packed their lunches, and hurried them off to catch the school bus. As I brushed my teeth, doubts crept in.

Am I doing the right thing?

Don't think about it. It will be done in an hour, and I won't have to think about this ever again. Soon I'll have the money I'm owed, and Ralph's child will get his procedure.

Backing out of the driveway, my palms began to sweat. I gripped the steering wheel tighter, watching my knuckles turn white from the pressure. As I drove down the winding back roads, I started to hyperventilate.

When I finally pulled into Lilly and Jacob's long dirt driveway, their house was eerily quiet. I noticed Lilly's car was not in the driveway as I shifted into park and turned off the engine. *Just breathe, take slow breaths, this will be over in an hour.*

I knocked on the door.

"Come on in. The door's not locked," Jacob yelled in a friendly voice. "I'm in the kitchen, Candy."

"Good morning, Jacob. I'm kind of in a hurry."

"No problem, your bag is over there on the table. Just drop the money by sometime this afternoon."

"Thanks, Jacob, I'll see you later." I grabbed the brown paper bag from the table and raced out the door, not wanting to open the bag to check what was inside. My nerves were barely holding it together. I didn't care what was in the damn brown bag.

I hate drugs.

I drove as fast as I could back to my house, tires screeching as I pulled into the garage. Grabbing the brown bag, I hurried through the door to the kitchen. As we'd agreed, Ralph was sitting at the kitchen table, waiting.

I handed him the brown bag. He glanced inside before saying, "Okay, let me run to my car and get the money." He turned and walked out of the front door. As I made my way back to the kitchen, I suddenly heard shouting from the outside.

"You're under arrest! Put your hands up!"

Startled, I quickly spun around, only to have a gun shoved into my forehead. It immediately brought me back to the moment Richard had fired a sawed-off shotgun at me.

My knees buckled. I lost consciousness as I collapsed on the floor.

"Stand up!" I heard them yell, their voices sounding as if they were coming from far away.

I felt hands slide under my forearms, pulling me to my feet, dazed and in shock. Everything around me blurred as I tried to make sense of what was happening. My eyes focused for a moment and I saw at least six large men wearing bulletproof vests that said TPD. Tampa Police Department. They were patting each other on the back, congratulating each other like they'd just scored a fucking touchdown.

"Great job, guys," one of them said, his voice cheerful.

"Yeah, we got her!" another one said.

"Do you know why you're being arrested?" one of the men yelled. I shook my head. "You're being arrested for distribution of a controlled substance."

Looking directly at Ralph, I screamed, "Ralph, why did you do this to me? You told me your child was sick."

He would not look at me. He just turned and walked away.

One of them began reciting my Miranda rights, while another roughly pulled my arms behind my back. Cold metal cuffs clicked so tight around my wrists I could feel them cutting into my skin.

"Guys, look around the house for any drugs or drug paraphernalia," one of them ordered, his tone authoritative.

"My children, what's going to happen to my children?" I asked in a low whisper.

"You should have thought about that before you bought drugs," one of them yelled.

"Why did you do this to me, Ralph?" I screamed at the top of my lungs. Then, whispering again, "What about my nursing license?"

"You'll probably never work as a nurse again," one of the officers snarked.

"I need to call my sister and ask her to pick up my boys."

"You can call her from the police station."

As they marched me outside, one officer on either side of me, my feet not touching the grass, I noticed at least five police cars parked in front of my house.

Just put your head down, don't look up.
Keep breathing so you don't die.

* * *

I have no recollection of what happened after I was shoved into the back seat of the police car until I found myself in a small room with no windows, plain walls, and the smell of old mildew. Ralph was sitting behind a cold gray metal desk with papers scattered all over it. He ordered one of the detectives to unlock the cuffs. He motioned for me to sit down in a chair in front of his desk. I sat and rubbed the raw, red skin on my wrists.

"Okay, give it up," he demanded, his voice low and smug. "I need some names. I know you know some drug dealers." He leaned back, arms crossed over his chest, a look of self-satisfaction plastered on his round face. His black belt was barely visible beneath his distended belly. The harsh fluorescent lights above reflected off his slick skin, his pores almost glistening with oil. His brown hair, streaked with gray, was combed back from his forehead with a part in the middle, giving him an oddly outdated look.

"Come on, give me some names, or you'll be spending a lot of time behind bars." His black boot tapped on the floor impatiently.

"I-I don't know any of Richard's dealers. I-I told you this before," I stammered, my voice trembling so much it was hard to get the words out. "Why did you do this to me?"

"You did this to yourself. Oh, I think you know a lot more than what you're saying. I need names now." He raised his voice. "If you give me some names, I'll speak to the district attorney and get your sentence reduced, but only if you cooperate."

Panic welled up in me. *I can't go to jail. What about my boys? I have no one to take care of them.*

"I have to call my sister," I blurted out. "I need to call my sister to ask her to pick up the boys after school and take them home with her for the night. I need to make this call right now."

"Fine, here's the phone." He slammed a phone down hard on the desk in front of me.

My hands trembling, I lifted the receiver and dialed her number.

"Sue, it's me. Um, could you please pick up the boys and let them spend the night at your house tonight?"

"What's going on?"

"I've been arrested, so I don't think I'll be home tonight. I'll explain later."

"Yeah, I'll pick them up."

I heard a click on the other end of the line. I knew there would be a price to pay later on.

Ralph began to badger me again, his voice rising as he slammed his hand down on the desk. My heart was pounding, but in that moment, something inside me shifted. I managed to clear my mind just enough to remember I had rights.

I've seen this on TV.

"Look, I'm telling you the truth, I don't know any dealers," I said, my voice becoming a little stronger. "I may not know much about the legal system. But I do know I have a right to an attorney, and I want to call one now."

"Fine, I'll step out of the room," he said in a curt tone, walking out and closing the door.

I didn't know any lawyers—but my boss would, she knew everybody. I'd told Gayle some small fragments of my home life with Richard and had mentioned his arrest. I never felt like I could share the whole story for fear she might question my competence as an effective nurse and also judge me. So, I kept the worst hidden.

"Gayle, it's Candy. I'm in a mess right now. I've been arrested. Do you happen to know an attorney I could call to help me?"

"What the hell? Arrested? For what? Did Richard do something to you?"

"I'm not sure, but I do know I've been set up. I can't lose my job, Gayle."

"Don't worry, this will all work out. Call Jerry, he's an attorney.

I've known him for years. He'll be able to help you. Call him right now. Do you have a pen and paper so you can write his number down?"

"Yes, I'm ready, give me his number, please."

"Tell him I referred you. Make sure you call me later and let me know how you're doing. I'll be waiting for your call. That bastard Richard, I'm sure he had something to do with this. Try not to worry."

* * *

I'd never spoken to an attorney before, but I knew I had no other choice. Pulling myself together, I dialed the number Gayle had given me. A pleasant woman answered the phone. I told her I needed to speak with Jerry right away.

A few seconds later, a man's voice answered.

I swallowed hard, my voice shaky. "My name is Candice, your friend Gayle said you would be able to help me." My voice broke. I was barely holding it together. "I've been arrested, I'm at a police station, but I don't know where it's located. This detective set me up for selling drugs."

"Okay, it's okay, just calm down. I'll take care of this. I'll find you, don't worry. Have you ever been in trouble with the law before?"

"No, just a couple of speeding tickets is all."

"It's pretty late in the day, but I'm going to see if I can get in touch with a judge I know and get you out on an ROR. So just hang tight."

"Will you get me out tonight? What does ROR mean?"

"I'm going to do my best to get you out of there tonight. An ROR is a release on your own recognizance. It means the judge doesn't think you're a risk for breaking any laws while being out of jail pending trial. You wouldn't need to put up any bail money, either. Just try and remain calm and I'll speak with you in a few hours and let you know what's happening." His voice was calm and reassuring.

The moment the line went dead, I started rocking back and forth, trying to keep myself from completely falling apart.

Just then the door swung open, and in strutted Ralph, dripping with smugness. It was as if he was trying to be theatrical, as though he was waiting for someone to acknowledge how important he thought he was. His khaki slacks kept falling, forcing him to tug them up every few steps. With a smirk plastered on his face, trying his best to intimidate me, he asked sarcastically, "Did you get in touch with an attorney?"

"Yes, I did, and he's going to help me."

"Then we're going to put you in a holding cell for now."

The next thing I remember, a tall man in a police uniform unlocked a heavy metal door. He pushed me into a dark, dirty cell with several metal bunkbeds crammed up against the concrete walls. No windows, just concrete everywhere. Walking into the cell, I saw an empty lower bunk bed to my right and quickly sat down, not making any eye contact with any of the several women in the cell. The slamming of the metal door made my body jerk.

"Hey, what are you in here for?" a woman asked.

I didn't want to answer. She said, "I asked, 'What are you in here for?'"

As she continued to press me for an answer, another woman came over and sat down as close as she could get without climbing in my lap. "You're really good lookin'," she said, curling a strand of my hair around her fingers. I couldn't move. I sat paralyzed with fear.

"Hey, bitch, leave her alone," another woman yelled out. "Can't you see she's never been in any trouble before? This is her first time in here. Come on, get away from her, bitch."

The woman reluctantly got up and walked to the other side of the cell.

I don't know how long I was in that cell, maybe a few hours. I lost all track of time. I recall that finally the heavy metal door was opened by a man in uniform who called my name. "Candice, you're being released."

I jumped up and walked out of that dark, dirty cell into a hallway. A man said, "Hi, Candice, I'm Jerry, your attorney." He was very tall, over six feet.

By the time all the paperwork was completed, it was past midnight. I had been released on that ROR thing, just as Jerry had explained.

"I have no means of getting home. They took my car, Jerry," I said, my voice tired and frustrated. "I live forty-five minutes north of here. I can't afford to pay a taxi to take me that far. What am I going to do? I need a car to work."

"Don't worry, my home and office are close by here. Why don't you stay at my place tonight, then I'll bring you to my office in the morning? I'll make some calls to some of the guys I know in the department, and I'll get your car released tomorrow."

"Okay," I replied reluctantly, feeling a knot in my stomach. I'd never spent the night alone at a male stranger's house before. I was frightened of everything and everyone, but I didn't see any other option.

"So how do you know Gayle?" Jerry asked.

"I work for her agency. I'm a registered nurse," I answered in a low voice, not wanting to talk.

"I've known Gayle for years. She's really a great gal. Here we are, I told you I lived close by." He pulled his car in the garage.

Sheepishly walking behind him into the kitchen, I hesitated for a moment before speaking. "Can I have some water? I haven't had anything to drink all day." My voice was barely above a whisper. As I stood there, I took in the room around me. His kitchen was large and impeccably clean, every surface spotless. Attached to the kitchen was an equally pristine family room, its walls covered in dark striped wallpaper that gave the space a formal look, almost stiff. In the distance, a long hallway stretched out, leading to what I assumed were bedrooms.

"Sure." He opened a cabinet, pulled out a glass, and filled it with tap water.

"Thank you." I immediately drank the entire glass.

"Let me show you where you'll be sleeping," he said, leading me down a short hallway. "This is the guest room, with an en suite bathroom. I'm sure you want to shower after being in that disgusting cell. Here's one of my T-shirts to sleep in."

"Thank you," I whispered, exhausted. All I wanted to do was shower in hopes of washing away this horrific day.

"Is there anything else you need? No? Good night." He closed the door behind him.

I walked into the bathroom and immediately locked the door behind me. Standing under the hot, streaming water, rinsing away the grime and fear, my nerves began to settle down. For the first time that day, my body was not trembling.

It will all be okay tomorrow.

Jerry will take care of everything so don't worry.
I'm safe now.

I walked out of the bathroom and stumbled toward the bed, desperate to stop my mind from racing. I didn't even think to lock the bedroom door. I just laid my head on the pillow and closed my eyes. I was about to doze off when I heard the bedroom door creak open. My eyes flew open. It was Jerry. He walked softly over to the bed, pulling back the sheet and blanket covering me. I froze as he climbed on top of me, spreading my legs apart. Pain shot through me as he shoved himself inside me. I couldn't move. I had no strength, no will in me to fight. I just lay there staring at the ceiling, tears streaming down my cheeks. *This will be over soon.* I could hear him breathing heavily as he continued to thrust, each second feeling like an eternity. When he was finished, he got up just as quietly as he entered and walked out, closing the door behind him.

He never said a word.

CHAPTER 25

The Mornings After

The next morning as I put on my smelly clothes from the day before, I told myself it didn't matter that he raped me. It didn't make a difference, because I wasn't worthy of being treated any better. That's what Richard had drilled into my head for years, so it had to be true, right? He always said I was nothing.

As I stood there, numb and hollow, Jerry yelled out, "Hey, are you ready? I need to get to my office."

"Yes, I'm ready." I opened the bedroom door and made my way to the kitchen. He stood there casually sipping his coffee. His eyes glanced at me then quickly looked away, as if I was worthless. Not a word, not even an offer of a glass of water.

It was clear that what he'd done to me the previous night didn't bother him in the slightest.

"Let's go," he said.

I followed him into the garage. The blast of the bright sun and humidity hit me in the face when he opened the garage door.

"It's going to be a hot one today," he said, starting the car.

Backing out of the driveway, he turned on the radio and began singing to a song that was playing, like it was just another day to him.

I sat in the passenger seat, shoulders slumped, my hands in my lap, pressing my body close to the door in hopes of creating some kind of barrier between us. I wanted to disappear, but there was nowhere to go.

Jerry's office was in a high-rise in downtown Tampa, located on one of the upper floors with a beautiful view of the city. The space had a modern décor with windows stretching from the ceiling to the floors.

"Good morning, Jerry. You're in the office early today. I thought you had to be in court this morning?" his receptionist said.

"I need to help this young lady get her car back. Hold my calls for about thirty minutes." His tone was calm but firm.

Jerry walked around his desk and sat in a brown high-back leather chair, gesturing for me to take a seat in the chair in front of his desk.

"Let me make some phone calls and see what I can do." A minute later he was chatting with someone. "Hey, James, how's everything going? I saw you at the courthouse last week, did you win that case? How's the wife and kids?"

I sat there dumbfounded, listening to this casual nonsense while my life had completely fallen apart. My world was in shambles, and here he was talking like we were at some social gathering.

Scared out of my mind, I couldn't comprehend if his chatty conversations with his buddies were helping me or not. After a few calls, he leaned forward, resting his elbows on his desk. "Looks like you're not getting your car back." His expression was full of smug satisfaction. "They said, 'No way are we releasing her car.'" He made it clear he was finished trying to help. He got what he wanted.

I fell back in my chair, my eyes welling up with tears. "What am I supposed to do now?"

Without a trace of compassion in his voice, he said, "I suggest you find a criminal attorney to see what they can do. I got you released from jail last night because any kind of attorney can do that. But from here on out, you're going to need someone who specializes in criminal law. I'll have one of my assistants drive you home. Goodbye and best of luck to you."

That's it? You're an asshole.

I never saw him again.

* * *

After Jerry's office assistant dropped me off at home, I trudged toward the front door, which suddenly felt miles away. Every step seemed heavier than the last. I was still trying to make sense of what had happened in the last twenty-four hours.

My feet moved on their own, disconnected from the rest of me as I unlocked the door and climbed the stairs to my bedroom. I had no control over my body.

Get in the shower. Wash away the filth.

Turning on the water as hot as I could bear, I stepped in, hoping the scalding steam would strip away the grime that clung to my skin—along with the shame and fear that had taken over. The water cascading down my back, I grabbed the wall, then slumped forward, sliding to my knees. I wrapped my arms around myself as if I could protect what was left of me from any more harm.

Tears poured freely, mixing with the steam and water, but no matter how hot the shower was, it couldn't wash away the overwhelming shame. It couldn't touch the fear.

No one is going to believe you were raped. Hell, they didn't believe you when you told them Richard bruised your body and broke your bones.

You have to get up off the floor now. Don't think about this right now, you will lose your mind.

* * *

That evening, the phone rang. "Candy, this is Gayle, how are you? Did my friend Jerry take care of you last night?"

I felt a lump in my throat, knowing there was no way I could tell her the truth, that Jerry had raped me. I said, "Jerry got me out of jail. He tried to get my car back, but the police said no. I don't have a credit card to even rent a car. I only have checks."

"Damn, that's horrible. I'll help you rent a car until you can figure things out. At least you'll be able to get back to work. Call this number. I know this guy at this car rental place. He'll help you. Make sure you tell him I sent you. I'll explain that you work for me and you'll be good for the rental fees."

"Thank you. I just need a couple of days to pull myself together. That was a horrific experience for me."

"Of course, I can only imagine how awful it's been. You just let me know when you're ready."

"Would you happen to know a criminal attorney you would recommend?"

"Sure, his name is Kolton. Give me a second and I'll look up his number."

The following morning, after getting the boys off to school, I dialed Kolton's number and scheduled an appointment with him for the next day. It was surreal to need a criminal attorney.

Just breathe, Candy, I told myself, trying to keep it together and not spiral out of control.

Next, I called the car rental company and told them Gayle had referred me. They were very kind and helpful. I explained I needed the car today but had no transportation to pick it up. They said they would deliver the car to my home that day and the weekly rental fee would be two hundred and ten dollars per week.

Okay, you now have transportation to get to Kolton's tomorrow, I reassured myself, realizing I'd have to work an extra twelve-hour shift each week in addition to my current sixty hours to pay for the rental car.

The next afternoon I arrived fifteen minutes early to my appointment with Kolton. When the receptionist ushered me into his office, I saw a short man behind the desk. He was leaning back in a large leather chair, both hands linked casually behind his head. His dark brown hair had distinctive gray streaks, but not the leading man kind of gray streaks. These were more like stripes. A rather large belly spilled over into his lap, and his tie hung loosely around his neck. There was something about him that made me think he was even older than he appeared.

"Have a seat, Candy. How can I help you?" he asked with a deep but firm voice. "Gayle called me this morning and said you were arrested a few days ago. What's going on?"

"I was arrested for selling cocaine to a detective."

"What? You were arrested for selling cocaine?"

"Yes, six officers barged into my house and arrested me. They took my car, too."

"All right, we need to start from the beginning." He leaned in closer and picked up the pen next to his yellow legal pad.

I told him everything from the time Richard and I moved to

Tampa, the beatings, being shot at, his control over me, the last time I saw him in North Carolina. I recounted how Paul owed me nine hundred dollars, and then how the detective called me, desperate, claiming his child was sick and that he needed money fast, asking me to help him find cocaine to sell, promising he would pay me my nine hundred dollars.

As I told my story, Kolton wrote frantically on his yellow legal pad.

When I finished, there was silence. Kolton leaned back in his chair, tossing his pen onto his desk. "You do know they entrapped you, right?" His tone was flat but firm.

"What's entrapment?"

"These guys reached out to you; you didn't seek them out. I wouldn't be surprised if your husband didn't have something to do with this, also. I'm going to get my private investigator on this to check some things out. He may want to meet with you sometime as well, but he'll call you if he does. Are you divorced from Richard now?" His tone was sharp and businesslike. "It's important we distance you from him since he's a convicted drug dealer. If you want any chance of a fair hearing or trial before the judge, you need to divorce Richard. If you're still married to him, the judge will not take kindly to this."

"I want to divorce that scum. I've been trying for years to get away from him."

"We'll get started filing the divorce papers along with the other legal issues. Have you heard from the Florida Board of Nursing?"

"No."

"You probably will soon. But we can't worry about that right now. Let's get the other legal problems addressed first."

"Mr. Kolton, I don't have a lot of money to pay you. I've never had to pay a lawyer before. I have no idea how much lawyers cost."

"My receptionist will get you set up with a payment plan. You just keep working as much as you can."

As I walked to my car, I felt a slight sense of hope creeping in, like maybe things were going to be okay. But then out of nowhere, a loud noise echoed through the air. It sounded like a gunshot.

I'm being shot at!

Absolute fear took over. I spun around quickly, only to see a car speeding by. I began running toward my rental car before my mind caught up. Frantically, I yanked the car door open and leaped inside, gripping the steering wheel hard to try to steady my trembling hands. Each breath came in a shallow burst.

Calm down, slow your breathing down. Come on, take a deep breath, now exhale, I told myself repeatedly.

After a few moments, my breathing slowed and the pounding in my chest began to ease. I realized it was just a car that had backfired.

* * *

A few days later, the private investigator Kolton told me about arranged to meet me at a local café. Walking into the café, I immediately noticed a young-looking man in his thirties, with brownish blond hair and a muscular body.

"I'm Matt," he said, handing me his driver's license. "That license is for you to see I'm really Matt. Take a look at it. Notice I'm also a highway patrolman. See my uniform?"

I looked down at the picture again, then back up at him. Terror came over me. *He must be here to arrest me.*

I got up and ran, not realizing there were three steps in front of me. I tripped on one of them and fell flat on my face in the middle of the restaurant. A waitress immediately came running over and helped me to my feet. I rushed into the ladies' room and began pacing back and forth.

Okay, okay. Call Kolton's office to make sure who this guy is. That's what you need to do. Go find a pay phone.

Do it now.

In my panic to find a pay phone, I bolted out of the ladies' room and stopped the first waitress I saw.

"Please, ma'am, I'm sorry to bother you, but do you have a phone I could use to make a quick call?" I asked.

She gave me a puzzled look, then gestured behind me. "Sure, there's a pay phone right there on the wall behind you."

The pay phone was right next to the ladies' room that I'd just come from. Embarrassed but grateful, I thanked her quickly and grabbed the phone, fumbling for a dime from my change purse.

"Attorney's office, Eileen speaking, how can I help you?"

"Eileen, this is Candy. I'm here at this café to meet Mr. Kolton's private investigator. This guy says his name is Matt. He says he's a PI. He says he's a Florida highway patrolman. Is he going to arrest me?"

"Don't worry, Matt's our investigator. It's okay to tell him everything. He's not going to arrest you or hurt you, I promise. You can trust him."

Pulling myself together, I walked back to the table, my legs feeling unsteady. I sat across from Matt, fear still heavy on my chest.

"I wasn't sure you were going to come back," Matt said, his tone calm and reassuring.

"I wasn't sure, either. I called Kolton's office to confirm you're really his investigator."

Matt nodded slowly. "I understand this must be very frightening for you, but you're safe with me. Please tell me what happened."

Steeling myself, I started from the beginning, and recounted my story. I told Matt everything, except that Jerry raped me. Somehow, in the twisted logic that had taken over my mind, I deserved it, like it was a punishment for picking up the drugs in the first place. I was worthless. If I hadn't made that choice, I wouldn't have been in that situation. So maybe, just maybe, the rape was the consequence I had earned.

* * *

In following the days and weeks, I was terrified of everything. Strangers asking harmless questions at the market made my heart race with fear. Even the mailbox was a source of anxiety, as I dreaded what might be waiting inside. Every strange sound in the middle of the night sent me into a panic.

The only place I had any relief from the constant fear was the hospital. There, I could compartmentalize and focus on my patients and their families. I felt confident and in control, knowing I was a damn good nurse.

But as soon as my shift was over, the struggles persisted. My stomach ached constantly. Every meal felt like a test of how much could I swallow without gagging.

I never told the boys what happened to me that night, the arrest or the rape. I wanted to shield them from this reality.

The only exception occurred a few weeks after my arrest when Jason came rushing in the house, his eyes wide open with concern.

"Mom, my friend told me his mother saw you being taken away

in handcuffs. Is that true?"

I struggled to find the right words. I wanted to protect him. I didn't want him dragged into this darkness. "Don't worry. This has to do with your father. They just wanted to ask me some questions."

Thankfully, he seemed satisfied with my answer.

Inside, I had a knot in my stomach.

My nerves were so on edge that I had little patience for the boys and their teenage attitudes. It was as if they were challenging me every day, testing the boundaries of my patience and control. This only fueled my frustration. Instead of having the patience and the ability to be their mother, I found myself snapping, reacting in anger. I yelled and screamed if they didn't obey me. It was as if I had become my parents.

One evening, I called them from the hospital and told them to take showers and get ready for bed before I got home. When I arrived, I could tell neither of them had showered, though they had their pajamas on.

"Did you guys take showers?" I asked sharply.

"Yes, we showered."

I raised my voice. "You guys didn't shower; your hair isn't even wet."

"Yes, we did, Mom."

Determined to prove them wrong, I marched upstairs, pulled back the shower curtain, and found the shower was bone-dry. The bar of soap wasn't even wet.

"You're both lying to me. The damn soap isn't even wet!" I yelled.

"Yes, we did, Mom!" Ben yelled back, his face flushed with anger.

"Mom, I showered, I really did," Jason snarked, his defiance growing.

After ten minutes of arguing and yelling, I'd had enough. "I'm going to spank you both with a belt unless you tell me the truth. I know you both are lying to me." I stormed into my bedroom, returning with a belt in my hand. "Are you going to tell me the truth now, or am I going to have to spank you?"

"Mom, I didn't shower, please don't hit me," Jason blurted out.

"Finally, the truth. Now go to your room."

Then I turned to Ben, who was still defiant.

"Ben, did you shower?" I asked again, staring him down.

"Yes, I took a shower!" he screamed, his face turning redder.

"Go in your room and lay across your bed." I was determined to make him tell me the truth. I stormed into his room after him and began swinging the belt, striking him on his buttocks. "Tell me the truth!" I screamed.

"I'm telling the truth!" he screamed back.

I kept striking him, but the truth I wanted never came. After several minutes, I couldn't hit him anymore. The weight of what I'd done made me sick.

I dropped the belt and walked out, heading to the kitchen where I gripped the counter, my whole body shaking as I began to sob.

Suddenly Ben stomped out of his room with Jason following him, screaming, "I'm going to call child abuse on you!"

"Oh, yeah," I shouted back, grabbing the receiver from the kitchen wall phone. "Here's the damn phone! Go ahead, call them! I'll even dial the number for you. Do you want me to dial the damn number?"

They both stomped back into their rooms and slammed their doors.

I made myself a rum and Coke and sat quietly, looking at the ugly rocking chair Richard used to sit in.

You disgusting piece of shit. You did this to us. I hate you!

* * *

It had been a couple of weeks since I had talked to Kolton. Finally, one day the phone rang and his receptionist told me Kolton would be by around lunchtime with some papers for me to sign.

When the doorbell rang, I knew who it was. I braced myself for bad news.

"Please, come in." I tried to sound steady. "We can sit at the dining room table. It's right this way."

"You have some nice antiques," he commented, glancing around the room. "I'd like to see the rest of your home. Do you have antiques upstairs?"

I thought it was a strange thing to ask but I said, "The boys have antiques in their rooms."

"Will you show me? I really like antiques."

I showed him. Then he asked, "Where is your bedroom? Do you have antiques in your room?"

I hesitated for a moment before motioning across the hall. "Here's my room. I don't have a bed, just the mattress on the floor as you can see. I do have an antique headboard, but I'll have to get a bed frame made when I can afford it."

"I like your headboard, and your mattress looks very comfortable, too." He walked into the bedroom and sat down on the mattress.

"Why don't you come over here and sit with me." He patted the mattress. "Come on, come sit with me, right next to me."

"I really don't want to. We can go downstairs so I can sign the papers you brought," I replied.

"No, I prefer you come and sit with me for a few minutes. Come on over here," he insisted, his tone more aggressive.

Reluctantly, I nodded. I sat next to him.

He reached over, pulling me closer, and started unbuttoning my blouse. Panic shot through me.

"What are you doing? I don't want to do this," I whispered, trying to stand, but he pulled me back down.

He didn't say a word. He slipped his hand inside my bra, roughly grabbing my breast. My heart pounded.

"I'm uncomfortable. I don't want to have sex with you," I managed to say, my voice trembling.

"This is how you can repay me for my legal services," he said coldly. "I know you don't have any money, and you won't find another lawyer to take your case without paying them. Now just lie down with me."

His words sent a wave of nausea through me as I lay there in fear and disbelief. Tears once again rolled down my cheeks. *I'm being raped again.*

There had never been any papers to sign. After he left, all I could do was curl up on my side, tucking my legs and feet tightly underneath my body as if making myself smaller could somehow erase what had just happened. My body convulsed in waves, but I wasn't cold. Chaotic thoughts raged in my mind, a storm of confusion and shame.

How am I going to survive? I'm worthless.
I can't go to prison; my boys need me.
What is wrong with me?
Why does this keep happening to me?
Is it me? Am I giving some kind of unspoken message that I want

to be raped? Is this my punishment?

Guilt wrapped around me like I was being suffocated. *Why would a man feel he has the right to rape me? Can't they see I'm mentally at my breaking point?* Clearly, they could see my fear and vulnerability, but they didn't care if I lost my mind.

Yet, here I was again, trapped, trying to make sense of how my life had unraveled.

I'm worthless.

* * *

The boys were growing more independent, still making their own money by finding and selling golf balls from the golf course. With me working so many hours, our lives began to feel like a blur. We passed each other like ships, connecting whenever we could, but drifting farther apart.

Pulling into the driveway after work one evening around eight pm, daylight still lingering in the sky, I noticed the garage door was already open and the boy's minibikes were gone. *The boys must be with their friends.* My eyes then focused on the mailbox at the end of the driveway. I hadn't checked the mailbox in days, too afraid of what might be waiting inside: another bill, or something worse, something I didn't want to face.

It's time to check the damn mailbox.

I dreaded what I would find. It was as if I knew instinctively there was something I didn't want to see.

Only one letter was inside. A sigh of relief came over me—until I saw the return address. It was from the Department of Professional Regulations, Board of Nursing.

My hands shook as I tore open the envelope and unfolded the letter. I scanned the subject line. *Your nursing license is being investigated for the reasons that follow.* I couldn't read anymore.

"They're going to take my nursing license," I whispered to myself. The one thing I'd sworn on the day I graduated that no one could take away from me. And now it was happening.

The next morning, I called Kolton's office and told him about the letter from the board. "I'm panicking, what do we need to do?"

"Calm down," he said. "Listen to me. We can't focus on the board investigation just yet. The state charges have to be our priority. We'll deal with the board later."

"What do you mean, later?" I asked, my voice breaking. "Isn't there something we can do to save my nursing license while dealing with the state charges? Please help me."

"Candy, listen to me. The board cannot take any action toward your license right now until the state charges are addressed first. You can still work, just like you've been doing. In fact, I want you to be working as much as you can right now."

"I'm already working sixty to seventy hours a week," I replied, pacing back and forth.

"That's great, keep it up. The more you work, the better things will look for you with both the state and the board. Hear me out. If the state drops the charges, the board will probably follow suit," he continued. "But if you're sentenced to prison, the board will almost certainly suspend your license or revoke it completely. Everything is dependent on what the state decides, and the board's ruling will follow. I need to get on another call. I'll keep in touch. Don't worry so much."

Click.

"This is so fucked up!" I screamed, my voice breaking with the force of my anger. "I loathe you! I hate you! Richard, Paul, Ralph, Kolton, Jerry, I hate you all!" I screamed louder, my fists clenched. I threw the phone across the room. Pure anger exploded. Every ounce of frustration, fear, and betrayal I had buried deep came roaring to the surface.

"Is there any other fucking thing you can do to me, God?"

* * *

The first state court hearing was set for December 1983, almost exactly ten months after my arrest. As the date approached, I continued to find comfort in a Bacardi and Coke every night. Alcohol had become my escape from the suffocating weight of it all.

There was a local bar a couple miles from my house that I would go to about once a week. I'd sit at the bar, drink, listen to the loud music, talk to strangers, and sometimes dance. It was an escape—I didn't have to be *me*. The men would approach me, I'd flirt, giving them just enough attention to keep them entertained. They would ask for my number, but I would play them along just for the distraction. For those few hours I didn't have to think about the looming legal troubles or constant arguments with the boys, and my mind didn't feel like it was going to explode.

The morning of my state hearing, Kolton walked up to where I was waiting on a bench outside the courtroom. "Come, we need to find a place to talk quietly," he said, taking my arm and briskly leading me to a corner of the courthouse. "Listen, I just spoke with the prosecutor. I told him you're going to enter a plea of nolo contendere. I also asked him if he would recommend probation. They agreed to recommend probation, but they've changed judges on us, so I'm not sure what's going to happen."

I just stood there with a blank stare as absolute terror took over. His voice sounded so far away.

He took my arm and led me into the courtroom, walking toward the bench. It was hard to breathe. The air felt thick and heavy. As I stood in front of the judge, my mind completely shut down.

Kolton and the judge exchanged words, but they seemed far away, like they were speaking through thick glass. I couldn't make sense of any of it until I heard the words, "I'm placing you on five years' probation."

In that instant my knees gave out beneath me, and I began to collapse. Kolton grabbed me, holding me up before I hit the floor. "Okay, you've got to walk over here. Come on, you have to stand." I could barely register his words, but somehow, I managed to find my feet.

"Now put your fingers out so they can take your fingerprints," he instructed, guiding me through the process as I struggled to keep myself together.

"You're not going to prison, Candy."

* * *

Later, I found out the whole story. Ralph and Pete, were, of course, detectives who had set up the drug buy. Paul, whom I'd let stay in my home, was a confidential informant for the Hillsborough County Drug Division. He worked for Ralph and Pete. This is what Paul meant when he'd cryptically said he "knew people." Out of his anger at me for kicking him out of my house, he had fed them the lie that I was a drug dealer and worked with my husband. They set me up in hopes of getting more information about Richard's drug dealers in Tampa.

It didn't stop there. I also learned Richard had told authorities I was involved in his drug dealings, which in turn helped him cut a deal at his sentencing hearing to get a lighter sentence.

Four years after I was arrested, the anger I had buried for so long boiled over. Closing my office door, I picked up the phone and called Ralph.

"Hello, this is Detective Ralph Wormley." Just the sound of his voice made me tense up.

"This is Candy. I'm sure you remember me," I said sarcastically. Feelings of hate and anger surged through my body, like a fire that couldn't be controlled.

"Yeah, sure, I remember you." His voice sounded chipper.

"First, I do not give my permission for this phone call to be recorded. Do you understand?"

"Yeah, sure."

"Second, you shattered my life and my children's lives."

"Well, you—"

"No, you are *not* going to talk. I'm talking now and you're going to listen, so shut up. You're going to hear what I have to say." My voice grew louder and more forceful. "You almost destroyed our lives. You put me and my children through pure hell. You knew I was struggling for money, and you lied to me, using your nonexistent child as a pawn. You believed your drug-addict buddy Paul, who fed you lies about me. The worst part is you believed him without a second thought. You didn't give a damn about what you were doing to me and my children. All you were interested in was putting another notch in your belt to set yourself up for a promotion. In the end, you found out I had no information to give you. How did you explain that to your supervisor, Ralph?"

He didn't respond. I was too angry to let him answer, anyway. "As a police officer, you take an oath to help and protect victims. You didn't protect me; you entrapped me. I don't know if you have any daughters, but if you do I hope to God they never end up with an abusive man because you sure as hell wouldn't have a clue how to save them. You wouldn't recognize the signs, just like you didn't with me."

I could hear a sigh on the other end of the line. "Well, you—"

"No, I'm still talking. Shut up! You're going to listen for once in your damn life. I suggest you take some classes in how to recognize the signs of an abused woman who has been beaten, shot at, raped, and had her bones broken. This way, hopefully, instead of patting your buddies on the back for doing a great job after you've entrapped her, you'd have some freakin' compassion for her and what she's had to do to keep herself and her children alive. That's your damn job, Ralph."

"Well, Candy, let me say something."

"Hell, no. I never want to hear your voice again."

I slammed the receiver down, ending the call.

CHAPTER 26

My Name is Candice

Shortly after the state's sentencing, I received notice my house was being foreclosed on. I knew we needed to leave Tampa—to get away from drug dealers, detectives, and especially Richard. Although Richard was still serving time in prison, I wasn't naïve enough to believe that meant we were safe. His reach could extend far beyond his prison bars.

I made the decision to move to St. Petersburg, just twenty minutes from St. Pete Beach—where the sound of the waves, the warmth of the sun, and the steady presence of Aunt Gen and Uncle Willis gave me the only feelings of safety I knew as a child. Life was simpler there, untouched by the chaos that would later consume so much of my world. Moving back felt like reaching for something I had lost—like trying to reclaim a small, sacred fragment of peace.

I hadn't told my aunt or uncle about my arrest, all the legal issues, or the pending problems with the Board of Nursing. I couldn't bear the thought of upsetting them. And deep down, I was still afraid—afraid because Richard had threatened to harm them, and some part of me still believed staying silent might keep them safe.

For the next couple of months, I saved every penny I could for our move, dedicating my days off to searching for a secluded house in a quiet neighborhood for us to live—and hide.

Thankfully, back then we didn't have the internet or social media, so disappearing was much easier. I created an alias. Cynthia would be my new name. It felt like a shield, a way to distance myself from the past. Of course, I had to use my birth name for employment, but I managed to navigate that. Working for Gayle helped, as she had work at hospitals in the surrounding counties, providing me with distance from my old life. This allowed me to slip into my new identity when needed.

* * *

It was just before Thanksgiving when one of the nurses I'd worked with insisted I join her for a small, casual Thanksgiving gathering. I really didn't want to go; my mind was consumed with everything I was dealing with. But after her persistent invitations, I finally agreed.

The moment I walked through her door, I locked eyes with a man sitting at the kitchen bar. It felt like a magnet pulling us together. He was a handsome man in his late thirties, with thinning brown hair and a strong muscular body. I was surprised by how drawn I was to him, given my fear of everything that moved.

The hostess introduced him as Chris. There was something calm and inviting about him, which eased my fears. As if reading my mind, he gestured to the empty seat next to him and asked me to join him. Despite the fear and anxiety that usually followed me, I found myself accepting his offer, curious to learn more about him.

We talked for the next few hours, completely lost in our own world. The conversation flowed effortlessly. It was as if no one else in the room existed. We talked about current events, sharing thoughts and stories. In that moment, it was hard to imagine anything outside of this connection mattered.

It didn't take long before we were inseparable. There was a comfort in his presence, a sense of safety I hadn't felt in a long time. Eventually, I told him all about my legal problems: the arrest, the pending Board of Nursing hearing, everything that was threatening to unravel my life. But I couldn't bring myself to tell him about the rapes. That part of me stayed hidden. He promised he would protect me and my boys, and I believed him. Chris was a Vietnam vet, having done two tours in the war, and there was a toughness in him that made me feel like he could handle anything.

Chris didn't have a successful career in the traditional sense but made his living doing odd carpentry jobs and construction around town. He took pride in his work, and one day he showed me some of the pieces he'd built. He even offered to build me a bed frame. Finally, I would have a real bed.

One evening, Chris and I had a long discussion about him moving in with us. We had officially become a couple, and it felt natural to take the next step. Chris opened up about his desire to pursue a formal education in HVAC (heating, ventilation, and air-conditioning). In Florida, where air-conditioning was essential, it was a stable and promising career.

I was proud of his ambition and excited for what this new chapter might bring us. "If you can keep working odd jobs and contribute to the household expenses, I'll work as much as I can to keep us going financially," I told him.

"Once I get my education, I'll be able to contribute a lot more," he said. "And you know I'll always make sure you and the boys are safe."

"It looks like we'll be moving in together," I said with a smile, reaching to pull him closer for a kiss.

During one of my rare days off, I decided to buy a small microwave to help speed up our dinner preparation. I carefully unwrapped it, placed it on the counter, and stood there, staring at it as tears welled up in my eyes. A wave of sadness came over me. *Would someone take this from me, too?* The thought lingered painfully, a reminder of how many things, both big and small, had been taken from me in the past.

The boys seemed to adjust to the move fairly well. I enrolled Ben in high school about two miles from the new house, and Jason started middle school within walking distance.

However, Ben had become increasingly curt and rude toward me. It seemed like no matter what I did or said he snapped back at me, defying me at every turn. Every interaction felt like a battle. His outbursts were often followed by him storming off to his room, slamming his door, and staying silent for hours.

I spent countless hours sitting beside him, trying to get him to open up about what might be troubling him, but all he ever said was "Everything is fine" and "I'm not mad." It was exhausting, never being able to break through to what was really bothering him.

One of the rare times I saw a spark of excitement in him was when Chris offered to teach him how to start the car and back out of the driveway. With his sixteenth birthday approaching, the idea of getting his driver's license was the only thing that seemed to lift his spirits.

One evening, I came home after a grueling day at the hospital, my heart heavy, nerves frayed, and legs aching from hours of standing. Chris was in the garage, where he spent most of his time when he wasn't in school. I'd spent my shift fighting to keep a twelve-year-old boy alive after he and his friend played Russian roulette with his father's gun. The young man had put the barrel in his mouth and pulled the trigger. The weight of that day was crushing.

Ben was in his usual snarky mood, snapping back when I told him it was his turn to put the dishes in the dishwasher. I had finally hit my breaking point. My patience was gone. I poured myself my usual evening rum and Coke, the ice clinking in the glass louder than usual. I stomped to my bedroom and called Ben's father.

"We need to talk, Scott," I said in a matter-of-fact tone.

"Why? What's going on?"

"What's going on? I'm going to put Ben on a plane this Wednesday and if you're not there to pick him up, I guess child services will need to take him."

"What are you talking about?"

"I believe I just said very clearly what's going to happen to your son if you don't pick him up at the airport," I said in a firm but loud voice. "I have raised him by myself, except for the three months you cared for him during my last semester of college. I'm sick and tired of doing this by myself."

"What has he been doing to upset you?"

"It's time for you to step up and be a damn father," I said, raising my voice. "He's rude, defiant, hateful, and downright mean to me and I'm not going to take it anymore. Now, are you going to pick him up at the airport or not?"

"Yeah, I'll pick him up, since you're threatening to send him to foster care and don't want to care for him anymore."

Fueled by frustration and exhaustion, I marched to Ben's room, where I found him lounging on his bed, eyes glued to the television. Without hesitating, I told him, "You're going to live with your father since you hate me so much." He didn't even flinch. He barely looked at me, just a brief glance before returning his attention to the screen, replying with a simple, "Okay." That single word cut deeper than any argument we'd ever had.

I took Ben to the airport that Wednesday morning, came home, and threw up.

In the days that followed, the guilt weighed on me. I couldn't shake the feeling I had failed, failed to raise my son in a nonviolent environment. Chris didn't have the skill to comfort or support me.

Two weeks after I sent Ben to his father, I received a call from Scott admitting he fully understood why I'd made the decision to send Ben to him. He confessed he was having trouble controlling Ben, too. The same defiance and attitude that had worn me down were now directed at Scott.

Hearing this didn't bring me any relief, only a deep aching sadness that maybe the problem ran deeper than I'd realized.

* * *

Jason didn't seem to mind that Ben had left; in fact, he seemed relieved. Without Ben's constant outbursts and tension filling the house, Jason seemed more relaxed.

I deeply loved both my boys. Putting Ben on that plane made me feel like I had failed as a mother, the ache of watching him disappear through those doors, knowing I wouldn't see him for months. I needed someone to share the weight with me, but Chris was emotionally unavailable, his attempts to comfort me falling flat, like he was reading from a script, rather than truly understanding my pain.

It broke my heart to think about how my boys had gone from being inseparable, always looking out for each other, to barely being able to stand being in the same room. Now they were apart. They used to be each other's protectors. I felt this rift between them stemmed from watching Richard hurt me. They had seen it all: too many moments of violence, fear, and helplessness. It changed them, hardened them in different ways, witnessing things no child should ever have to see.

The conflicting emotions weighed heavily on me; the heartbreak of losing Ben, of watching him drift away, was almost unbearable, yet his deep resentment toward me filled me with pain. Strangely, a small sense of relief washed over me when he left. It was easier without the constant reminder of his hatred.

One evening as the sun was about to dip below the horizon, I stood in the kitchen, looking out the window. I noticed Jason pulling a cage full of blue crabs from the water. I walked out to the dock to see what he was doing.

"Mom, I figured out how to catch blue crabs. Look how many I just caught! See, see, look, Mom." His face glowed with excitement as he stood there, his bright-colored beach shorts contrasting with his tanned skin.

I couldn't help but smile, watching his enthusiasm and the simple beauty of the moment.

"That's enough crabs to have a nice crab boil for dinner one night. Tell me how you catch them."

"Mom, there's a whole process you have to do," he said proudly. "You see, I have to attach a piece of a hot dog on a string and throw it into the canal to catch a small fish. When I catch the fish, I let the fish die and get real smelly, then put the dead fish in the crab cage, throw it in the canal, and wait for the crab to come in the cage to eat the fish. Then they're trapped and can't get out. That's how you do it." His face beamed with pride.

It made me so happy, seeing him relaxed, having fun, and just being a boy.

* * *

I continued working sixty to seventy hours a week, but no matter how hard I pushed myself, it felt like I was running on a treadmill—exhausted and getting nowhere. Even though Ben was living with his father, I still had to support Chris, who was finishing up his last year of HVAC school. The rental car fees were eating up nearly half of my weekly earnings, and I knew I had to address the problem sooner rather than later.

Determined to find a solution, I began researching cars that were both highly rated for safety and efficient on gas. This was crucial since I was driving close to seventy thousand miles a year. The fuel costs alone were becoming overwhelming. I found the Ford Taurus to be the best option for what I needed. However, I visited two different car dealerships and was turned down both times. My credit was too damaged, and Chris had no credit history.

Frustration and desperation began to set in, leaving me no other choice but to reach out to my Uncle Willis to see if he would cosign a car loan for me. It was the last thing I wanted to do—my father's warnings about not bothering my aunt and uncle with my problems still echoed in my ears—but I had no other choice. I dreaded the conversation, but I knew I couldn't keep pouring money into this rental car. I never wanted them to think that asking them for money was the reason I adored them. I wanted them to know my affection for them had nothing to do with their wallets; it was their love that meant everything to me.

I detailed all the research I had done on the car and scheduled a time to meet with him. As I nervously laid out the situation, he surprised me. Without hesitation, he said, with a smile on his face, "I'll do this for you. Just make sure you make the payments on time."

His simple act of trust meant more to me than just a car loan; it was the first time a member of my family had faith in my ability to handle things and keep moving forward. It gave me a sense of strength I needed so badly.

Two days later, I happily returned the rental car and proudly drove out of the dealership with my Taurus.

* * *

We'd been living in St. Petersburg for almost two years. Jason was thriving in high school, even making the diving team in his sophomore year. I was still working as many hours as I could, always pushing myself to keep everything together. It often felt like Jason was raising himself, and I was just existing beside a man who never once asked me, "How can I help you?" Chris had been to Vietnam as a marine, but I had been in my own Vietnam, a different kind of battlefield. We were both survivors of wars with deep-rooted scars.

In mid-March, I received a notice of hearing from the Board of Nursing. Ripping the letter open, I read: *A hearing will be held in this case in The School Board Administration Building, 1960 E Druid Road, Clearwater, Florida at 2:00 p.m. on April 14, 1986. Issues: Whether respondent's license to practice nursing should be revoked, suspended or otherwise disciplined for the reasons set forth in the Administrative Complaint filed on January 24, 1984.*

I walked back in the house, trying to steady the anxiety building inside me.

Just breathe, take a breath.

I knew I couldn't face this alone. I needed a lawyer. I was reluctant to ask Gayle for recommendations, considering how her other recommendations had turned out, but she was my only resource. There was no internet then, no easy way to research or verify anything. She referred me to a man named Stewart who had done work for another nurse.

I called Stewart's office and scheduled an appointment with him for the following week. I'd been setting aside some money for a while, knowing this day would eventually come. It felt both nerve-wracking and relieving to finally get the board hearing date. The reality of it all was coming to a head.

Please, God, don't let them take my nursing license away.

I met Stewart the following week as planned. Though I was extremely nervous about trusting another lawyer after the last two, it felt different this time; I felt stronger.

I hesitated, then forced the words out, recounting everything that had happened over the last few years: Richard, the arrest, probation, the anxiety of waiting for the nursing board hearing. As I spoke, I noticed his expression shift, his eyebrows lifting and his eyes widening.

"I've dealt with these types of hearings several times," he reassured me. "First off, it's always a good idea to have legal representation with you during the hearing. You'll have the chance to present your side of the story directly to the board, and they might ask you a few questions to clarify things. The whole process usually takes about thirty minutes or so. Now, don't expect a decision right then and there; they won't give it to you that day. Instead, they'll meet afterward, discuss everything, and make their decision collectively.

Afterward, you'll receive their final verdict in the mail. Sometimes it takes a couple of months."

"For the love of everything holy, this is torture," I muttered, running my hand through my hair in frustration. "More waiting, more uncertainty; it's unbearable."

Everything rested on this hearing, on him, on the board, and on decisions that were completely out of my control.

"I'm sorry, but this is how they work," he replied with a firm voice. "I think I have everything I need here. My secretary will send you a bill for my legal services. I'll meet you at the hearing in Clearwater on April fourteenth." He stood up. "Call me if you have any questions. Oh, also, wear conservative clothes the day of the hearing, nothing flashy."

The day of the nursing board hearing finally came. I don't recall what I wore that day, but it certainly wasn't anything flashy; I didn't own anything flashy.

The drive to the hearing took about forty minutes, but I left ninety minutes early. As I pulled open the door to the building, I said a little prayer: *Please, God, help me. I can't lose my nursing license.*

I spotted Stewart standing in the lobby. He'd arrived early, too, which I was grateful for. His presence, though stiff, was reassuring.

"Now, listen," he said, leaning in slightly, his voice firm but measured. "When you walk in that room, you tell them your side of the story in a calm and confident voice. There's usually a panel of at least eight board members that you'll be sitting in front of. Look each one in the eye as you're speaking, but the main thing is: *do not cry.*"

"What? I'm about to tell the damn nursing board that I was beaten, shot at, isolated, and then arrested and you're telling me don't cry?"

"Yes, that's exactly what I'm telling you. Crying could show weakness." His words cut through me. It was as if he put the fear of God in me. If I cried, they would take my license. Didn't *anyone* even want to try and understand the mental anguish and torment of a domestic violence survivor?

"They're calling your name. Now go in there and tell them your side of the story."

As I opened the tall, heavy door, I was taken aback at what I saw. There must have been over one hundred and fifty people packed in the room. I focused on the long tables arranged in a straight line across the stage. A panel of eight professionals, both men and women, sat with an air of authority, their expressions unreadable. The sheer size of the audience made my stomach hurt. I had expected something smaller, more intimate.

All eyes turned toward me as I walked to the front of the room, my body visibly trembling with every step. My legs started to buckle underneath me. *No, you can't fall in front of all these people. Come on, put one foot in front of the other. You can do this.*

I was walking into a spotlight I never wanted. I sat down in front of the panel, my hands clammy. One of the assistants pulled the microphone closer to my mouth. I could feel the weight of every stare pressing down on me. I felt exposed, vulnerable, like a public spectacle in front of all these strangers, as if my entire life was being laid bare for judgment.

"State your name, please."

Tilting my head back, looking up at the stage, I said, "My name is Candice."

"Candice, as you can see, we have quite a few attendees here today. There are students from two different nursing schools in attendance."

Mortified, I wondered, why did this have to happen to me?

One of the panel members, a man, addressed the other panel members and the audience. "Let's proceed. We are here to determine if your license should be revoked or suspended or if you should be otherwise disciplined for the reasons set forth in the administrative complaint filed on January twenty-fourth."

The man turned his attention toward me and said, "Now, Candice, tell us your side of the story."

I swallowed hard before speaking. "I was in an abusive marriage for thirteen years and went to nursing school during that time. My ex-husband was arrested for selling drugs and implicated me in his crimes after his arrest so he could get a lesser sentence." My voice wavered. I was barely able to force the words out.

"Okay, let's stop here," another male panelist interrupted. "Why didn't you just leave the marriage?"

What? I wanted to scream at him. I couldn't believe he had the audacity to ask such a ridiculous, ignorant question. My jaw locked, teeth grinding as I fought to keep my composure, but inside, a storm was raging. How could anyone think it was that simple?

"Let's not get into all that," a female panelist interrupted. "What have you been doing since your arrest? Have you been working as a nurse?"

"Yes, ma'am, I've been working anywhere from sixty to seventy hours per week as a nurse."

"Good. Have there been any complaints from your employer regarding your performance?" another panelist asked.

"No, ma'am, all of my yearly evaluations have been excellent."

"Are you still on probation with the state?" another panelist asked.

"Yes, but I've requested an early release and I'm waiting to hear back from them."

"Okay, I think we've heard enough. You'll receive our response through the mail. Is there anything you would like to add?"

Sitting up straight in my seat, I said confidently, "The one thing I do know is I'm a good nurse," putting a firm emphasis on *good*. "I give my patients the best care with dignity and respect."

Holding back tears, I forced myself to look at each one of them, searching their faces for any sign of compassion. Most of them stared back at me sternly, with unreadable expressions, except one, a female panelist sitting to the far left. She gave me a half-smile. In that moment, I felt a flicker of hope. She believed me.

I knew out of all those women at that hearing, there had to be at least one, if not several, who had experienced physical, mental, or sexual abuse at some point in their lives. It was impossible to believe otherwise. Yet, no one was talking about it. It was like a silent agreement: "Don't say the word 'abuse.'"

The reality is, so many of us lived in that fear and silence.

After the hearing, I was still pissed off at the guy who questioned why I hadn't left the abuser. But then it occurred to me that there were a lot of women in that room. Perhaps, I was put in that room for a reason—so that another woman in a similar situation could hear my story and gain the courage to get out.

CHAPTER 27

Reclaiming My Life and Career

On October 24, 1986, I received notice from the state granting me early termination of probation, a moment that felt like a long-awaited victory. But just three weeks later, the nursing board delivered a blow, placing me on probation for three years, starting November 14, 1986, with a list of stringent requirements. I was ordered to undergo an in-depth psychological evaluation, provide evaluations of my work performance from employers for the last three years, and successfully complete courses in assertiveness and the legal aspects of nursing. Additionally, I had to submit quarterly reports on my progress.

I tackled everything head-on, completing all the board's requirements within the first three months, eager to prove I wanted to move forward.

I was working the 7 a.m. to 7 p.m. shift at one of the hospitals in St. Petersburg. I'd just finished a late lunch when my beeper went off. Uncle Willis.

Frightened, I picked up the phone and called him back immediately. "Are you okay?" I asked, attempting to sound steady. "Is Aunt Gen okay?"

"We're fine, but there's something you need to know. Richard just called me. He's out of prison and living in a halfway house in Tarpon Springs."

My stomach dropped. Tarpon Springs, Florida, was about fifty miles north of St. Petersburg.

The thought of Richard calling and involving them made my blood boil. He had already threatened to harm them. I wasn't sure what to do. Telling them Richard was a danger to them seemed risky; what if their anger pushed them to confront him? That would give Richard an excuse to act on his threats. The thought was unbearable.

"He's looking for you," my uncle continued. "He asked me where you were living and wanted your phone number, but I didn't tell him anything. Please take care of yourself and be safe."

"Don't you worry, I'm going to take care of this. If he ever bothers you again, you let me know and I will handle it."

That fucking bastard.

The next morning, I called the prison in North Carolina. They confirmed Richard was released to a halfway house in Tarpon Springs and gave me the telephone number.

I immediately called the halfway house. "Hello, ma'am," I said to the receptionist who answered. "I've been in hiding from my ex-husband and his drug dealers for several years. And he just called my elderly uncle's home looking for me. If he finds me, he'll kill me. I am telling you he will kill me," I repeated in a firm, but shaky, voice.

She was very empathetic and seemed to understand my fears. "I think you should come here as soon as possible to speak with the administrator. Can you come tomorrow at eleven?"

"Yes, I'll be there, but will Richard be gone then? I don't want him to see me or the car I'm driving."

"The prisoners are taken to their work programs very early in the morning, so he won't be here. But if you'd feel more comfortable, stop at a pay phone on your way and call me to confirm."

"Thank you, this makes me feel better. I'll call you tomorrow."

The next morning, I was so nervous I could barely function, let alone get myself in the car. My mind raced as I drove, my stomach in knots, but I knew I had to do this.

About ten miles from the halfway house, I found a pay phone next to a gas station. I parked and fumbled through my change purse, looking for a quarter for my call. My body was shaking so badly I needed both hands to pry open the phone booth door. I grabbed the receiver, but my hand trembled too much to hold on, and the quarter slipped through my fingers, clattering to the floor. My knees buckled, and I had to steady myself against the glass. Pure fear and anxiety had taken over, gripping me so tightly that even a simple act of retrieving the coin felt insurmountable.

"Hello, ma'am, this is the lady you spoke to yesterday. You told me to call and make sure the prisoners are gone."

"You're safe to come now, they're all gone from here."

"I'll be there in about fifteen minutes."

Immediately after I walked in the door of the halfway house, this kind woman greeted me and took me directly to the administrator's office, a makeshift space in an older mobile home. The space felt cramped and dingy, with an old, scratched-up desk and two metal chairs. The dark wood-paneled walls added to the gloom. Papers were scattered everywhere on the desk. I couldn't help but wonder how he managed to keep track of anything, let alone prisoners.

This is probably how Richard was able to get away with calling Uncle Willis.

Just then an older, gray-haired man walked in and took a seat behind the desk. "So, I understand you're concerned about one of my prisoners," he said in a deep, gruff voice, leaning back in his chair.

"This man will kill me if he finds me. Do you understand?"

Fumbling through the papers on his cluttered desk, he eventually pulled out a manila folder with Richard's name on it. Opening it up, he waved his hand over the documents inside as if trying to emphasize his point.

"Look here," he said, almost casually, "he's been a model prisoner." His words sent a chill through me. They were meant to reassure me, but all they did was make my heart race faster. *A model prisoner?*

No file could erase the fear I carried with me every single day.

Once again, no one believed me.

I straightened my back with a surge of determination. "Listen, sir, perhaps you didn't understand me the first time. This man will kill me if he finds me." I leaned in closer, locking eyes with him. "He has beaten me, broken my bones, bruised my body, and even shot at me with a sawed-off shotgun." My voice was firm and forceful, leaving no room for misunderstandings. "He has called my elderly uncle's home trying to find me. Maybe *The St. Petersburg Times* newspaper might like to hear my story of how you're allowing an inmate to harass a senior citizen looking for the woman he fully intends to kill."

His eyes widened as he looked back at me, the weight of my words finally sinking in. "I understand." His voice was lower now. "I'll see to it that he doesn't bother you again while he's still here."

In that moment I felt a flicker of relief, but I knew better than to trust so easily. I had heard too many empty promises before.

I nodded. Walking out of his office, a sense of exhaustion washed over me. As I headed for the door, I stopped to thank the kind woman at the front desk. She had seen the fear in my eyes and quietly helped me. Her gestures of kindness made a difference in a way she might never realize, offering me a flicker of humanity in a world that had often been so cruel.

Later I wondered if she'd ever been abused, if her empathy came from a place of knowing.

* * *

Chris graduated HVAC school and made the bold decision to start his own company. I supported him fully, knowing how skilled he was at his craft. His customers loved him. He was loyal, dependable, and trustworthy. Word about his good work spread quickly. What thrilled me most was that he was now contributing to our living expenses, easing some of the financial burden I'd carried for so long. I was getting burned out working twelve-hour shifts. Factoring in commute time, this sometimes led to fifteen- and sixteen-hour work days.

His success felt like a light at the end of a long, exhausting tunnel, offering hope that I could soon catch a breath. Our relationship seemed to improve once he started contributing to the finances. The tension between us eased; there was a sense of balance, like we were now a team.

In December 1985, I began to feel confident that I knew enough about the homecare business to start my own nursing agency. The idea had been growing in my mind for about a year, but I had to wait until Chris graduated. With years of experience behind me, I recognized a growing need in the St. Petersburg elderly population.

Many of them were determined to remain in their homes, fiercely resisting the idea of going into a nursing home. But they needed more than just a nursing assistant to help with their morning routine, meals, and doctor appointments; they needed a comprehensive plan of care, including a weekly in-home visit by a registered nurse. This approach would ensure each client received the appropriate level of medical supervision, tailored to their individual needs.

At the time, no other companies offered this kind of care. The gap in the market gave me the confidence my agency could fill a critical role, offering something unique.

But I was lacking in the finance department. I knew I needed help. I drew up a detailed five-year business plan to present to my uncle's financial planner. Henry had been in the financial business for years and was very successful. His expertise and reputation in managing money were well-known. He had helped numerous clients build and sustain profitable ventures.

I scheduled an appointment with Henry and pitched my business plan, giving him strict instructions not to approach my aunt or uncle for investment; the last thing I wanted was for them to feel obligated or think I was taking advantage of their love for me. I wanted this venture to stand on its own merits.

I would describe Henry as a gentle giant. He was in his early sixties and had a commanding presence, tall with broad shoulders, but his demeanor was always calm. He was someone I had grown to respect.

Included in my business plan were rental space, an office manager who could oversee the internal operations and knew accounting, and as many 1099 employees as I could recruit to build up a solid roster. My role would encompass multiple titles: president, medical supervisor, and marketing director.

Henry said he was very impressed with my plan and felt this business would fill a niche in the market. A few weeks later, he called to ask me to stop by.

Once we were seated in his conference room, he said, "I have some good news and some bad news. Let me explain. I pitched your plan to several of my clients. They really didn't want to take the risk."

"I understand." My feeling of letdown was palpable. My shoulders dropped as I leaned back in the large leather chair.

"I do have some good news," Henry added, a hint of excitement in his voice. "I know you forbade me from speaking with your uncle, but I didn't have any other choice. I truly believe in your plan and felt it deserved backing. Your uncle didn't hesitate when I explained everything to him; he immediately said he wanted to invest in your company. How does this make you feel?"

"That is great news. Thank you so much. But I'm a bit nervous since it's my aunt and uncle investing."

"I'm sure you will make them proud. I can't wait to watch you succeed in your venture. I'll get the papers drawn up so we can get this plan moving. I'll be in touch soon."

I walked to my car, still in shock from the wonderful news, and sat there in a daze. The air-conditioning blasted in my face, but I barely noticed. I gripped the steering wheel, feeling the weight of the moment.

My uncle and aunt lived through the Great Depression. As a result, they were cautious with money. Uncle Willis was in charge of their finances and always made careful, calculated decisions. His meticulous approach to money management was the backbone of his success. For him to believe in me and invest in my vision meant the world to me. His backing felt like a validation, a confirmation that I was smart. His belief in me proved that I was capable of so much more than I once thought.

The following year, I secured contracts with a few large, progressive retirement facilities, hospitals, and nursing homes. The growth of the company was rapid and profitable, far exceeding my initial expectations. By the end of the first year our revenues were close to one million dollars. Despite the success, I took a minimal salary, just enough to cover half of the household expenses. I was more focused on reinvesting in the business and ensuring its long-term stability than immediate gain.

* * *

Chris and I had set our wedding date: February 13, 1988. Chris was born and raised in Tennessee and most of his family were still there. I agreed to marry in his hometown because I knew only a couple of my family members would want to attend.

It was a small, intimate ceremony with mostly family held in a quaint country church in Tennessee. I wore a beautiful white dress full of ruffles. Chris and Jason were dressed in white tuxedos, accented with red cummerbunds and red bow ties. It was simple, yet perfect. Ben, now twenty years old, was still living in Michigan and unable to get time off from work. It was difficult not having him there, but I understood.

Aunt Gen and Uncle Willis came to the wedding and seeing them there filled me with happiness. My father came, too. It wasn't until later I learned the full story: Uncle Willis had firmly told my father he had better attend. And my father, fearing the possibility of being written out of Uncle Willis's will, wasn't about to take any chances.

The small country church was filled with warmth and laughter. There was a simple charm to the day that everyone seemed to enjoy, the beautiful setting, the heartfelt vows, and even the fun little moments during the reception.

Later that same year, we celebrated Jason's high school graduation. A sizable flag marking his achievement with the words "Congratulations, Graduate!" proudly adorned our front door.

My relationship with Jason became strained during his last year of high school. The disagreements between us seemed constant as his defiance of the house rules grew. He had started dating a young lady who had dropped out of high school, and there were troubling rumors that they were experimenting with drugs. To make matters worse, her parents were pressuring them to get married as soon as Jason turned eighteen. I was losing control, and my heart was breaking, watching him make the same bad choices his father had.

* * *

By the following year, 1989, I had completed more than two of the three years of probation required by the nursing board. While I was finally free of state probation, the weight of the nursing board restrictions felt unbearable, and I was desperate to be finally free from them. Every day under probation was a constant reminder of Richard.

Determined to reclaim my life and career back, I decided in early February to write a letter to the nursing board, requesting an early release from probation. To my surprise, I soon received a response informing me my case had been added to the docket for the board's annual April 14th hearing. However, there was one condition: I would need to travel to Miami and attend the hearing in person.

Hell, I would have travelled all the way to Alaska if that was what it took to finally be free from any lingering restrictions.

The hearing was much different from the last one. This time, I felt confident walking in, steady and more sure of myself. My stomach wasn't in knots, and, for once, I wasn't consumed by anxiety. There was no lawyer warning me not to cry, no need to stuff my emotions down and prepare for the worst. I felt calm, ready to face whatever came my way, knowing I'd done everything required of me. It was a small but powerful shift, a feeling of quiet strength I hadn't felt before.

This time there were only a few people in the audience, and I didn't have to speak into a microphone. When they called my name, I stood as they quickly reviewed my file, noting that I had completed all the requirements for early release. One of the board members asked if I was still working in the nursing field, and I replied "yes." They thanked me, then informed me that they would discuss the case privately and notify me by mail in the coming weeks.

And that was it. It was over. As I walked out of the building, a weight I'd carried for years finally lifted, replaced by a quiet, almost surreal sense of hope. For the first time in my life, I felt free: free to look forward, free from my constraints. The world seemed a little brighter, and I couldn't help but breathe in deeply, savoring the feeling of a new beginning before me.

A few weeks later, I received a letter in the metal mailbox—the same box that used to scare me with what might be inside. This time it held something different. The letter from the board read, "Upon consideration, the Board determines that the probation has been satisfactorily completed. Wherefore, it is hereby ORDERED that Respondent's probation be terminated on May 5, 1989."

Tears began to fill my eyes as I pressed the letter against my chest, the weight of it all hitting at once. Relief washed over me as I read those words again. It was finally, officially over.

* * *

During my first year in business, I received a call from Uncle Willis, who was eighty-six years young at the time, informing me he needed heart surgery and wanted my opinion. He was diagnosed with an aneurysm in the superior vena cava, meaning the blood vessel was blocked or squeezed, impeding blood flow to the heart. The size of his aneurysm was ten centimeters, quite large, and if it ruptured it could cause severe hemorrhaging, even death. I explained this was a big surgery, but I felt it would be okay and I would be there for him all the way. I was extremely concerned, but I didn't let him know.

However, the surgeon was unable to remove the aneurysm as planned due to a bowel blockage that was discovered during the surgery. The bowel blockage posed a serious threat, and the surgical team had to shift their focus, leaving the aneurysm untouched.

He came through the surgery quite well, but when he returned home it was a different story. Knowing that the aneurysm could burst at any time was a tremendous mental burden, but he had made the decision not to have another surgery. Five days a week I went to their home to care for him.

We had our arguments in the beginning of his recovery. He was sharp as a tack and could roar like a lion. I would snap back at him, "You're not going to die today on my watch." This would usually get his attention.

It was the best two months for both of us. Every afternoon, I would drive him around St. Pete Beach, and we'd talk about his mother, father, and sister. We passed by the house they used to live in, and we visited the cemetery where they were buried. He shared stories about the motel he and Aunt Gen had owned, recounting the ups and downs of running the business, the challenges they faced, and the moments of joy. These conversations brought us closer, giving me a deeper understanding of my father's side of the family. It was a time of healing for both of us and he got to relive precious memories with someone who adored him. During one of our outings, he asked me if I would make sure Aunt Gen was okay if something were to happen to him. Without hesitation, I gave him my word.

Two years later, I got a call from Aunt Gen, telling me Uncle Willis was having severe pain in his back. I knew immediately that the aneurysm had ruptured, and he could hemorrhage in a very short time. I instructed her to call 911. I would call his physician and meet them in the emergency room.

When Chris and I arrived in the emergency room, Uncle Willis was on a gurney with several medical providers working urgently on him. The surgeon approached Aunt Gen and me with a question that stopped my heart: "Do you want us to try and save him?" Aunt Gen quickly turned to me for the answer. Though she was technically the one responsible for making the decision, she always leaned on me for medical advice. Not only because I was family, but because she trusted that, as a nurse, I would know what was best to do.

I didn't want him to suffer, but I wanted him to have a chance. "Yes, please try and save him," I answered.

It was impossible to get close to him as they hurried him to the operating room. I wanted to push everyone away, run to him, and tell him how much I loved him, but there was no time. As they wheeled him away, our eyes locked for a brief heartbreaking moment, and in that instant, it felt like we both knew this would be the last time we would see each other on this earth. The sadness I saw in his eyes that day will never leave me. When they pushed him through the doors, my heart shattered into a thousand pieces.

I pulled myself together enough to ask Chris to take Aunt Gen home. He nodded and said he would. I turned to Aunt Gen and gently told her, "It may be a long night, and I don't want you waiting around here." I could see the concern in her eyes, but she understood. "I'll call you just as soon as I know something."

I'd barely sat down in the waiting room when one of the OR nurses approached, carrying Uncle Willis's belongings in her arms. Her face was solemn, and before she even spoke, I felt the air leave my lungs.

"I'm so sorry, Candy," she said softly, "but he didn't make it." I looked down at his belongings in my hands, the reality sinking in. He was gone.

I walked out of the hospital in a daze and sat down on the nearest bench, clutching his things tightly to my chest, as if holding a piece of him would somehow make this easier.

"How am I going to tell Aunt Gen that her husband of almost sixty-five years is gone?" I looked up at the stars. My heart ached for her, for what I had to tell her, and I whispered, *Please God, give me the strength I need right now.*

I took a cab back to their apartment, dreading what I had to do. As the cab pulled up, I could see Aunt Gen through the window, quietly puttering around in the kitchen, like she always did when she was nervous. My heart sank as I gently opened the kitchen door. The moment she saw me, she knew he had not survived. We hugged tightly and the tears came as I whispered in her ear, "I'm so sorry, but I will keep you safe."

I had not been in touch with any family members in a very long time, but I knew all too well my father and other self-serving family members would soon be circling Aunt Gen, either at the funeral or later, asking for money.

I sat her down and said, "If any family member comes around asking for money, tell them to call your financial adviser. I promised Uncle Willis that I would protect you, and I will, always."

A week after the funeral, an idea came to me about how to memorialize both Aunt Gen and Uncle Willis. When I went to Aunt Gen for my weekly visit, I shared my idea: "Education has always been important to both of you, and you've often said how a college education opens doors and creates opportunities for people. My hope is that the Doyle name will never be forgotten. You kind of know the challenges I faced when I was in college, right?

"Yes, you had some hard times, I know."

"What do you think about us creating the Mr. & Mrs. Willis Doyle Nursing Scholarship, dedicated to helping a single mother pursuing a nursing degree?"

With a big smile on her face, she said, "This is a great idea! Let's do it."

I'm very proud that this scholarship at St. Petersburg Community College (now St. Petersburg College) has helped so many women achieve their dreams.

CHAPTER 28

Death, Documents, and Deception

By 1991, I'd been running my business for almost four years, and it was steadily growing, showing consistent profitability. Chris's business was also expanding, and he was thriving in his work. On the surface, everything appeared to be going well, but the demands were intense. We both worked seven days a week, leaving almost no time for each other.

Meanwhile, shortly after graduating from high school, Jason had joined the navy. But his service was cut short by a medical discharge and life had moved quickly for him as well; he married the girl he'd been seeing, but their relationship ended in divorce only a few months later.

Ben's father had been killed in a tragic boating accident. Despite the shock and sadness, Ben was firm in his refusal to let me come to Michigan to support him through his loss. He wanted to grieve in his own way, and I respected his decision, though it wasn't easy. I, too, was mourning; I had shared a chapter of my life with his father, a marriage that, though brief, had given us Ben.

One afternoon, I said my own quiet farewell to Scott at the beach. Sitting in the sand, watching the waves roll in and out, I thanked him for giving me Ben and wished him happiness and peace wherever he was now. I couldn't help but wonder how life might have been different had we stayed married. "Goodbye, Scott," I whispered.

Not long after, as I was getting ready for work, my phone rang.

"I've been up all night with a stomachache," Aunt Gen said in a frantic voice. "I've been sitting at the kitchen table in pain."

"I'm coming right over," I assured her. Without waiting for a response, I hung up, gathered my things, and jumped in the car.

When I arrived, I found her still sitting at the kitchen table with a heating pad. I threw a sweater around her shoulders and told her we were going to the emergency room, suspecting she had a bowel blockage.

After blood work and a scan, the same physician who had treated Uncle Willis pulled me aside to show me the results. There, clear as day on the screen, was a tumor wrapped around her intestines. He gently informed me it was more than likely cancer. The news came as a shock.

Back at her home, I settled her in her favorite chair, hoping to give her a moment of rest. But as soon as she was comfortable, she looked at me with that familiar, determined gaze and became insistent, demanding to know what the doctor had said.

I kneeled down in front of her chair, placing my hand on her leg. "Aunt Gen, the doctor said you have a tumor wrapped around your intestines. It is operable. You'll need surgery. It's more than likely cancer."

"I'm ready to be with Uncle Willis," she blurted out in a firm voice, leaning back in her chair and taking a breath.

Her words caught me completely off guard. A deep sadness settled over me. As a nurse, I understood the gravity of her diagnosis and realized our time together would be heartbreakingly short. Yet, with my sadness there was a feeling of gratitude; knowing how deeply she missed Uncle Willis, it gave me comfort to believe she would find peace in reuniting with him.

"I'll have the surgery, but I'm not doing any of that chemotherapy or radiation," she told me. "I want to live my last days not taking a bunch of medications." Her decision was firm, unwavering, and I could see she'd made up her mind long before today.

A look of quiet determination mixed with concern crossed her face. In a soft, almost pleading tone, she said, "Candy, I don't want anyone to know about this. Please keep all those family members away from me. I don't want to deal with them. And I want to die in my home, peacefully, on my beach, no police, no firetrucks, and no ambulance." Her request was clear. I nodded, promising to honor her wishes.

Within a few days Aunt Gen had her surgery, and she came through without any complications, but the final diagnosis was cancer. Though surgery had been challenging, she showed remarkable strength, just as she always had.

Her cancer symptoms progressed quickly, starting a few months following her surgery. I had nursing assistants with her twenty-four hours a day. A few months later, Aunt Gen was completely bedridden. I knew it would only be a matter of weeks.

Honoring her wishes for a peaceful passing without the disruption of emergency personnel, I sought special permissions. I visited the fire department, police department, and ambulance services, carrying her medical records, a letter from her physician, and proof she was receiving round-the-clock medical care in her home.

After explaining the situation and showing them my documents, each department granted approval not to respond to her home when she passed. Then I coordinated with the funeral home, ensuring I could call them and they would come and take her body peacefully and quietly, just as she asked me to do.

I decided I needed to prepare for the inevitable, my family invading her home after her passing. I knew too well they wouldn't be searching for sentimental keepsakes but for anything valuable to satisfy their greed. I couldn't bear the idea of them picking apart cherished pieces of her and Uncle Willis's lives.

Chris and Jason helped me remove all their belongings and put them in storage, leaving only what she would need for her medical care.

I visited her several times a week and the nursing assistants called me daily with any updates or changes in her condition. She had become confused and nonverbal; I knew it wouldn't be long before her passing.

One day, I'd just arrived home from work when the phone rang.

"Ms. Candy, I think you should come quickly."

I felt my heart sink as I gripped the receiver. "I'm on my way. Is she comfortable? Is she suffering?"

"She's comfortable. She's having the death rattle, though."

"Please turn her head to the side. I'm on my way now."

It took me less than twenty minutes to get there, but she was already gone by the time I arrived. I stood at her bedside, feeling the weight of her absence wash over me. Then I heard a gentle voice whisper in my ear, *It's okay. Don't be sad. This is just my body here; I'm with Uncle Willis.* Tears filled my eyes. Comfort settled over me, but it was heart-wrenching at the same time.

I watched as the funeral home director spread the navy velvet cover over her body and ever so gently placed her in the hearse. I sat silently in the driveway, tears streaming down my cheeks, lingering for a few moments after everyone had gone. I needed to feel the presence of my beloved aunt and uncle around me just for a little longer.

How am I going to live without them near me?

Over the last eight years, we had formed a deep and loving relationship. They were the first two people who had truly believed in me, who loved me unconditionally, and now I had to say goodbye. It wasn't fair; I needed more time.

After arriving home, I immediately called their financial advisor Henry to tell him of Aunt Gen's passing. I asked him to call the family members.

A few minutes later, he called back to say, "I just wanted to let you know I spoke with the family members, and just as you predicted, they're already on their way to Aunt Gen's house."

"Thank you for letting me know, but the only thing they are going to find is a hospital bed and medical supplies," I replied, a bittersweet satisfaction in my voice.

"Candy, you've brought this full circle now, and they were very proud of you. Thank you for watching over them these last years. You brought them so much joy."

I felt a lump rise in my throat. "I wouldn't have had it any other way. I loved them both so deeply."

Aunt Gen's funeral took place the next day. All eyes were on me, filled with accusations, as if I was some sort of villain who deliberately kept them away from her in her final days. They had no idea it was her dying request, and I didn't bother to tell them. I held my silence, letting their words fall away, through the whispers that I overheard and the shouts from across the gravesite, "You're going to hell, bitch." Yet I stood firm, honoring her wishes.

That evening, I couldn't sleep, tossing and turning, questioning myself. *Did I do everything right for her? Did I carry out her wishes like she wanted me to?*

Finally, I got up and went to lie on the couch, hoping to quiet my restless mind. As I began to doze off, a bright beam of light appeared from the hallway directly in front of me. I opened my eyes and saw a silhouette: a woman in a pure white, flowing dress, gliding effortlessly through the air. Startled, I quickly closed my eyes. *Is this real? Am I imagining this?*

With my eyes still closed, I felt a gentle touch, a delicate flutter caressing both sides of my face, and trailing softly down the left side of my body. When I opened my eyes again, I knew I wasn't dreaming. A deep sense of relief and peace washed over me. I understood it was Aunt Gen, reassuring me of her love and gratitude. She gave me my answer, I could rest now, and I fell asleep. She was at peace and so was I.

A month after the funeral, I held a successful garage sale of their belongings. What I didn't sell, I donated, finding comfort in knowing their possessions would go to others who could cherish them. I took the cash from the sale and delivered it to the college financial aid department as a contribution to the Mr. & Mrs. Doyle Nursing Scholarship, turning their life remnants into something meaningful that would help others.

Today, thirty-five years later, the Mr. & Mrs. Willis Doyle Nursing Scholarship has continued to help single mothers graduate with their nursing degree. Because of this generous foundation, over thirty-five nurses have successfully graduated and now care for others. To this day, I'm so proud to say a plaque hangs in the halls of the St. Petersburg College with their beautiful names on it.

They may not be walking this earth anymore, but the Doyle name lives on, giving hope.

* * *

By early 1996, my marriage to Chris had become strained. We traveled a couple times a year to his hometown, but our visits had become increasingly uncomfortable for me. One of his family members had started to corner me in the hallway of the house and grope me. At first, I tried to brush off his advances, making excuses and gently pushing him away. But I grew tired of dealing with him and decided it was time to tell Chris.

I broached it one Sunday afternoon, when Chris was lying on the sofa watching sports. "I need to talk to you about something, do you have a minute?" I asked, almost embarrassed to bring this up.

"Yeah, sure. What do you want to talk about?" he replied with one eye on the television.

"I need your full attention, Chris, please."

"Okay. What is this about?" He sat up straight on the couch, his expression tense.

My chest tightened as I forced air into my lungs, knowing he wasn't going to like what I had to say about one of his "perfect" family members. "This problem has been going on for a while now. It's happening every time we go to Tennessee."

His eyes narrowed. "What are you talking about?"

I tried to explain gently, hoping he'd understand. But before I could finish, he stood abruptly, putting his hands on his hips.

"Are you crazy? This never happened. I don't even know what you're talking about," he snapped. "Just because you say you were abused before, you think everyone is out to abuse you."

My anger surged, overtaking my restraint. "Are you calling me a liar? You think I'm making all this up? Really! You're a fucking asshole!" I screamed, the anger and betrayal boiling over.

He barely flinched, simply sat back down, his eyes fixed on the television as if I hadn't said a word.

This was the end of our marriage. I filed for divorce.

* * *

Around this time, I began to notice significant changes happening in the market. My company's success had attracted the attention of larger competitive homecare companies. As the time approached to renew the contracts I had secured with various retirement facilities, these larger companies swooped in, offering lower prices and bundling additional services that I simply couldn't compete with.

I began exploring different avenues to diversify. A noticeable and alarming rise in the number of young men being diagnosed with HIV and AIDS meant there was a need to provide registered nurses for home visits (to administer medications intravenously). I began looking into how I could expand into pharmaceutical services.

I soon realized the upfront investment needed to get started was significant, but the margins for profitability were promising. Diversifying into pharmaceuticals would require me to sell off the homecare side of the business to focus on this new venture.

Moving forward with my plan, I set up the pharmacy and hired personnel to get operations going.

Fortunately, I had a great relationship with Dr. Hill, a physician whose primary practice was treating HIV and AIDS patients, and he quickly started referring patients. I developed a close friendship with him.

Within a week, the homecare side was sold. I took the money

and immediately reinvested it in the pharmaceutical side, excited for this new adventure. But it didn't take long for problems to crop up. I needed to increase my cash flow due to the fast growth of the business. Most of the revenue came from Medicaid, which could hold payments for as long as nine months. This put considerable burden on my cash flow, especially since the drugs were extremely expensive. One dose could cost as much as fifteen hundred dollars and the drug company I purchased the drugs from required payment within three business days.

I decided to partner with two men from Tampa. Walter had been in the home pharmaceutical business before and knew the business well. Clarence, a friend of Walter's, on the other hand, had never been in the healthcare business, but had become extremely wealthy when a railroad company bought his family farm for millions.

The agreement we reached was that I would retain fifty-one percent of the company, holding the title of CEO and president, and they would split the remaining forty-nine percent between the two of them. This would allow me to maintain control of the business.

Shortly after the documents were signed, I met with the investors.

"I think we should start securing other physicians in other counties, like Sarasota," Walter said. "Candy, you need to be freed up from working with Dr. Hill so you can market to the other counties. Clarence can spend time at Dr. Hill's office and let you know if he needs help."

"What? I don't think that's a good idea. Dr. Hill trusts me completely. He knows I will go above and beyond to ensure his patients receive the best care and that their treatment plans are executed properly. I don't think you truly understand the complexity of this disease—"

"I think Clarence will do a good job with Dr. Hill," he snapped back, while Clarence sat, unmoved by the conversation.

"Clarence, you're from the Midwest, and you've never worked in healthcare, let alone with a young man with AIDS, correct?" I asked, looking at both of them.

"Yes, that's true." Clarence replied.

"Walter, this is not a good idea."

"Let's just try it for a few weeks and see how things go," Walter said.

Within three weeks, I was receiving calls from Dr. Hill. "Candy, what is this guy Clarence doing here? Why did you send him?" Dr. Hill's voice was sharp with frustration. "He sits in my waiting room, trying to have a conversation with my patients. He's upsetting them and acting like he can tell me how to run my practice. Nobody is going to tell me how to treat my patients or manage my office. You know how important my patients are to me. You need to get him out of here now."

"I'm so sorry, Dr. Hill. I will take care of this," I replied, trying to calm him down.

"Look, I've been dealing with this guy for three weeks now, and it's clear he has no understanding of this disease or the care these patients require. I know he's one of your investors, but if you don't dissolve your partnership with them, I'm going to get another company to care for my patients. I can't have my patients subjected to this kind of disruption or insensitivity. My patients' well-being comes first, and I won't compromise that," Dr. Hill said firmly. "Goodbye, Candy."

Dr. Hill's referrals were seventy-five percent of the company's revenue and losing his business would be devastating. I needed to save this relationship desperately. Beyond the financial impact, I'd built personal connections with his patients over time, visiting them every week to ensure they were receiving the best possible care delivered with dignity and respect. This wasn't just a business to me, it was about the trust and care I had cultivated with these young men and their families.

One afternoon, Dr. Hill called me with news that Nick, who had full-blown AIDS, had been admitted to the hospital with difficulty breathing. Without hesitation I rushed to the hospital, knowing how critical it was to be there for him, both as a nurse and a familiar face. The respiratory therapist was trying to calm Nick down as he struggled to breathe, attempting to place a C-PAP mask on his face, but he was fighting her.

His diagnosis was Pneumocystis Carinii Pneumonia or PCP, and his body was covered with lesions from Kaposi's sarcoma, a kind of cancer (now called Kaposi sarcoma) that creates discolored patches or nodules on the skin. His frail frame and sunken face were heartbreaking.

I walked over to his bed and gently touched his arm. His eyes were the bluest blue I'd ever seen and they lit up the moment he saw me. He had always trusted me. I sat with him, held his hand, and spoke to him softly, trying to help him calm his breathing. He was fighting so hard to live. I could relate to his struggle so well; I had fought to live for many years with Richard.

Later, I stood up, leaned into his ear, and whispered softly, "It's okay for you to go now, Nick. I don't want you to suffer anymore. I'm so thankful to have had the privilege of knowing you. You don't have to fight anymore." Soon after, he passed away, quietly and peacefully.

Another funeral.

* * *

The families of these brilliant men were so giving and so deeply appreciative of how their sons were cared for in their final days. Although many people stayed far away, gripped by fear of contracting AIDS, I was never afraid. I was honored to walk with these young men through their final moments, offering them the dignity and respect they deserved when others would not.

Even after my strongest efforts, I couldn't salvage my relationship with Dr. Hill, which caused the revenues to plummet. Walter decided we needed to have a company meeting to address the situation.

I arrived at the office after a long day out in the field. When I stepped inside, I was met with an unsettling sight. Clarence was sitting behind my desk, in my chair, while Walter sat across from him in another chair. The shift in the dynamic was unmistakable, as if they were silently asserting control over a company I had built for the last ten years. I steadied myself, bracing for whatever conversation lay ahead, already sensing this was no ordinary meeting.

"You are aware of our revenue numbers, correct?" Walter began, his tone cool and measured.

"Yes, I'm aware of the numbers, especially since we lost Dr. Hill's referrals," I replied, my voice steady but stern.

Clarence didn't flinch. "We've decided that you need to step down as president of the company. You can stay on as a marketing rep if you want. We can offer you that position."

"What?" I felt a wave of disbelief. "I built this business from the ground up. I was the one who brought you both into my company. I warned both of you it was not a good idea to have Clarence overseeing Dr. Hill's office. That's why the revenues are down. It's because of both of you, not me."

"We don't see it that way," Walter replied with a smirk, his tone dripping with condescension.

I took another deep breath, anger rising. "I still own fifty-one percent of the shares in my company. You can't do this to me."

Walter leaned back, smug. "That's not the case anymore. We have documents saying something different."

"Let me see your documentation," I demanded, refusing to back down.

"We'll send you a copy in the mail. Now do you want to stay on as a marketing rep or not?" Walter snapped back. "You can apply for unemployment if you need to."

I stood up, shaking my head in disbelief. "I'm not staying on as a marketing rep for my own damn company," I said. "I'll see both of you bastards in court." Without another word, I turned and stormed out, slamming the door.

Yanking the car door open, I threw my bag into the passenger's seat. I was too mad to cry, anger coursing through me like fire. Gripping the steering wheel tightly, I peeled out of the parking lot, tires screeching against the pavement.

What different documents are they talking about?

* * *

After arriving home, I threw my purse on the floor, rushed into my home office, and began tearing through my files, desperate to find a copy of the documents we'd signed at the attorney's office. My mind raced with confusion and anger.

How could they even suggest they owned the majority? How could they think they could just take my company away?

Finally, I found the file and frantically began flipping through the pages. Relief washed over me when I spotted the clause stating that I retained fifty-one percent ownership. It clearly said I owned the majority of the company. There was no way they could simply take it from me. What documents could they possibly have saying otherwise?

I didn't want to wait to find out. After dark, I drove back to the office. As I neared, I saw the parking lot was empty. I parked directly in front of the main entrance. They hadn't even bothered to ask for my office keys. I unlocked the door, the silence thick and unsettling. The air-conditioning was off, leaving a stale, heavy stillness in the air. I made my way to my office, flicked on the light, and stared at my chair behind my desk, a surge of anger building inside me at their audacity.

Just hours ago, Dumb and Dumber had been sitting in my office, behind my desk, telling me I could stay on as a marketing rep. *The nerve.* My fists clenched as I stood there. *This is my space, my work, my vision.*

I rummaged through the files on my desk, pulling open drawers, tossing papers in my frantic search. Finally, there it was, a copy of the documents. I shoved them in my bag, flicked off the light, took one last look at my office, and hurried out, locking the door behind me.

Sitting at my dining room table, I spread out both versions of the documents in front of me, painstakingly comparing each page, each line, word by word. The truth hit me hard. The attorney—their friend—had manipulated the original agreement, altering the ownership percentages to shift the control to their hands. As I examined it closer, I noticed that all the original signatures were untouched, mine included. They'd been careful, calculating, and deceptive in a way that would leave the documents looking legitimate. My anger burned deeper, knowing they'd played me.

I sat there, feeling the weight of it all crash down on me. I grabbed my head with both hands, my fingers digging into my scalp. I began rocking back and forth trying to make sense of all this. *How did this happen? I'm such a fool. It's all gone. My company is gone.*

It would take months, maybe years, and cost a fortune in attorneys' fees to show that they'd stolen my company from me—if I was even able to do it. They knew that. They knew I'd been drawing a minimal yearly salary of just thirty thousand dollars a year, just enough to barely cover my household expenses.

They'd counted on me not being able to defend myself, banking on my lack of savings to keep me trapped. I couldn't wrap my head around this kind of evil. I felt like I couldn't breathe, like I was drowning. I just wanted to die.

In the days that followed, there were no words to capture the depth of my despair, the rawness of the betrayal, the cruelty of it all. I was paralyzed, unable to muster the strength to take a single step forward. Unable to eat, to swallow without throwing up, I began losing weight again. My entire world had collapsed around me: no money, no way to keep my house, my car, my company gone.

Not even during the brutal thirteen years enduring beatings had I felt this lost, nor during the years that followed as I struggled to build and find my place in the world. But now, I didn't know if I had the strength to keep going. My company wasn't just my business, it was the living proof of my Aunt Gen and Uncle Willis's faith in me, a legacy I had poured every part of my being into. Without it, I was empty. There was no Candy left, just a hollow shell where my identity used to be.

The suicidal thoughts and the overwhelming weight of the pain seemed endless, stretching like a dark tunnel with no light at the end in sight. Each day bled into the next, a never-ending loop of emptiness. I wasn't working; I couldn't work. I spent my days lying in bed, motionless, as if any movement might shatter what little I had left to hold onto.

Mornings became my enemy. As light crept in through the drapes and the birds began their cheerful song, I hated those sounds. I hated hearing those birds. It felt as if the world outside my bedroom was mocking me, carrying on as if my pain didn't matter. I found myself waiting for the night to fall because only in sleep could I find relief from the excruciating pain. But each morning, as the sun rose and those birds started singing again, the pain returned, raw and relentless.

Some days, I would move to the couch, sometimes staring blankly at the television, though even that noise felt like too much. The silence of the night became my only refuge.

About a month later, I filed for unemployment. I wouldn't receive my first check for a few weeks and my mortgage was due in just a few days. I knew the unemployment payments wouldn't even cover the basics.

Ben's grandmother had sued the company that had caused the boating accident that had killed Ben's father. Ben had received a substantial sum from the lawsuit. At the time, his grandmother asked if I wanted to claim any of the money and I said no; I wanted it all to go to Ben.

But the situation was different now. I hoped he might understand my need for help. He hadn't offered and I'd never asked him for any financial support. Shame and embarrassment weighed heavily on me. A mother should never have to ask her son for money, but I had no other choice.

Ben agreed to lend me some money and we made repayment arrangements to start once I was able to go back to bedside nursing.

Early in 1997, nine months after I was thrown out of the company I had built, Walter (Dumb) and Clarence (Dumber) were forced to close its doors due to lack of business. The news stirred a mix of emotions within me: vindication, sadness, and an enormous sense of loss. Everything I had poured into that company, all my hard work and vision, was gone. But knowing that they hadn't succeeded in sustaining it reminded me that it was my dedication and passion that had kept it thriving all along.

I carried an enormous weight of guilt, feeling as though I'd let Aunt Gen and Uncle Willis down. I was unable to shake the thought that I had failed them. The disappointment in myself ran deep, and I would spend years beating myself up for trusting the wrong people to invest in my vision.

Until one day, years later, something shifted. A quiet realization dawned on me: *Look at all the people you helped.* I had given so many elderly individuals the chance to stay in their homes, to live with dignity rather than be placed in a nursing home. I supported young men with AIDS and their families in their final days, allowing them to pass with grace and dignity. I hadn't let anyone down except myself, carrying this guilt for years when those I'd served were so deeply grateful. In that moment, I began to forgive myself and see this journey for what it was: one of purpose and compassion for others.

CHAPTER 29

An Unexpected Visitor

"Candy, this is Lisa. I just heard about what happened. Are you okay? You must be devastated, honey. What can I do to help you?"

Lisa was a dear friend, a nurse about twenty years older than me, with beautiful curly blonde hair that framed her face perfectly. She was always impeccably dressed when not in her nursing uniform, radiating a sense of grace and warmth. Her presence was like a bright ray of sunshine. She was always ready with hugs and a comforting word. Lisa had a way of making everyone feel cared for and supported, offering kindness that felt rare and genuine.

She lived on Treasure Island, directly on the Gulf of Mexico, where the waves rolled up a few steps away from her wooden deck. Just a couple of miles from there was the place where I used to swim with Aunt Gen as a child.

"I'm so glad you called," I said. "I'm having a difficult time right now. This is so hard. I don't want to get out of bed. I can't continue to live with this pain."

"Now, you listen to me, all right? Are you listening?"

"Yes, I'm listening."

"I want you to get out of that bed right now and get in the shower, because I can't have you smelling up my house," she said with a laugh, her tone both playful and firm. "Then drive here. We're going to have a nice dinner on my veranda, then take a walk on the beach. I'm not going to take no for an answer. Do you hear me?"

"Yes, I hear you. I'll be there in a couple hours," I said, my voice steady despite the turmoil churning inside. I hung up the phone, the sharp click resonating in my quiet bedroom. I shuffled toward the shower, stepping over clothes scattered across the floor, dishes piled beside my bed, remnants of forgotten food. The stale air in the room clung to me, a reminder that it had been some time since I'd last brushed my teeth or run a comb through my hair.

Lisa literally kept me alive. She helped me through countless days when getting out of bed felt impossible. We spent hours at her house, walking on the beach, sometimes stopping by a hotel bar for drinks. She became my lifeline, her unwavering support and motherly love filling the emptiness that had swallowed me whole. I'm certain I wouldn't be here today if it weren't for her gentle strength and constant presence.

Lisa loved to dance. One evening she invited me to join her to hear a beach band playing at a local hotel bar. The place was lively, filled with music and laughter, and Lisa seemed to know everyone there. She introduced me to some of her friends, and just as I was beginning to relax, I felt a gentle tap on my right shoulder.

Turning around, I saw a handsome man with gray hair and kind eyes.

"Hello, my name is Gary. Would you like to dance?"

I hesitated for a moment, then replied, "Okay," a bit unsure but curious. His touch was gentle and his hands soft as he led me to the dance floor.

The band began playing a slow song. At one point he gently

tried to pull me closer, but I hesitated, subtly pulling back to keep a comfortable distance. He seemed to understand, and we settled into an easy rhythm, swaying to the music while sharing a pleasant conversation. I found myself relaxing and enjoying the dance and the company more than I'd expected.

As the night was coming to an end, Gary leaned close, his voice barely above a whisper, and asked, "Can I see you again? I've really had a good time tonight. You are so beautiful."

"I would love that," I replied with a small smile as I handed him my number. A quiet spark of hope flickered within me, something I hadn't felt in so long. There was something genuine and kind about him that made me feel comfortable.

During the next few dates, I began to learn more about him. He'd spent most of his career as a general contractor and had owned his own company building residential homes. Recently, he'd moved to Florida from the Northeast, seeking a change in pace and scenery. He told me he'd attended Dartmouth. I saw a depth and warmth in him that drew me in even more. Each date felt easy and natural.

It didn't take long before we started talking about moving in together. I was ready to sell my house and leave behind the shadows of the past, along with all the negativity I'd been carrying. Gary had his sights set on a new development in Beverly Hills, Florida, where he wanted to start building residential homes. The idea of a fresh start, combined with the excitement of working together, felt like exactly what I needed. I was exhausted working in the healthcare system. We decided I would handle all the office duties while he would manage his external subcontractors. It was a new chapter waiting to be written.

To fully commit to this new path, I'd even decided to invest some of the proceeds from the sale of my house into Gary's business. With the booming housing market, investing in real estate seemed like a smart, stable move. It was a choice that gave me a sense of purpose and hope, as if I were finally creating a future.

My St. Petersburg home sold pretty quickly, and we found a charming house to rent on an acre of land in the new development. But not long after we settled in, I noticed Gary was drinking more often. At first, I brushed it off, thinking it was just part of unwinding. But soon he was drinking during working hours, and my concern grew, leaving me with a nagging feeling.

What had once felt like a promising partnership was starting to fall apart. We argued mostly about his drinking, which was escalating, no matter how much I tried to address it. His dedication to his business was slipping, with project delays and responsibilities ignored. Somehow, despite sharing a home and a life, Gary and I felt further apart than ever.

Needing comfort, I found myself looking at ads for basset hounds. I had such a soft spot for their sad eyes and their big floppy ears. Jason had always loved basset hounds, too, and the thought of bringing one into my life felt special, almost like a small connection to him, even though he'd been absent from my life for quite a while.

A couple weeks later, I heard a distinct *woof woof* coming from the front of the house. Curious, I went to the door. To my shock, there stood a basset hound, looking up at me with those soulful eyes, as if to say, "I've been looking for you." I couldn't help but smile, feeling an immediate connection with this unexpected visitor who seemed to think she belonged in my life.

I brought her into the house, wondering who she could possibly belong to. She seemed so calm and playful. I gave her a bath and then fed her some leftover chicken I had in the refrigerator.

When Gary arrived home, he walked into the kitchen, immediately spotting her. "Where did this dog come from?" he asked as he made himself a cocktail.

"I don't know." I shrugged. "She just showed up on the doorstep this afternoon. We need to find out who her owner is. Could you ask around tomorrow?"

"Yeah, sure, I'll find out who she belongs to."

The next morning Gary found her owner, who lived a mile away, and took her back.

A few days went by. I was sitting in the office doing some computer work when I heard that familiar *woof woof* at the door. My heart skipped a beat as I went to open the door. And there she was again, perched on my doorstep, looking up at me with those soulful eyes, as if to say, "I'm back, and I'm here for you." It felt like she had chosen me. I couldn't help but smile and welcome her back inside.

I went to the phone and immediately dialed her owner's number, a mix of exasperation and amusement bubbling inside me.

"I wanted to let you know your dog was just on my doorstep again," I said.

There was a brief pause, then a chuckle on the other end. "Well, I guess she likes you better," the owner replied with a hint of resignation. "So, you might as well keep her."

For a moment, I was speechless. I hadn't expected that. But as I looked down at the dog's hopeful eyes, a warm feeling washed over me. Maybe this was exactly what we both needed, a loving home for her, and a little unexpected companionship for me.

I named her Molly. I'm not exactly sure why, but the name seemed to fit her, us, perfectly. Molly & Me. We became inseparable. From the moment Molly trotted into my life, it was if she instinctively knew the void she was meant to fill. Her companionship brought a calm I hadn't felt in a long time, and her gentle presence became a quiet strength I could lean on. She listened without judgment, her soulful eyes seeming to understand more than words ever could. Molly was my confidante, my comfort, the loyal friend I needed. She'd come into my life at precisely the right moment.

One evening as I waited for Gary to get home, I decided to make myself a vodka and soda with a twist of lime. I poured a shot of vodka into a glass of ice, added the soda, and took a sip. But as the cool liquid hit my tongue, I noticed something odd; I couldn't taste the vodka. Frowning, I took another sip, but the taste was unmistakably diluted. Suspicion rose within me. I went to the vodka bottle, unscrewed the cap, and took a careful sniff. The usual strong smell was faint, watered down.

Then it hit me. I'd been gently suggesting to Gary that he should cut back on his drinking, and now it seemed he'd been topping off the vodka with water to hide just how much he'd actually been drinking.

He'd been lying to me.

The anger simmered beneath my skin, but this time, it felt different. I decided to confront him when he got home, determined not to repeat the mistakes of my past.

I'd been seeing a therapist for a few years, working through the pain of my marriages and the ongoing struggles with my sons. Therapy helped me understand I deserved honesty, respect, and integrity from the people in my life—and I would never again tolerate lies or deception. But even with all that healing, there was still parts of my story I had kept buried. I had never told anyone the full extent of what I had endured with Richard—or the rapes. Until I wrote this memoir.

The door opened, and Gary called out. I took a steadying breath, then walked out of the office and into the kitchen.

I could see it in his eyes; he'd already been drinking. I was determined not to back down this time.

"Gary, why did you put water in the vodka bottle?" I asked, folding my arms across my chest, my tone firm.

He scoffed, his expression turning cold. "What the fuck are you talking about? Water? You're crazy."

"Gary, there's water in the vodka bottle," I said, each word deliberate, my gaze fixed on his. "And I believe you put it in there to cover up the amount of vodka you've been drinking lately."

The sharpness of my tone seemed to catch him off guard, and for a fleeting moment, I thought I saw guilt flash across his face. But that moment vanished as quickly as it had come. His expression twisted into rage, his face reddening, eyes bulging with fury. Before I could process the shift, he lunged toward me, hands reaching for my neck.

I stumbled backward, instinctively raising my arms to shield myself. "You bitch!" he screamed, his words slicing through me. I struggled to keep my balance, my mind racing for a way to diffuse the situation to protect myself. I'd never seen this side of him before, and in that instant something inside of me shifted. This wasn't just a boundary he'd crossed; it was a line I refused to overlook. The days of tolerating abuse, of being broken down, were over. I had come too far, grown too strong to let anyone pull me back into that darkness. I was done allowing this kind of chaos to infect my life.

I raced to the office and grabbed the phone, frantically dialing 911.

"911, how can I help you?"

But before I could respond, Gary stormed into the room, snatching the phone from my hand and slamming it down. "You're not calling 911 on me!" he yelled. "I did nothing to you."

"Yes, you did!" I screamed back. "You tried to put your hands around my throat!" I stood my ground, refusing to let him rewrite history the way Richard used to do.

Just then, the doorbell rang, and a firm voice called out. "This is the police, please come to the door."

Gary's face twisted, his eyes narrowing with a glare of hatred. A wave of fear washed over me, mingling with a sharp realization that I was seeing a side of him I hadn't known existed. He leaned close, his voice a low whisper. "You better not tell them anything, do you hear me?"

A chill ran down my spine and a mix of fear and defiance swirled inside me as I watched him walk to the front door and open it.

"Yes, officers, how can I help you?" Gary asked with a polite, steady voice.

One of the officers nodded, his expression calm but serious. "We got a call from this number that someone needed assistance."

"Yes, that was me, I was the one who called," I blurted out, trying to contain the mix of fear and frustration inside me. "He tried to put his hands around my throat."

The officers exchanged a look before one of them asked, "Okay, what's going on? What happened?" Both stepped inside, dividing us; one took Gary aside while the other turned his attention to me.

I began explaining, the words coming in a rush, but then he cut me off, his gaze focusing on my neck. "Have you been drinking?" he asked in a condescending manner while continuing to inspect my neck.

"I took a few sips of my cocktail tonight." This was beginning to feel like déjà vu.

"I don't see any marks on your neck."

"You don't see any marks because I defended myself," I replied firmly, meeting his gaze. "He didn't get the chance to put his hands fully around my neck." I could sense the doubt, but I held my ground, determined to make sure they understood what had happened.

Leaning slightly to the side to look past the officer standing in front of me, I caught sight of Gary and the other officer engaged in what looked like a friendly conversation. They were talking about how many houses Gary had built in the area, his tone relaxed, almost casual, as though nothing serious had just taken place.

I felt a knot of anger tighten in my chest. I turned back to the officer in front of me, gathering every ounce of strength, determined not to let my voice be dismissed again.

"Officer, please believe me," I pleaded. "He really did try to grab my throat."

"I can only go by what I see, and I don't see any marks on your neck."

"Are you calling me a liar?" My voice echoed through the room.

The officer's expression barely shifted; he looked at me like I was just another woman making a baseless accusation. "Let me give you a pamphlet about domestic violence."

I threw up my hands in exasperation, the weight of disbelief pressing down on me. I turned and walked away. In the bedroom, I tried to calm down, feeling the walls close in around me.

After the officers left, I took a moment to collect myself, feeling a mix of anger and hurt, but determined not to go through this again. I walked out of the bedroom only to see Gary standing in the kitchen with a smug smirk, casually pouring himself another drink.

"You bastard!" I yelled, my voice cracking with emotion. "How could you do this to me?"

He shrugged, slowly lifting his eyes while taking a gulp of his cocktail. "Do what? I didn't do anything. You brought this all on yourself."

His words cut deep. "I'm leaving you, Gary. I will not go through what I did before with Richard. I'm going for a drive."

His face darkened. "Oh, you're not going anywhere."

I squared my shoulders, locking my gaze with his. "Watch me." Without another word, I grabbed my purse and car keys, and stomped out, slamming the door behind me.

I didn't have any idea where I was going, I just knew I had to get out of there. I drove aimlessly, the shock and adrenaline slowly fading to an ache of confusion and anger. After a while, I pulled over in a quiet residential area. As I sat, everything that had just happened replayed in my head. *I won't put up with this anymore.* Feeling the weight of my words sink in. But then, another thought surfaced. *What about the money I invested?*

Startled by the ring of my cell phone, I fumbled as I pulled it out of my purse. "Candy, this is Gary," he began, his voice unsettling. Before he could finish, I cut him off, my voice sharp and steady. "I know who this is."

"The police are here, and they want to talk to you. So, they want you to come back to the house."

"What? What are you talking about? What do they want from me?" I asked, my voice laced with frustration and confusion.

"I'm not sure, they just want to talk to you," Gary replied, his tone evasive.

"Why are they back at the house? Did you call them, Gary?"

I could hear one of the officers in the background, his voice firm and insistent. "We need to talk to you, ma'am."

A surge of anger came over me. "I'll think about it," I said coldly, pushing the end-call button on my phone.

My mind began to race, questions tumbling over each other in a frantic rush. *What has Gary told them? Should I go back? No, don't go back, stay here.* But another thought gnawed at me: *If I don't go back, will they send other police officers out to find me? God, my stomach hurts.*

I've done nothing wrong, but I don't know what Gary told them. He could have told them anything. Anger rising in my chest, I decided to go back and try and defend myself again. *I'll make sure they listen this time.*

A few minutes later I walked in the house, my heart pounding, and saw the same two police officers that were there before standing in the living room talking to Gary, who looked calm and collected. The room fell silent as I stepped in, the officers turning to face me.

"Ma'am, you're under arrest for domestic violence," one of them announced, with an authoritative voice.

"What! Domestic violence?" I stammered, my voice rising in shock. "What do you mean?"

"Gary has a couple of scratches on his left arm. He says you bit him."

"Bit him?" I repeated, staring at Gary with disbelief. His expression was cold and smug. I realized he'd woven a story that turned everything against me.

"Officers, this man is making this story up to get back at me," I said, my voice shaking but resolute. "He's a contractor, he's going to have scratches on his arms. Look at me! I'm not even five feet tall and weigh a hundred pounds. Look at him, he's almost six foot tall and muscular."

Before I could say another word, one of the officers cut me off. "Ma'am, he's filed a complaint, saying you attacked him and bit him. We're going to take you to the police station for the night. You're under arrest."

CHAPTER 30

I Have a Voice

Sitting on the curb outside the police station the next morning, waiting for a cab to take me home, a whirlwind of questions and frustrations flooded my mind. I'd stood my ground with Gary, spoken up for myself, yet somehow, my voice had gone unheard. Why was I the one spending the night at the police station? Why didn't they believe me?

I replayed the scene in my head. How much clearer could I have been? Why did it seem like the police always fell for the manipulation of an abuser? Were they truly that blind, or was it easier for them to dismiss my pain? The injustice stung deeply, and I knew I couldn't ignore the broken system.

When I arrived home, I found Gary in the kitchen, casually making himself a cup of coffee. He looked up, a smirk spreading across his face.

"What are you doing here?" he sneered, his voice dripping with sarcasm.

A surge of rage boiled up inside me, and I didn't hold back. "My name is on the lease of this house," I shot back. "And yours is not."

He leaned against the counter, that smug smile unfazed. "I have a restraining order on you."

"Guess you better start packing then," I replied, my voice unwavering. "And once I tell everyone in this community, your subcontractors, and the people whose homes you're building that you tried to choke me, then lied to the police, claiming I bit you, I'm pretty sure your reputation will end up in the toilet. Unless, of course, you decide to drop these ridiculous fabricated charges that I tried to assault you."

It felt good to speak up for myself, a power I'd never felt. I'd lived in pain and fear all my life, always terrified of the consequences, but this moment, I stood tall, facing this disgusting abuser with defiance instead of fear. The years of silence, the layers of fear, pain and helplessness, began to peel away, revealing a part of me that I didn't know existed.

Damn it, I am somebody and I have a voice!

I watched as his smug smile faded, replaced by a flicker of uncertainty. For the first time, he seemed to realize that I wasn't going to be his silent victim. I found my voice and I was prepared to use it.

"All right, I'll drop the charges," he muttered, the confidence draining from his face.

I crossed my arms, meeting his gaze with strength. "Good," I said, refusing to let my guard down. "And don't think for a second that I'll stay quiet about what happened here if you decide not to pay me back the money I invested in your company. If you try to pull anything on me, everyone will know exactly who you really are."

He looked away. For the first time, I saw him for what he really was, weak and powerless in the face of someone who'd reclaimed her own.

A few days later, I met with an attorney named Collins to discuss representation for the assault charges. His secretary led me into his office where he was finishing a call. I was a bit surprised by his appearance. He didn't quite fit the image I expected. He was a short, stocky man in his mid-forties, dressed in somewhat rumpled clothes that gave him a casual, approachable air. His demeanor was warm and pleasant and he greeted me with a smile.

"I need representation for an assault charge."

Before I could even finish, he interrupted. "Ma'am, I represent criminals, not victims of assault. I'm a criminal attorney."

I paused, gathering my words before speaking. "Um, you see, I'm the one who has been charged with assault."

He looked at me, eyebrows raised in genuine surprise. "What? You?" he said, clearly shocked. His expression hovered somewhere between disbelief and confusion. "Wait a minute, you're the one who was charged?" he repeated, then let out a laugh as his eyes scanned me, a petite woman he clearly hadn't expected to hear this from. "I'm sorry for laughing. Please tell me what happened."

I explained the entire situation, giving as much detail as I could, recounting every painful memory of that night. When I finished, he leaned back, running his fingers through his hair, his face a mixture of disbelief and frustration.

"This is ridiculous and unbelievable," he said, shaking his head. "I can't believe they charged you and not Gary. Don't worry, I'll make this all go away quickly. I'm going to get Gary to say in court that he's dropping the charges. This is going to give the judge a good laugh."

His confidence was comforting, giving me hope.

* * *

I'd been speaking with my brother Asser over the last year, reconnecting in ways I hadn't expected. He'd been going through a tough divorce, and I empathized with his pain and struggles. Our conversations often drifted into discussions about our past relationships, the shared craziness of our dysfunctional family, and how it had shaped us, sometimes in ways we were only beginning to understand.

I was feeling closer to him, but there was always a subtle distance that lingered beneath our conversations. It was as if he'd built walls so high and fortified that no matter how close we got, I could never quite reach him, leaving me both connected and isolated from him at the same time.

During our calls, he often encouraged me to move to Montana, offering his home as a place to stay until I bought a place of my own.

"Are you sure this is okay with you?" I asked repeatedly.

"Yes, I'm sure," he'd say with conviction. "Sis, you can get a job anywhere since you're a nurse."

Each time, I'd respond with a cautious, "I'll think about it." But after the ordeal with Gary, Asser's words began to resonate differently. I found myself seriously considering it. *Maybe he's right, maybe a fresh start is what I need.* But the thought of living in Montana felt daunting. Could I really fit in there? I was a lost soul, searching for a purpose, and Montana began to seem like a place where I might finally fit in.

After giving it much thought I decided that once the assault charges were settled, Molly and I were moving to Montana. It felt like a leap into the unknown, but something about the idea of starting fresh in a new place brought a sense of relief. I was ready to leave Florida behind.

* * *

My attorney and I arrived at the courthouse the day of the hearing; it was packed with people. As we waited, he reassured me, "Don't worry, I'll have these charges dismissed."

I watched Gary enter the courtroom and take a seat on the opposite side. I pointed him out to my attorney. "Don't worry, I've got this," he replied, giving my arm a comforting pat.

When the judge called our case, my attorney rose confidently, stepping forward to address the judge. He launched into a series of legal terms that I struggled to follow, his tone calm and authoritative. Finally, he concluded, "Your honor, I have an affidavit from the plaintiff. He's requesting that all charges against my client be dropped."

I held my breath waiting for the judge's response.

"If the defendant and the plaintiff are in the courtroom, please stand," the judge ordered.

Both Gary and I rose to our feet. Suddenly all eyes were on us. The judge glanced down at the documents before him, then fixed a puzzled gaze at Gary. "It says here that you're the plaintiff. Is this correct, sir?" he asked, an eyebrow raised in confusion.

"Yes, your honor," Gary replied, clearly unaware of the reaction he was about to spark.

In that instant, the entire courtroom, judge, attorneys, even the spectators, burst into laughter. The absurdity of the situation wasn't lost on anyone. A wave of relief washed over me, knowing the truth of my case was undeniably on display.

"This case is dismissed."

That was the last time I laid eyes on Gary.

CHAPTER 31

Molly & Me

Molly and I arrived in rural Montana in the spring of 2001, brimming with excitement for our new adventure. Remnants of snow lingered on the ground, a stark contrast to the warm sunlit landscapes we'd left behind in Florida. The trees stood bare, not yet touched by the spring's green leaves. The starkness of the scene heightened my sense of change and new beginnings.

My brother's home was a sprawling ranch-style. It seemed to have a lot of history within its walls, having been built in the early 1900s. With its multiple levels, the layout offered a sense of openness, although it was furnished with only the necessities. The house sat on an expansive piece of land, surrounded by acres of open fields, with a horse barn nearby, a few horses roaming, and cattle grazing peacefully.

For the first time in what seemed like forever, I felt safe, truly safe, in a sanctuary where I could finally let my guard down and breathe freely.

While waiting to hear back from the hospital about the director of nursing position I'd applied for and anticipating the arrival of the truck with my belongings, I found myself reflecting deeply. Questions kept surfacing: *Why didn't my parents love me? How had*

I ended up with Richard? Why did I lose my company? How had I picked Gary, another drinker and abuser?

Since I had limited access to in-person therapy sessions, I began reading articles on abusive relationships, hoping to understand the patterns and choices that had led me here. I tuned into talk shows that frequently featured discussions on abuse and women's rights, drawn to the voices of other women sharing their stories. I read books about women's issues, but my dyslexia and ADHD often made it challenging. I found myself rereading paragraphs and losing focus, struggling to retain what I had just read. Yet, despite these hurdles, I pressed on, determined to gain insight and understanding.

My newfound sense of security didn't last long. As the days went on, I noticed a shift in Asser's demeanor. He began to seem distant, almost indifferent, which left me feeling confused and wondering if I'd done something wrong. I tried approaching him, gently asking what was going on, hoping he might open up.

But every time, I got the same dismissive response: "Nothing's wrong." When I pressed him for an answer, wanting to understand, he'd grow irritated, his voice tense, until he'd storm out the door. His reactions left me feeling more unsettled and hesitant, unsure how to bridge the gap between us. Within days of my arrival, the warmth I thought I'd found in his home no longer existed.

About ten days after I arrived in Montana, I was offered and accepted the position of director of nursing at the local hospital. Then the day I had been eagerly waiting for, the day my furniture and belongings would finally arrive, came. I was given the day off to handle it.

That morning, the driver called to say he'd made it.

"Vince, you're here?" I called out with excitement, catching sight of his truck parked in the driveway. "I'll be right out."

Slipping on my shoes, I noticed Molly stirring from her nap. She trotted after me, tail wagging as we headed outside to greet Vince.

"Vince, I'm so happy to see you got here safely."

"Had a few rough spots, but I'm used to driving through bad weather," Vince replied, stepping down from the truck. "Where do you want it all to go? You said your brother would be around to help unload, right? Where is he?"

I hesitated, feeling embarrassed. "Unfortunately, he's not here. When I asked him this morning, he said, 'This is not my deal.' But I've been on the phone trying to find some guys who want to make some extra money."

Vince sighed, giving me a reassuring nod. "All right, no worries. Let's figure this out." Despite Asser's refusal to help, Vince's demeanor remained calm and supportive.

Pointing at the house, I said, "See that door over there? I'm going to store my belongings in that room."

As Vince and I unloaded the truck, I heard the crunch of gravel. Asser's truck pulled into the driveway. He stepped out, a look of displeasure etched across his face, and started walking briskly toward the front door of the house.

"Hey, man," Vince called out hopefully. "Could you give us a hand unloading?"

Asser didn't even pause. He barely glanced our way before turning and snapping, "This is not my deal." Without another word, he disappeared into the house.

Not long after my desperate calls for assistance, three men showed up to help finish unloading my belongings.

In the weeks that followed, Asser's demeanor grew more menacing, his eyes fixed on me with chilling, hateful intensity. It was as if he were a predator stalking his prey, watching my every move with a cold, calculated focus that could strike at any moment. If I wasn't working, I would retreat to the bedroom with Molly and lock the door.

Asser had mentioned a friend named Jim, someone he'd confided in during his divorce, so I decided to seek Jim out, hoping he might offer some insight into my brother's sudden, disturbing change in behavior.

A few days later we met, sitting across from each other in a quiet room at his office. I explained what had been happening with Asser, describing his cold, hateful stares and the tension that now filled the house. When I finished, Jim looked at me intently, and said, his tone serious and unwavering, "Get out of that house now."

I stared, taken aback. "Are you telling me my brother would hurt me?"

He held my gaze, his expression grim. "Get out of that house now. That's all I'm going to say."

His words left me shaken, and I knew I couldn't ignore the warning. Without hesitation I contacted a realtor and began the process of finding a place of my own. It wasn't as if I could find a hotel nearby, but within a few weeks I closed on a house near the hospital and moved my furniture in. I felt a renewed strength in taking control of my safety.

I never saw or talked to my brother again.

* * *

I worked at the local hospital for less than a year. It became clear early on that they didn't care much for the progressive short blonde from Florida coming and pushing changes. I introduced accountability for employees who frequently missed shifts, advocated for repairing or replacing outdated medical equipment, prioritized creating professional relationships with the physicians, and implemented a plan that corrected staffing shortages. In the end, pushback from the administration made it difficult to accomplish lasting change.

One afternoon, the administrator called me into his office, his tone impersonal and firm. He informed me that I was being let go because, in his words, I was "creating too much turmoil." Despite my efforts to enhance patient care and foster professionalism, my vision wasn't welcome.

The one thing my past had taught me was, document, document, and document some more. Determined to stand up for myself, I sought out an attorney who specialized in labor laws, intent on filing a wrongful termination lawsuit against the hospital. At first, he seemed skeptical, saying, "Everyone tells me they've been wrongfully terminated."

But as I presented my detailed documentation, his demeanor shifted. After reviewing my record, he took my case, and the hospital ultimately settled with me for ten thousand dollars. My attorney was so disgusted by the way I had been treated, he offered his services pro bono. It wasn't just about the money, it was about standing up for what was right and proving to myself that I wouldn't be silenced.

I accepted a position with a nursing agency and was assigned to Fort Peck Indian Reservation located in Montana near the Canadian border. It was a four-hour drive from my house, so my schedule was structured around six consecutive twelve-hour shifts, followed by eight days off. The hospital provided housing for both me and Molly, conveniently located directly across the street.

The hospital was small, with just over fifty beds, including one intensive care bed and one emergency room bed. Despite its small size, I found myself truly enjoying the staff I worked with. Their dedication to patient care was evident; their primary concern was always "What can we do to help?" There was always a physician available on call, and on the weekends, a physician would fly in and spend the weekend.

After nine months of working on the reservation I found myself growing restless, weary of the relentless extremes in weather, especially the brutal winter drives on ice- and snow-covered roads, with temperatures sometimes plunging as low as forty to fifty below zero. I knew it was time for a change, time to pursue something I'd always dreamed of experiencing: New York City.

One evening after a long shift, I sat down to eat my dinner. Molly, as usual, stared up at me with those familiar, soulful eyes. I looked at her and asked, "Molly, how would you like to go to NYC?"

She tilted her head as if to say, "Mom, as long as I'm with you I'll go anywhere." We had made our decision. We were bound for New York City!

* * *

The summer of 2002, Molly and I landed at LaGuardia airport, both of us filled with excitement and anticipation for our new adventure. We arrived with just two suitcases and Molly's travel house, only the essentials to get us by. It felt like a fresh start, the kind that leaves you both nervous and exhilarated.

Before moving, I'd made the deliberate choice to close up my house in Montana, leaving it untouched. Selling or renting it didn't seem right, not yet. I wanted to give myself time to decide where I truly wanted to settle. For now, my focus was on discovering what life in the bustling city might hold for me and my loyal furry child.

I initially rented a home on Long Island, but with a coworker's help, I soon moved to a studio apartment in Manhattan, closer to my job on the Upper East Side. One of the windows faced First Avenue, bringing the city's sounds into our little space. Though compact, the apartment felt just right for the two of us, a small, warm haven that became our own slice of the city.

On my days off, I pored over *TimeOut*, *The Village Voice*, and *The New York Times* to see what was happening. Armed with a list of must-see spots and events, I'd carefully map out my day before leaving my apartment, determined to make the most of my time.

One unforgettable day, I joined a six-hour line at the Park Plaza Hotel (now called The Plaza) during its pre-renovation auction, eager to snag a few pieces of history. Standing in that iconic space, I even got to see the Queen of Soul, Aretha Franklin, and her entourage at the hotel picking up a few treasures.

"I hope all of you find something special," Aretha shouted as she walked out the door. Inspired by her words, I carefully roamed through the collection, searching for the perfect memorabilia for myself and for my family. Among my finds were elegant bed linens and bathmats embroidered with the distinctive blue PP, as well as wine glasses that made me wonder if a famous actor or even a diplomat had sipped from them or slept on the linens.

I felt a deep connection to the history and glamour of the hotel, making my six-hour wait entirely worth it. To my disappointment, when I sent some of these treasures to my family members, they didn't seem to appreciate the history and significance that had captivated me, leaving me to cherish the connection alone.

I enrolled Molly at her doggie gym and on the days I worked at the hospital, a pet taxi would take her there. After work, I took the subway to the stop closest to her gym and we'd walk home together.

I absolutely loved the ritual of picking out a new recipe, then heading to the market with my rolling cart. It became an experience that awakened my senses and brought me genuine joy I could share with my coworkers. The vibrant colors of the fresh vegetables and their crispness promised something delicious. I loved stopping to chat with the butcher and pausing to take in the aroma of fresh-baked bread. I always made one final stop, the flower stand, to add a touch of beauty to my apartment.

I would then push my cart home, navigating the bustling city streets with excitement. When I arrived at my building, I'd position my cart and begin the climb up to my fourth-floor walk-up, building a new life one step and one recipe at a time.

Manhattan was a mosaic of cultures with many different ethnicities living side by side. Their traditions, languages, and customs were endlessly intriguing to me, each offering a glimpse into a world beyond my own. Watching children from different backgrounds play lovingly, their laughter bridging gaps. Families gathering for dinner in a bustling restaurant, their conversations flowing freely, with bursts of laughter, clinking glasses raised in celebration. Observing these moments of joy drew me in. I found myself captivated by their warmth, longing for that sense of belonging. I couldn't help but wonder how different my life might have been if I'd grown up knowing such ease.

There was always something to do, and the endless energy and opportunity made living in the city exciting to me. It marked a milestone on my journey of healing, a time when I discovered the power of joy and endless possibilities.

But I feared joy. I feared it because I feared losing it again, like

I always had. It was as if I were trapped under a manhole with its heavy cover pressing down on me. Each time I began to feel joy, I lifted the cover just enough to glimpse daylight, to let in a sliver of hope, only for someone to come along and stomp it shut again, trapping me in the darkness once more.

I realized that joy and fear could coexist, that feeling happiness didn't mean it would be stolen away. I had the power to embrace the light, to refuse to let the shadows define me. I was shedding the fear of fear itself and learning to embrace joy.

I wanted to stand in the middle of the street and throw my hat in the air, like Mary Tyler Moore, and shout, "I made it!"

* * *

It had been nearly five years since I'd last spoken to Jason. He'd disappeared, not wanting to be found, leaving a void that I'd learned to live with, though it never stopped aching. Ben, on the other hand, visited me about a half dozen times during the six years I lived in the city. By then, he was in his mid-thirties and deeply committed to his work at the golf course, so his visits were always brief, three or four days at a time.

I was always thrilled to see him, cherishing every moment we spent together, but I couldn't help noticing a pattern. After a day or two, something would shift. He would become irritable or retreat into complete silence, leaving me wondering what I'd done wrong. Whenever I asked him what was bothering him, his response was always the same response I got when he was a child: "Nothing is wrong."

It was a wall I couldn't get past, no matter how hard I tried. The unspoken tension created a heavy burden, leaving me feeling both confused and heartbroken.

Before my move to Montana, I'd spoken frequently with Sue and Asser, hoping we could all reunite and support one another during a time when we each needed to heal from the horrors of our childhood. I believed by breaking the silence and learning to express our true feelings, we could begin to dismantle the pattern of emotional isolation—and in doing so, offer something healthier to the next generation.

One afternoon, it all exploded. Ben, along with Sue's daughter Nora, had come to visit me for the Thanksgiving Day parade. The day should have been filled with joy and celebration, but Ben had been giving me snarky remarks since the morning, his irritation barely concealed. Nora decided to run an errand, leaving us alone for a short while.

As soon as the door closed behind her, Ben's sharp comments started up again. Finally, unable to hold back any longer, I turned to him, frustration clear in my voice. "What is wrong with you? Why are you being so hateful to me?"

"Nothing's wrong," he replied in a curt tone that only fueled my frustration.

"There *is* something wrong," I pressed, my voice rising and my patience wearing thin. "You're being very rude, and I want to know what the hell did I do to you? I know I wasn't the best mother when you were growing up, but I kept us alive, and I've been trying ever since to make it up to you. I work my ass off, standing on my legs for twelve hours several days a week, to have money to pay for your flight to come here, pay for dinners and entertainment, and all you can say is 'nothing is wrong.'"

He just stood there, his posture stiff, his jaw tight, staring at me with a defiance I had come to dread. His pupils were dark and wide, dilated with anger. Sweat rolled down his forehead as he refused to respond.

My voice cracked under the weight of my emotions. "When was the last time you bought me a birthday or Mother's Day card? When was the last time you showed me you cared? You think your father was so wonderful? Let me remind you, I didn't get any child support from him to help raise you, except for one lousy time. I did it all on my own."

"Shut up, shut up!" Ben roared, his voice echoing in my small apartment. "Shut up! Don't you ever mention my father!" His face twisted with rage. It felt like the room was about to explode as I watched him pack his bag and storm out the door.

I sat on the edge of my bed, my hands shaking, trying to make sense of what had just happened. For years, I had tiptoed around Ben's mood swings, never daring to confront him, but this time it all spilled out.

Why was his father so great?
I was the one who kept him alive.
Why does he hate me so much?

* * *

After our argument, I called Ben within the week to apologize. I admitted that I should never have brought up his father and expressed my regret for upsetting him. He accepted my apology, though he never addressed his own rudeness or unwillingness to explain why he was so rude to me. It hurt deeply, but I told myself it was important to maintain a relationship with my son, in hopes one day he would open up and share why he treated me the way he did. Then we could finally begin to heal and rebuild our relationship.

One evening a few weeks later, he called and said, "I have something to tell you."

"Oh, no, is it bad news?" I asked, bracing myself.

"Actually, it's good news," he reassured me. "I wanted to tell you before now, but I've been going to college."

It took me a moment to process his words. "I'm so thrilled to hear this. I'm so proud of you. But why did you wait so long to tell me?"

"I don't know why," he admitted. Then he added, "I'm majoring in physical therapy."

"I'm making a promise to you," I said, my voice filled with emotion. "No matter where I am or where I'm living, I will be at your graduation. I will be so proud to watch you walk across the stage to receive your degree." It wasn't just a promise, it was a declaration of how much his achievements meant to me and how deeply I wanted to celebrate this milestone with him.

"That would be great, Ma. I'll talk to you later."

I'd always told my boys I loved them, and they could be and do anything, and I meant it every time, but for years those words carried the weight of my fear, fear of loss, fear of rejection, fear of not being enough. Now as I was healing and slowly shedding that fear, those words flowed out with a lightness I hadn't known before. They were no longer bound by anxiety or desperation but instead came from a place of genuine love and confidence.

* * *

In 2006, I was standing in the middle of the emergency room on one of the busiest days I could remember. The air buzzed with urgency as gurneys filled every available space and physicians and nurses shouted, "I need some help over here!"

Every part of me was working in overdrive, every brain cell and every muscle in my body moving as fast as it could go. Suddenly, I paused, looked around at the overwhelming scene, and thought, *I don't want to do this anymore. I need to do something else.*

That evening, sitting in my Upper East Side apartment, I began exploring new opportunities in nursing. I began researching possibilities on the internet. One ad caught my eye: an aesthetic training class in New Jersey. *This may just be my doorway to a different kind of future.*

The class came with a hefty price tag, twenty-six-hundred dollars, but I knew it was time to invest in myself and the new path I was determined to pursue. It felt like a leap of faith, but one I was ready to take. Without hesitation, I signed up and paid the fee.

On the day of the class, I boarded the ferry from Manhattan to New Jersey, watching the city skyline fade in the distance as I embarked on what I hoped would be a transformative journey.

* * *

Molly was aging, now thirteen years old. Her once boundless energy had given way to a slower, more deliberate pace. Our walks to Central Park, which used to feel effortless, now took much longer as she often paused to rest. She was starting to show signs of aggression toward her furry friends at her gym, a stark contrast to her usually friendly demeanor.

One day, while I was talking with Sue about Molly getting older, she gently suggested, "Maybe it's time for you and Molly to leave the city. Maybe you could come live near me in Georgia."

Her words stopped me in my tracks, sending a wave of fear through me. The idea of leaving New York City, the place that had shaped me, taught me about love, courage, and my own worth, was terrifying. This city had shown me that I was smart, capable, and deserving of a full life. If I left, would I lose all that I had gained? Would the lessons stay with me, or would I be stepping away from the person I had become? The thought frightened the hell out of me.

But Molly deserved a backyard full of sunshine to warm her belly in her final days.

I woke up the next morning feeling overwhelmed. As I took Molly for her morning walk, I thought about all that was in front of me: leaving the city, moving and buying a house in Georgia, selling my house in Montana. It felt like too much to take in at once.

Sue and I had many conversations about my moving to Georgia. She'd recently relocated there from Florida after her youngest daughter graduated from college. During one call, she said, "You could stay at my house for a few months until you save up some money for a down payment."

"Thanks, but I can't handle a repeat of what happened with our brother."

"We won't let that happen."

"I'll think about it. I don't want to jeopardize our relationship in any way. It would break my heart if the same thing happened to us."

Soon I started making a list of all the tasks I needed to accomplish. Surprisingly, the most difficult one was finding a moving company that would allow me to take their van out of the city. The few companies that did charged outrageous fees. Frustrated but determined, I made countless calls.

Finally, I found a U-Haul office willing to help, but there was a catch—they didn't have a van large enough to fit all my belongings. Instead, I had to rent two smaller vans to make it work. It wasn't ideal, but it was the best option I could find.

I asked Sue if she would mind coming to the city to help me by driving one of the vans. I offered to pay for her flight. To my relief, she said yes, and I felt a small sense of comfort knowing I wouldn't have to tackle this journey alone.

When the day arrived for me to leave the city, the scene was chaotic as we loaded up the vans on bustling First Avenue. The constant horns honking, the hum of the traffic, and the hurried pace of the pedestrians served as a backdrop to our frenzied packing. After the last items were placed in the vans and the doors closed, I took one final walk up the four flights to say goodbye to my apartment.

Standing in the now-empty space, I whispered a prayer.

Thank you for being my safe place.

Thank you for so many wonderful memories.

Please help me to not lose what this city has taught and given me.

Now as I walked down the steps for one final time, the weight of leaving my little apartment, a sanctuary that had nurtured my growth, pressed upon me, making each step more poignant than the last.

As we drove through the Lincoln Tunnel, leaving the city behind, I whispered, "Until next time, New York."

* * *

We broke the drive up into two days. On the second day, I began to feel ill. I brushed it off as nerves and sadness about leaving the city. I didn't have time to be sick; my house in Montana had sold and I had just a few days to pack up and move all of those belongings to Georgia.

I asked Nora if she could fly with me to Montana to help me pack and she graciously agreed.

Once we arrived, the reality of packing up a full house of belongings and furniture hit us hard. It was absolute torture. By the end of the three grueling days, the sound of tape ripping to seal the boxes was enough to drive us mad. When the eighteen-wheeler was finally loaded, car included, I felt nothing but relief as I waved a cheerful goodbye to that horrific mistake.

By the time we arrived back in Georgia, I was feeling utterly miserable, plagued by a relentless cough and a low-grade fever that left me drained. All I could think about was crawling into bed and sleeping for days. Thankfully, I had a couple weeks before starting my new travel nurse job in Atlanta, which gave me a little time to recover.

Being a nurse, I recognized the symptoms of walking pneumonia, and tried to manage it on my own, but after a few days, it became clear that rest and over-the-counter remedies weren't enough. I reluctantly made the decision to see a physician, knowing I needed proper treatment to get back on my feet.

"Sis, would you mind taking me to the doctor tomorrow?" I asked, my voice barely a whisper.

"No, you can go by yourself. I'll be too tired when I get off from work." Her words were sharp and dismissive.

Her refusal cut deep, leaving me hurt and bewildered that she wouldn't help me in such a vulnerable moment. Still, I didn't want to rock the boat. After all, she'd offered to let me stay with her.

Swallowing my disappointment, I mustered what little energy I had, pulling myself off the sofa and forcing myself to get dressed. Each movement felt like a monumental task. As I fumbled with my shoes, I couldn't help but wonder how I was going to manage the drive to the doctor's office a few miles away.

I gathered just enough strength to see the doctor, get my prescriptions filled, and make it back to Sue's house. It took a good week of rest and medication before I started to feel like myself again. I couldn't remember ever being that sick before.

Ironically, a couple weeks later, Sue came down with pneumonia, too. Watching her struggle like I had made me wonder if she regretted not helping me when I needed her. Despite the hurt I felt during my own illness, I couldn't bring myself to ignore her. I cared for her as best I could, preparing soups, making sure she took her medications, and checking on her often. At the same time, I kept my distance as much as possible, wary of falling sick again. It was a strange dynamic, offering her the support I had hoped for but hadn't received.

In the end, there was no gratitude, no acknowledgment of the care I had provided during her illness. Instead, Sue chastised me, blaming me for giving her pneumonia. Her words stung, but they also served as a painful reminder of how we were raised: taught to bury our emotions and withhold compassion, even in moments when it was most needed. It was a cycle I had worked hard to break away from, striving to show kindness and vulnerability. I hoped that, in time, Sue might find it within herself to do the same, breaking free from these barriers.

It was a small hope, but one I held onto, nonetheless.

* * *

In the fall of 2007, a few months after moving into Sue's house, I purchased my own home. The cathedral ceilings in the open kitchen and living room created a bright and spacious atmosphere, much different from my tiny apartment in New York City. Molly even had her own paradise, a backyard where she could lie in the sunshine to warm her belly.

The house was located between the hospital and Sue's house and I hoped the proximity to Sue would help strengthen our relationship. I wanted so desperately to have some sense of family.

From time to time, I asked Sue to come and help me unpack or to help with painting the kitchen, trying to make it a fun experience.

"I'll come, but I'm only staying from twelve to three," she would say, her tone clipped and final. There was always a condition, a limit, something that made her help feel more like a begrudging obligation than a genuine gesture.

I would give suggestions of activities or adventures we could do together, hoping to spark some excitement or connection. But her response at times would be, "You need to find some friends to do things with besides me." Her words were confusing, cutting through me with a mix of anger and hurt. I couldn't understand why she felt the need to push me away when all I wanted was to spend time together. It left me questioning if I was asking too much or if she simply didn't care.

For Easter 2009, we decided to have dinner together. Sue's daughters were coming up from Florida with their families and a couple friends, making for a lively and crowded gathering.

With so many of us, it was clear we couldn't all fit at the dining room table, so we decided to serve the meal buffet style. Sue insisted on using flimsy paper plates, the kind that bend under the weight of the food. I couldn't help but cringe at the thought of juggling those plates while trying to enjoy the meal, but I bit my tongue.

After I almost dropped my plate in my lap, I said, "I'm sorry, but I can't eat off this paper plate, I need a real plate." I reached in the cabinet to get a ceramic plate.

Sue shot me a sharp look. "You're the only one who can't eat off a paper plate, everyone else is fine with it. I don't know why you can't."

Later, as we cleaned up the kitchen, I mentioned in passing that I needed to have a television hung on a wall at my house.

Before I could say more, Nora chimed in enthusiastically, "My boyfriend can do that, no problem. If you want, we can go to your house after we finish cleaning up and hang it for you."

Relieved and grateful, I said, "I would really appreciate it, thank you."

But this simple exchange didn't sit well with Sue. Her mood shifted noticeably, her expression tightening as she avoided eye contact. By the next day she refused to answer my calls. I wanted to have a conversation about why she was so upset with me. I couldn't understand how such a small gesture of kindness from Nora or my wanting to eat off a ceramic plate could spark such a reaction.

It took three months for Sue to finally address her feelings, and even then, it was through an email, not a phone call. Her message was filled with anger, frustration, and blame. She accused me of taking her daughter and boyfriend away from her at Easter, comparing me to our mother, who she felt had controlled her. She even brought up the ceramic plate incident, calling it rude and unnecessary. In the end she said our relationship was important to her, but we were very different and wished me well.

Confused, shocked, and angry after reading her email, I found myself spinning in a haze of emotions. I needed time to make sense of it, to untangle the hurt and disbelief that I felt in my chest. Her words on my screen were like a final blow, shattering the fragile hope I'd carried for so long. I cried for days, mourning the loss of my sister. I'd hoped we would grow old together, breaking free from the ugly cycle of our dysfunctional family, loving and supporting each other in ways we'd never been taught.

In the following days, I began to think with a clearer mind, trying to understand what the hell happened. I replayed the email over and over in my mind, dissecting every word. Slowly, I concluded that reconciliation is impossible if two people don't communicate in a loving and respectful manner. No matter how deeply I wanted to mend the rift, it would take two of us and only one was willing.

Not long after I received Sue's email, I picked up a voicemail from Nora, requesting I return her mother's garage door opener by mail. Sue couldn't pick up the phone and ask me herself; instead, she chose to involve her daughter. It was very clear she was now playing the role as the victim.

I didn't send the garage door opener back. Instead, I got in my car and went for a drive. I rolled down the window and threw the opener out, watching it tumble into the ditch like she had carelessly thrown away our relationship. "Goodbye, sister," I said aloud to no one. "I refuse to play these games anymore." The words hung in the air, bittersweet but freeing as I drove away.

CHAPTER 32

Divorcing My Family

Moving to Atlanta and getting out of bedside nursing had helped me start down a new path. Determined to move forward, I found a therapist close to my house and began seeing her a couple times a month. Those sessions became a space where I could process my frustrations and focus on my goals in aesthetics. I was committed to carving out a career even if the road ahead felt challenging.

With few aesthetic classes being offered in Atlanta at that time, I took matters into my own hands. On my days off from the hospital, I dedicated myself to taking as many online courses and in-person classes as I could find, determined to build my knowledge and skills in the field.

While attending an aesthetic conference, I learned about a physician who was looking for a part-time aesthetic injector. It felt like a breakthrough, a chance to finally step into the career I'd been working toward, blending my medical expertise with my passion for beauty.

After nine years working in the aesthetic arena, pouring my energy into mastering the skills and knowledge needed to train and inspire others, I became an aesthetic educator. My goal was to instill in others the same confidence and inner beauty I had worked so hard to discover within myself. I traveled across the U.S., training physicians and mid-level providers. It fed my soul.

* * *

While checking my email one spring morning in 2009, a message stood out to me. It was from Ben. The subject line was simple, but the content made my heart skip:

Hello, I just thought I would send you an email telling you that I have graduated with my bachelor's degree. I also will be walking on June 14th at Perani Arena. If you would like to attend, call me. Up to you, Ben.

Though we spoke at least once a month, he hadn't mentioned anything about his upcoming graduation, so his message surprised me, especially since our conversations were always focused on what was happening in his life. Rarely did he ask about mine. There was an unspoken tension between us, a lingering undercurrent of anger I felt he held toward me for his childhood. I continued to try and get him to talk about his feelings, always attempting to get him to open up, but he never would. Each attempt ended the same way, with his distant reply: "Nothing's wrong."

Despite the walls he kept up, I vowed to keep the doors of communication open, in hopes one day he would finally share his true feelings with me. I longed for the chance to tell him I was sorry he had endured such a horrific childhood. I wanted him to know that his pain mattered, that I acknowledged the weight it carried, and I wished I could have shielded him from it all. Until that moment came, I resolved to be patient, to be present, and let him know that I loved him and that I was there for him.

I immediately called him and left a voicemail telling him I would love to attend his graduation. We talked a few times before his graduation ceremony, but each conversation felt increasingly strained, a reminder of the emotional distance between us. Still, I made my plans, determined to keep my promise to be there.

On one of those calls, I said, "My flight lands around lunch time, will you be able to pick me up?"

"I have to work," he said, coldly. "I can't pick you up."

"All right, that's fine. I'll rent a car." When I asked for hotel recommendations or ceremony details, he replied curtly, "I'll let you know."

When I arrived, I found a charming café close to the hotel to have some lunch and texted Ben.

He called a minute later and I said, "I'm at a cute little café across the street from the Hilton hotel I told you about, having some lunch."

"I might stop by, but I don't know."

"I would love to see you," I said, keeping my tone light and hopeful.

"I'll try, but I don't know," he replied sharply and hung up.

Not long after, the café door opened, and Ben walked in. His expression was guarded, with a hint of irritation etched across his face. I stood up immediately, smiling as I reached out to hug him. "I'm so happy to see you."

When we were seated, I handed him the menu. "Are you hungry?"

"No, I'm fine."

"Are you excited about your graduation ceremony? I'm so proud of you!"

"Yeah, it's fine," he muttered, avoiding eye contact.

Trying to make conversation, I said, "Will your grandmother or your uncle be coming to the graduation?"

"No!" he snapped. "I told you my grandmother died."

A lump formed in my throat. "You never told me that," I said gently. "I'm sorry to hear."

"Yes, I did tell you." His voice rose with irritation. "Now, what did you do to Aunt Sue?"

I drew in a breath, trying to remain calm. "I'm not here to talk about that, I'm here to celebrate your graduation."

His face twisted in anger. "You're such a bitch! Why do you always have to be a bitch?"

His words hit me like a punch in the gut, leaving me stunned and struggling to maintain composure in the middle of the café. I quickly pulled some cash out of my wallet to pay the bill, placed it on the table, and gathered my things to leave. But when I stood up, Ben stood up, too, blocking my path. He screamed, "I hate you! What did you do to Aunt Sue? You better tell me, bitch!"

"Ben, you need to get out of the way so I can leave," I replied in a soft but firm voice. "Now, please step aside."

Ignoring my plea, he followed me as I moved to the café door. Once again, he blocked me, his rage escalating. White foam began to gather at the corners of his mouth as he shouted, "You better not show up at my graduation, or something bad is going to happen! Do you hear me?"

"Yes, I hear you," I said trying to keep my composure even as my fear increased. "Now, please, let me leave." My voice wavered as memories of Richard's abuse flashed in my mind. The same sense of helplessness gripped me. I became terrified of what Ben might do.

The café was bustling with activity but not one person was

offering to help me.

"Ben, stop. Stop yelling at me," I pleaded. My hands fumbled to swing the door open, and I finally stepped outside into the daylight. The fresh air hit me, but it did little to calm my pounding heart. Without looking back, I raced toward the rental car. Behind me, his voice continued to echo through the parking lot. "Bitch, you better not show up at my graduation! I'm telling you, you better not show up or something bad will happen."

I quickly jumped in the car, locking the doors. I drove around to the back of the restaurant to hide. Once parked, I let out a breath, my body still shaking. I leaned forward, resting my head on the steering wheel. The tears came in a flood.

"How could my own son do this to me? How has it come to this?" I whispered through sobs.

The hurt cut deeper than I could have imagined, a pain that only a child's rejection could bring. I had come to support him, to celebrate one of the most significant achievements of his life, and yet here I was hiding from him behind a restaurant.

I left the next morning to fly back to Georgia. Even though I didn't get to see him receive his diploma, I kept my promise.

Five months later, I received an email from Ben:

I will be graduating with my master's degree next June and I do not even know if you are going to be there. That is upsetting to me.

Running my hands through my hair, I stared at the screen, shocked as I read this unemotional, nonapologetic email. The cold detached words felt like a slap in the face, void of any acknowledgment of the pain he had caused or the fear he had instilled. My heart sank as I read it over again, hoping I had somehow misunderstood. I couldn't help but wonder, did he even have a conscience? How could he casually dismiss everything that happened?

The son I once knew, the one who saved his hard-earned money as a young child to treat his brother and me with tickets to see *On Golden Pond* seemed like a stranger now, leaving me to wrestle with an ache so painful I couldn't put it into words.

I responded to his email, congratulating him for being the first person in the family to complete a Master's program. This was the last time I heard from him.

* * *

It was the fall of 2011. I had just finished cleaning my dinner dishes and was packing my lunch for the hospital the next day when the phone rang. It was late, and I wasn't expecting any calls, especially from an unfamiliar number. I hesitated for a moment, but curiosity got the better of me, and I decided to answer.

"Hello," I said tentatively.

"This is your son, Jason."

I froze, startled. "Who, Jason?" I repeated, my voice rising with disbelief. "Did you say Jason?" It didn't sound like him at all. His words carried a heavy southern drawl, something I'd never associated with him before. My mind raced as I tried to reconcile the voice on the other end of the line with the son I hadn't heard from in so long.

"Yes, this is me, Mom," he said, his voice steady but unfamiliar. "I know it's been almost a decade since we've talked."

Still unsure, my heart pounding, I needed to confirm. "What is your date of birth?"

"It's December twenty-ninth," he replied without hesitation.

The answer was right, but I still struggled to process the moment.

My mind was a whirlwind of emotions: relief, confusion, and a guarded hope this was the beginning of something I'd long prayed for. Ten years had passed without a word, and now suddenly here he was.

"It's really good to hear from you, Jason," I said, my voice quivering with a mix of excitement and nerves.

"Yes, it's good to hear your voice," he said warmly. "I'm a registered nurse, just like you. And I've been living in Georgia for the last several years."

"That's wonderful!" I exclaimed, feeling a swell of pride. "What areas of nursing are you working in?"

"I usually like working in the emergency room," he said confidently. "I like the fast pace and the challenges that come with it."

We talked for a few minutes, catching up with the basics of life and work. Before we said goodbye, we made plans to meet at a restaurant in Atlanta the following Saturday. My heart felt lighter with the prospect of seeing him again, but it was tinged with unease. I hoped this reconnection could mend our relationship and finally provide answers to the questions that had haunted me for so long. Why had he disappeared? I tried so many times to find him, searching every website online, but always came up empty. What had I done to push him away? The pain of not knowing had weighed heavily on my heart. Now, with the chance to see him again, I clung to the hope this meeting might bring the understanding and closure I had been yearning for.

As the day of our meeting approached, my nerves grew stronger with each passing hour. Would he still love me? I wondered what he looked like. How much had he changed, and how much of the boy I remembered would still be there? I could still hear his southern accent in my mind.

Just go with the flow, Candy.

I felt the rush of possibility—and the weight of everything that could go wrong.

Let him take the lead in the conversation. Don't say anything that might push him away.

As I opened the restaurant door, I immediately saw him sitting at the bar. He hadn't changed as much as I'd imagined. His smile was still the same, that lopsided grin where one side of his mouth curled up just a little more than the other. He dressed sharply, and though he'd gained some weight, it suited him, giving him an air of maturity.

I took the empty seat next to him at the bar, my heart pounding with a mixture of joy and nervousness.

"It's really good to see you, Momma," he said, his southern accent prominent.

"It's wonderful to see you, too, son," I replied softly, reaching out to pull him into a hug. To my relief, he reciprocated, holding me tightly. For a moment, it felt like no time had passed at all, and I let myself savor the feeling of having my son close again.

"What would you like to drink?" he asked, casually, his tone light but with an edge I couldn't quite place. "I'm not drinking, I've quit." He paused just long enough for me to feel the weight of his words. They struck a nerve, dragging me into a flashback of his father's hollow declarations. *See, I quit drinking,* he'd say, only to start beating me again days later. The memories clawed at the edges of my mind, but I forced them away. *Don't think about that right now. You're here with your son, not his father.*

"Would you mind if I had a glass of wine?" I asked, trying to sound nonchalant but unable to mask the hesitation in my voice. I didn't want to upset him, but I could really use a glass of wine to calm my nerves.

He said, "Have whatever you what. I don't mind."

I tried to keep our conversation light, steering it away from anything too personal or heavy. We talked for several hours, reminiscing about our experience as nurses in the emergency room. Sharing these stories came easily: moments of triumph, humor, and heartbreak that only another nurse could truly understand. We laughed at the absurdity of some situations, like patients arriving with the most bizarre injuries, and fell into a quieter reflection when recalling the tougher moments, the ones that lingered long after our shifts ended.

"Would you like to come to my house for dinner next Friday?" I asked, my voice tinged with hope, silently pleading for him to say yes.

"Sure, Momma. I would really like that," he replied, and relief washed over me.

* * *

We had a few dinners together after that initial evening, each one a step toward rebuilding our relationship. Over time, he began to share more details about how his life had been over the past ten years. One evening, he finally let it all spill out, his words tumbling over one another in a rush of confession.

"I've been living in a hotel room for the last few months," he shared. "I've been in and out of rehab for drugs and alcohol. I've been diagnosed with a mental health issue, too. I'm trying to get a job at this hospital in town. I've applied and I'm waiting to hear back. I haven't been drinking for the last few months."

"Okay," I said, taking a deep breath to steady myself. "That's a lot of information all at once."

I could see in his eyes he truly wanted to turn his life around. Feeling the sincerity in his voice, I resolved to help him—not financially, but emotionally. I wanted to be a steady presence in his life, someone he could trust and rely on. The guilt I carried for raising both of my sons in such a horrific, violent household weighed heavy on me, and this felt like a chance to make amends. I couldn't erase the past or undo the pain, but I could be there for him now, hoping this would begin the healing for both of us.

I began carefully. "You said you're on medication. Do you have enough of your medication now? And does your physician specialize in treating people with your diagnosis?"

He shifted uncomfortably. "I've got enough medication for about another month," he admitted. "But my doctor doesn't really know how to treat me, so I've been pretty much telling him what drugs I need. The medications have caused me to gain a lot of weight."

I frowned, concern rising. "First, I think you need to find a specialist physician because you can't work if you don't have the proper medications. That's nonnegotiable."

He nodded reluctantly, and I pressed on. "Second, I suggest you contact human resources at the hospital to see what is taking so long to process your applications. This delay doesn't make sense to me given the current nursing shortage."

He hesitated, avoiding my gaze. "There may be a problem with the background check. I have a DUI conviction."

I sighed. "Okay, that's something we'll need to address. It's not ideal, but it's not the end of the world, either. You've been working on turning your life around, and that's what matters most. You have to take this one step at a time."

In the coming weeks, he was hired by the hospital, with full benefits enabling him to schedule an appointment with a physician specializing in his disease. However, there were still challenging moments. He would call me during times when his mental health wasn't being managed well, his thoughts racing and his words tumbling out in rapid succession. During these calls, I did my best to remain calm and supportive, gently encouraging him to take his medication.

A few months later, I grew concerned. I hadn't heard from Jason in a few weeks, which was unusual because he typically called at least a couple times a week. But I knew he'd started working the evening shift, seven to seven, so I didn't worry too much.

On my day off, I got a call from him. "Momma, it's me, Jason. Um, I got in an accident and totaled my car. I'm not hurt, but I checked myself into a rehab center. I've been here for the last six days."

"Come again? You're in rehab after totaling your car? What the hell happened?" My mind raced to connect the dots.

"They're discharging me today. Would you mind coming and picking me up?"

"Of course, I'll pick you up. Text me the address."

When I picked him up at the drug rehabilitation center, he was unusually quiet. I could see the weight of his shame in the way he avoided eye contact with me and in the slump of his shoulders as he climbed in the car.

"Momma," he said after a long silence. "I need to make an appointment with my doctor to see if I need my medications adjusted or changed."

Not wanting to stir up any conflict, I nodded. "That's probably a good idea."

He sighed and shifted in his seat. "I'm not sure how I'm going to get to work now, since my car was totaled."

"Why don't you buy a moped?" I suggested. "You can use the back roads to get to work."

He looked at me, the hint of a smile breaking through his somber expression. "A moped, huh? Maybe that's not a bad idea."

A couple months went by, and things seemed to be going well. Until he called again.

"Momma, you know when I totaled my car a couple months ago?" he began hesitantly.

"Yes," I said, bracing myself. "What's going on?"

"I have a court hearing next Thursday for sentencing. My attorney said I needed to be there, and I don't have a car."

I felt my stomach drop. "Sentencing? What for?"

"It's for when I wrecked my car a couple months ago. I was arrested for DUI. This is my second DUI in Georgia, and I might get sentenced to jail."

I closed my eyes, trying to suppress the frustration bubbling up inside me. Another DUI. Another mess. And now, jail time might be on the table.

"I'll come and pick you up at 4 a.m. on Friday. It looks like it's about a three-and-a-half-hour drive to the courthouse," I said, trying to keep my voice steady.

I knew he'd been making an effort, and I couldn't ignore that. Despite the frustration and worry, I felt like I needed to support him in any way I could. Maybe this court hearing would be the wake-up call he needed.

We arrived at the courthouse with plenty of time to spare, found our way inside, and took a seat. As we waited, I felt the familiar pangs of anxiety creeping in, stirring my PTSD from my own past court hearings. I tried to steady my breathing, but the atmosphere, the murmurs, the formality, felt all too familiar, bringing up memories I'd long tried to suppress. Yet, I couldn't let Jason know. I'd never told him about my own experiences with the court system.

When the bailiff finally called Jason's name, he and his attorney stood up and approached the bench. Then came an unexpected blow. The judge announced that there was another DUI in the state of Florida, which meant jail time was unavoidable.

Jason's attorney, visibly taken aback by these new revelations, quickly requested a moment to speak with his client. The judge granted the request, while Jason turned, motioning for me to follow them into a small room across the hall from the courtroom.

While waiting for Jason's attorney to return, I looked at Jason and said, "I'm so sorry you experienced what you did during your childhood, and I know it's played a role in leading you to this mess. But I want you to know, I'm here to support you in any way I can, and I love you very much."

Just then his attorney came into the room. "Jason, did you know about the DUI in Florida?" he asked firmly, his tone edged with disbelief and a hint of disgust.

Jason hung his head, his voice low. "Yes, I knew about it, but I didn't think it would come up."

At that moment, I interrupted, my voice calm but urgent. "Excuse me, sir, may I speak?"

He glanced at me, then nodded. "Yes, go ahead."

I took a deep breath, choosing my words carefully. "I know what my son has done is absolutely horrible. He should never have been driving while drinking and I understand the seriousness of his actions; he could have injured or even killed someone. But in the last few months, he's taken real steps to turn his life around. He's gone to rehab. He's working full time. And he's under a physician's care to manage his health. I'm in no way excusing his behavior, but I'm asking the court to consider the progress he's made and give him a chance to build on it."

To my relief, it worked. The attorney used my argument to appeal to the judge and in the end the judge sentenced Jason to probation, several hours of community service, and fines.

During one of our phone conversations following the court hearing, Jason said he had something to tell me. My first thought was *What has happened now?* I braced myself and said, "Okay, what is it?"

I could hear him take a deep breath. "The other night, I was talking with my dad and he told me out of the women he abused, he abused and beat you the worst." Jason paused, his voice shaking slightly. "And he had a smirk on his face when he said it."

A surge of anger and pain rose within me, but I forced myself to stay calm. My left fist clenched at my side, and my voice, though steady, was laced with fury. "He said that? With a smirk?"

"Yes, he did, Momma."

I wanted to scream. I couldn't believe the callousness, the complete lack of decency or remorse. Richard didn't even have the mental capacity to acknowledge the damage his abuse had inflicted, how it almost destroyed me and left a profound lasting impact on two innocent children.

"What a horrible thing to tell his son."

* * *

Jason had been asking me about life in New York City, curious about the stories I'd shared from my time there. One day, during one of our conversations, he mentioned, "I'd love to go to New York City with you sometime."

We decided to visit in the fall. One of my friends, Frank, whom I met while working at a hospital in Manhattan, invited us to join his family for Thanksgiving dinner on Long Island, and Jason and I happily agreed.

During the train ride to Long Island, I noticed subtle but troubling signs in Jason. His curt answers to Frank's friendly questions, his irritability, and the anxious energy radiating from him were hard to ignore. It wasn't anything I could clearly pinpoint, but it stirred an unsettling feeling in my stomach. Then, just as suddenly as the irritability had appeared, he leaned back and fell asleep mid-conversation, leaving an awkward silence.

"What's wrong with him?" Frank asked, his voice laced with genuine concern.

I hesitated, unsure how to respond. Instead, I shrugged my shoulders and said quietly, "I don't know." It wasn't the full truth, but it was all I could manage in that moment.

Frank's family, who were warm and engaging, made me feel right at home. But as the conversation flowed, I noticed Jason had disappeared. At first, I thought he might be exploring the house or had stepped outside for some air, but as time passed, a knot of unease began to form in my stomach. Something didn't feel right.

"I need to speak with you privately about Jason," Frank said, quietly, his tone serious. "It looks like he has locked himself in the bathroom, refusing to come out. My uncle, who is elderly, can't climb the stairs to use the upstairs bathroom."

I felt a wave of shame and panic wash over me. "Oh, for the

love of everything holy," I muttered, my voice breaking. "This is horrible. I'm so sorry I brought him, Frank. I'm so embarrassed."

Before Frank could respond, we both saw Jason stumble out of the bathroom, looking disheveled and dazed. He made his way to the living room and collapsed onto their pristine sofa without a word.

Turning back to Frank, my face flushed with mortification, I whispered, "I'll take care of this."

Frank shook his head gently and placed a reassuring hand on my shoulder. "No, don't, let him sleep until you're ready to leave. It's better this way."

When we arrived back to the hotel, Jason barely made it through the door before collapsing onto the bed. Humiliated and furious, I couldn't hold back my need for answers any longer. I began rummaging through his suitcase, desperate to find something to explain his despicable behavior.

And then I saw it: a nearly empty bottle of Percocet tucked under his clothes. I examined it, noting the prescription date. It had just been filled. He must have gotten an ER doctor to write him a prescription, manipulating the system to feed his addiction. Just like his father, manipulative, cunning, always using people for what he could get out of them.

I took the remaining pills and flushed them down the toilet.

The next morning, I hailed a yellow cab back to the airport. Jason slumped in the seat beside me, still acting as though he were drugged. It was clear he must have had more pills hidden somewhere.

While going through TSA, I kept my distance from him, my anger and fear building. I didn't want anything to do with him. I was furious with his reckless behavior, but more important than that, I was terrified of being associated with him.

If the TSA pulled him aside and started searching him or his belongings, and found illegal drugs, or deemed him unfit to fly, I was afraid that I could be implicated, just as his father had dragged me into trouble years ago. The possibility of going to jail again or jeopardizing my nursing license was unbearable. My career and my freedom were hard-won, and the thought of losing them sent waves of panic through me. Silently I prayed to make it to the plane without incident, willing the moment to pass without catastrophe.

Fortunately, we got on the plane without any problems. As the cab from the airport pulled into my driveway, I looked at Jason and said, "I love you. But I hate your drugs. If you decide to get help, give me a call. Until then, goodbye."

I unlocked my front door and stepped inside, pushing it shut with a firm click. The words broke free before I could even think, rising from somewhere deep and final as my hand pressed hard against the door:

Not one more day.

Not one more hour.

Not one more second.

It was my promise to myself. No longer would I accept anything less than healthy, respectful relationships.

I will no longer be manipulated, used, or abused.

I was finished trying to mend my family, finished striving for the love and approval I would never fully receive. At that moment, I made a decision. My energy, my love, and my healing would no longer be sacrificed for the sake of a family that had caused me so much pain. It was time to choose myself.

That night I divorced my family.

CHAPTER 33

Goodbyes

Molly was getting older; she was fourteen now. Her days of chasing anything that moved were behind her, replaced by quieter moments of rest. Still, she remained my world. Every evening as I pulled into the garage, I would pause, holding my breath, waiting for her familiar, reassuring *woof woof*. It was her way of telling me she was glad I was home.

One night, Molly met me at the door as usual, her tail wagging faintly, and I could tell something was off. She didn't want to eat her dinner, a clear sign something was wrong. I was exhausted from a long day at work, but I gently made her a comfortable place next to the bed with an old T-shirt of mine to sleep with. I was glad I had the next four days off from the hospital so I could spend some time with her and figure out what she needed.

The next morning when I got up, I found her lying on the cool floor in the kitchen. I bent down to pet her, hoping for even a small wag of her tail, but she just looked at me quietly, her energy fading. My heart sank as I realized this was the end. I wanted to hold her one last time, to give her the comfort she had always given me. Gently, I walked her over to the chair we had shared so many times before and pulled her onto my lap. She rested there quietly, her soulful eyes locked on mine as if to say, "My work is done here, Mom. I can't go on, but you will be all right now." Tears streamed down my face as I held her close, knowing she was giving me her final gift, her love and reassurance, even as she prepared to say goodbye.

I had always promised myself when it was Molly's time, she could leave this world with dignity, free from pain or suffering.

I couldn't lift her on my own, so I carefully picked up her front paws, placing her body between my legs, and gently walked her to the car. Once there, I eased her in the front passenger's seat, where I could watch her closely, making sure she wasn't in any pain or struggling to breathe.

The sky opened up as we drove, a torrential rainstorm flooding the streets, adding to the weight of the moment. My hands gripped the steering wheel tightly as I navigated through the downpour to get her to her veterinarian.

When we finally arrived, the clinic was still closed, the front doors locked. Without thinking, I drove around to the back, leaped out of the car, and began banging on the door, my voice breaking as I called out, "Somebody please help my dog, she's dying. Please, please!"

Suddenly the door opened, and a young man in scrubs stood before me, his face a mix of confusion and concern. "Can I help you?" he asked, his tone cautious but kind.

"My dog is in the car and she's really sick. She's too heavy for me to carry. Can you please go get her? She won't bite, she's a basset hound and her name is Molly."

Hearing the desperation in my voice, the young man didn't hesitate. He yelled, "Hey, Dad, I need you, there's a lady here with a sick basset hound" and ran out to my car.

The young man carefully placed Molly on the exam table, her

body limp but her eyes still searching mine. I immediately reached out, my hand gently stroking her soft head, my fingers tracing her floppy ears. Tears blurred my vision as I leaned closer, whispering, "It's okay, my sweet Molly, I'm here."

Moments later, the veterinarian entered the room, his years of experience evident in the calm yet focused way he approached her. After a quick but thorough exam, he looked at me and thoughtfully said, "Candy, I can do some tests and probably give her a little more time."

Before he could finish, I interrupted him, my voice firm despite the tears streaming down my face. "I will not keep her alive to suffer just because of my selfishness for wanting more time. That's not right. I will not do that to her." The words felt heavy, but I meant them with every fiber of my being. Molly had given me a lifetime of unconditional love, and now it was my turn to let her go with the dignity she deserved.

"Candy, I commend you for doing this. She shouldn't suffer," he said softly.

His son entered the room, holding a syringe. He quietly handed it to his father. The vet looked at me with compassion and explained, "I will gently inject her with this medication and her heart will stop beating very quickly. Are you okay?"

"I'm okay. I'm going to be here with her. She's never left me and I'm not about to leave her now." I wiped my nose on my sleeve and then leaned down, caressing her face as I gazed into her eyes. "It's going to be okay, my sweet baby. I love you more than you could possibly imagine. Thank you for always being by my side." As I whispered those words, I felt her body go limp. In that quiet, heart-wrenching moment, Molly was gone.

My voice barely was audible as I asked, "Where will she go now?"

The vet placed a comforting hand on my shoulder and said, "We'll cremate her. You can come back and pick up her ashes when you're ready." He paused for a moment. His expression softened again. "And there is no charge for today. You've been through enough and I'm proud of you for making the selfless decision not to let her suffer."

I managed to nod. "Thank you for your kindness." Slowly I walked out of the office to my car, the world around me blurred by my tears. The drive home felt impossibly long, and when I finally arrived, I sat in the driveway for a moment, dreading the silence that would greet me inside, knowing I would never hear that *woof woof* again.

Summoning all my strength, I opened the door and stepped inside, my heart heavy. I made my way to our special chair, the one we'd sat in together a few hours ago, and curled up as if her warmth might still be there. My mind drifted back to the day fourteen years before when Molly walked over a mile and ended up on my doorstep. She had chosen me to be hers.

I would rather have endured another one of Richard's beatings than feel this kind of loss.

* * *

I had left my position at the hospital and was now working with another nursing agency in an outpatient surgical setting, a role that provided me with the flexibility to pursue my growing interest in aesthetics. On the days I wasn't scheduled at the surgical center, I filled in at various aesthetic offices, stepping in whenever I was needed.

I had also moved to be closer to work and nearer my friend Julie.

Julie had introduced me to several physicians' offices and med spas in the area that occasionally needed a part-time injector to help with demand or fill in when someone was out on maternity leave or with an illness.

Each day brought opportunities to meet wonderful providers. Their expertise and enthusiasm inspired me, and the connections I made fueled my excitement for this journey. It was invigorating to be a part of a field where creativity and care came together to make people feel confident and beautiful.

One morning, as I was gathering my things to head out the door, a voice stopped me in my tracks halfway down the stairs leading to the garage. It was so unexpected and yet so familiar, it froze me mid-step.

I don't know why you're doing this. You're too stupid to do aesthetics, the voice sneered, laced with the same cold disdain I'd heard my entire life.

I knew instantly it was my father's voice. Though he'd been dead for years, the weight of his judgment filled the room like a thick fog.

But I wasn't the same woman I once was.

Without hesitation, I answered back, my voice firm and unwavering: "Shut the fuck up! You're not going to do this to me anymore, so just shut the fuck up!"

The words echoed in the silence, defiant and liberating, as if they carried the full weight of all those years of silence, now finally shattered. In that moment, I felt as though I had reclaimed a part of myself, standing up not just to his memory, but to the doubts and fears that had haunted me long after he was gone.

* * *

Since moving into my new townhome, I'd been itching to dive in and make it truly my own. It was time to renovate the kitchen, living room, and the primary bedroom. I'd always dreamed of a walk-in shower, the kind you'd find in a luxurious spa, with sleek tiles, rainfall showerhead, and multiple jets. This was more than just a home-improvement project, it was about creating a space that reflected the life I had worked so hard for, a place of comfort, safety, and peace.

"Candy, the plumber just informed me it's going to be really expensive to run plumbing all the way up to the third floor for your shower," the designer said cautiously, clearly bracing for my reaction.

Without hesitation, I replied confidently, "I don't care what it costs, I deserve that shower with all the shower heads. I want it to be like a human car wash."

That shower became so much more than a luxurious addition to my home, it became a symbol of self-care and indulgence. It reminded me, every time I stepped into its soothing cascade, that after years of pain and hard work, I was finally investing in myself and the life I deserved, claiming joy, one drop of water at a time.

* * *

Julie traveled frequently, training other aesthetic providers, but when she was home, we always made time to get together. Whether it was a shopping excursion or cozy dinner, we cherished our moments together. Since I loved to cook, Julie would often put in requests for her favorite dishes, and I'd prepare them with care. Our dinners became a ritual filled with laughter, heartfelt conversations, and stories about our adventures in the aesthetic world. Those evenings were a comforting reminder of our bond, a blend of friendship and shared professional passion that made every meal and every moment special.

One evening, Julie and I were out taking a walk when she shared some unexpected but wonderful news.

"I met this guy the other day, and I think I like him. We went to dinner and had a great time." Her face lit up.

"I don't think I've ever heard you say that before," I replied, a teasing smile on my face. "What's his name?"

"Mike. He's from the Midwest. We're going on another date tomorrow." Her eyes sparkled with excitement as she added, "He's picking me up about seven. You'll need to look out your window and check him out when he comes to pick me up."

I laughed. "You know I will. Can't let you head out with just anyone without my stamp of approval." It was refreshing to see her so excited.

The following evening, right at seven, I found myself with my nose pressed against the window, eagerly waiting. When I saw a tall, handsome man with dark brown hair ring Julie's doorbell, I couldn't help but smile. He carried himself with confidence, and I could already tell there was something special about him.

A couple dates later, I finally met Mike in person, and my first impression was confirmed: he was charming, kind, and clearly smitten with Julie. I absolutely approved, and seeing her happy made it even better.

Since Julie had found her love, she was determined to help me find mine. Her enthusiasm was relentless, and as we spent hours together enjoying long girl talks about life, love, and everything in between, I began to see something I'd never truly believed before. Julie and I had developed a bond unlike anything I'd experienced, a relationship that wasn't just surface-deep but rich with understanding and mutual care. This was new territory for me. Every other relationship I'd had in my life seemed to end in disappointment or fracture, leaving me with the sinking belief that lasting connections simply weren't possible for someone like me. But Julie proved me wrong.

Our friendship wasn't perfect. We had our disagreements, moments where life tried to pull us in different directions. But somehow, we always found our way back, weathering the storms with a resilience I never thought relationships could have. It was a major turning point for me, a realization that relationships, real relationships could survive hardship and thrive despite imperfections. Julie's unwavering belief in love, for herself and for me, made me start to believe, too. It wasn't just about finding romance; it was about finding the courage to trust in the strength of connection.

"You're too cute and too wonderful to be single," Julie announced one afternoon, her eyes sparkling with determination. "I'm going to create a profile for you on Match.com."

"This should be interesting," I replied, raising my eyebrows and crossing my arms. I had not shared the details of my abusive childhood or my horrific marriage with her, so she didn't understand why I approached dating with such caution.

Over the next several months, I met over a half dozen men, all very different from one another, but only gave two of them a second or third date.

"So, how's the Match going?" Julie asked one evening during

dinner. "Any exciting prospects yet?"

Rolling my eyes, I said, "Julie, I've met over a half dozen men, and let me tell you, it's been educational. This is a full-time job! Listen to some of the shit I was told or asked."

Julie leaned in, clearly intrigued. "Oh, this should be good."

I held up a finger, counting off. "First, there was the guy who asked, 'What is oregano?' Seriously, how do you not know what oregano is?"

Julie burst out laughing. "Maybe he was sheltered."

"Oh, it gets better. There was one who said, 'Candy, I don't know whether to push you away or kiss you.'"

"What did he mean by that?" Julie asked, clutching her stomach, laughing. "That's terrible but hilarious. Keep going."

"Then there was the one who said, 'Yep, came home from work, and she had packed her things in a U-Haul and left me.' And he couldn't figure out why."

Julie was now bending over, laughing. "That's hysterical."

"Oh, I'm not done," I said, shaking my head. "There was the guy who said, 'I gave my ex everything, trips, money, a big house and she still left me.'"

Julie groaned. "Why do they always act like they're saints?"

"And then my personal favorite," I said, throwing my hands up for emphasis, "is the one who said, 'Oh, you're a nurse. I've hit the jackpot.'"

Julie wiped tears of laughter from her eyes. "Please tell me this is the end."

"Not quite," I said. "One guy actually told me, 'You don't know it yet, but you're going to be my wife.'"

We laughed so hard about my dating experiences, tears streamed down our faces. I decided it was time to shut down my profile. If meeting someone was truly meant to happen, it would be the good old-fashioned way, through chance encounters and genuine connections, not curated by algorithms and cheesy pickup lines. I was content to focus on my own newfound happiness and let the universe take care of the rest.

* * *

Julie and Mike married a couple years later at a stunning ceremony in South Carolina. Not long after the wedding they bought a home there. While genuinely happy for both of them, I couldn't help but wonder how things might change between us. Mike had become the first man I truly trusted, and Julie and I had grown so close, I didn't want to lose them.

One afternoon, during one of our usual girlie conversations, I told her, "Honey, if this move is what will make you happy then I support you one hundred percent. You have to do what makes you and Mike happy."

She smiled and replied, "We already have a bedroom designated Candy's Room in the new house."

CHAPTER 34

This Is *My* Life Now

Two of my biggest challenges while traveling were finding food and getting to and from the airport in Atlanta. I relied so heavily on granola bars for dinner that, after months of this routine, the mere sight of one nauseated me.

Adding to the strain, the rising crime rate in Atlanta made driving to and from the airport a nerve-wracking experience. One particular early morning, I scheduled an Uber to avoid the stress. When the car pulled up, I was pleasantly surprised to see a Mercedes. The driver stepped out, placed my luggage in the trunk, and even opened the door for me.

"Good morning, sir. Thank you for putting my luggage in the trunk," I said with appreciation.

"You're welcome, ma'am," he replied humbly.

As I settled in the backseat, I couldn't help but notice how spotless his car was and how the top of his head almost touched the ceiling.

Should I ask him if he would be interested in driving me to and from the airport every week? Why not? Just ask him.

"Don, would you be interested in driving me to and from the airport? I fly every week, though," I said, half expecting him to hesitate.

Before I could finish asking, he handed me his card.

"I'd be happy to," he said. "I injured my knee after working for twenty-seven years on the night shift and I had to have surgery. I got bored sitting at home."

From that day forward, Don has never been late picking me up and he's always sitting at the airport when I land. After that first ride, he stopped driving for Uber entirely.

There wasn't a time that Don didn't share a joke or a story that made me laugh during our trips. Whether it was six in the morning or midnight, his humor was always ready.

One night, with a mischievous grin, he said, "You know, Candy, I told this boy who picked up my daughter the other night he better bring her back looking the same way as she left."

I burst out in laughter.

Don's booming voice and storytelling were as comforting as they were entertaining, a glimpse into the protective and loving father he was, a six-foot-three man with a heart that somehow managed to be even bigger.

During another ride to the airport, Don glanced in the rearview mirror and said, "Guess what I did this week, Candy?"

"What? Did you go out on your motorcycle with your buddies?" I teased.

"No," he said proudly, "my daughter started college on Monday, so I went to the college and introduced myself to each of her professors."

"Oh, wow, Don, what a wonderful father you are," I exclaimed. "You're the epitome of a great dad. You know your daughter will never move out of your house, even after she gets married. She will never leave her daddy."

Don just giggled, clearly delighted by the thought. Moments like these reminded me how special he was, not just as a driver, but as a person with a deep love for his family. Don's reliability, kindness, and the effortless way he made me feel at ease gradually broke down those walls. He became a reminder that trustworthy people still exist and could show up in the most unexpected ways.

After Julie's husband Mike, Don was the second man in my life I learned to trust.

* * *

After nine years and training over four thousand aesthetic providers, I began to weary of the constant travel. The providers had fed my soul for so many wonderful years and my journeys included numerous trips back to my beloved New York City, where I'd retraced the steps Molly and I used to walk.

But as fulfilling as it had been, I knew it was time to change my life's direction. Not long after I survived the Tahoe accident in North Dakota, I was walking down the hallway of a hotel, utterly exhausted, pulling my Tumi luggage, when my mind began to race.

I don't want to travel anymore, but what will I do? I want to keep training providers.

Why don't you write a book? a quiet voice within asked.

I pushed back instantly. *I can't write a book, I have no idea how to write a book, I'm dyslexic.*

People need to hear your story. It's time, the voice persisted.

Maybe I can *write my story.*

That night, in the quiet of the hotel room, I opened my iPad and began typing. The words came slowly at first, hesitant and raw, but they carried the weight of years of pain, survival, and healing. I wasn't sure where it would lead or if I'd have the courage to finish, but deep down, I knew this was the start of something important. This wasn't just about telling my story, it was about showing those who have been or who are still being abused that there is hope.

It's about letting them know they aren't alone with their pain, struggles, guilt, and shame. It's about offering them hope, healing, and freedom, knowing a better life is possible.

Today, I only travel the state of Georgia training providers. My home has become a sanctuary, a place where I can recharge and find comfort. It's a reflection of the life I've built, a space filled with warmth, resilience, and the quiet joy of knowing I am finally free to live life on my own terms.

I love to explore in my new kitchen, experimenting with a new recipe. I especially enjoy preparing a beautiful meal and inviting my friends over for dinner. There are moments when I step back, watching them talk and laugh, enjoying my home-cooked food, and I feel a wave of disbelief wash over me.

This is my life now.

I have the freedom to welcome friends into my home, without the constant fear of the table being turned upside down, or without the terror of being beaten, or the chaos of fighting, yelling, and screaming. I have the privilege of this creative haven.

When I enter my bedroom and light a lavender candle on my nightstand, breathing in its calming fragrance becomes a sacred moment. As I run my hands over the beautiful wallpaper, admiring the blue, soft gray, and cream colors, I'm no longer scanning the walls for a bullet hole that almost ended my life.

Instead, when I pull back the blanket and find cookie crumbs from the indulgent snack Julie taught me was perfectly okay, I smile. A simple reminder of the comfort and safety I've created.

Pictures of my Molly are displayed throughout my home, each one a reminder of her unwavering love and loyalty. I continue to feel her spirit around me, a comforting presence that seems to whisper, *I'm still here.* It's almost as if she knew when she passed that her job on this earth was done. She'd seen me through difficult times and knew I would be okay.

I haven't had the courage to get another fur baby. Molly's loss, even after sixteen years, remains deeply painful, but as I look at her pictures and remember the joy she brought, I remind myself: never say never.

I grieve for that young girl I once was, who always knew she was different but didn't yet understand her own strength. She couldn't see the small spark of tenacity and fierceness buried deep inside her, a spark that, despite everything, refused to be extinguished. Over time, that spark grew, fueling her determination to persevere through many hardships, searching for a better life, shaping me into the person I am today.

Through years of therapy and unwavering support from close friends, I've discovered peace, resilience, and joy in ways I never thought possible.

While writing my memoir, one of the most profound realizations was the presence of numerous angels who were sent to me when I needed them most. Some appeared only briefly: a kind stranger, a gentle word of encouragement, a simple question like, *Why don't you go to college?* or a quiet act of kindness that left a lasting imprint.

Others stayed, becoming steady lights in my life, guiding me. Each one gave me hope when I felt hopeless, and strength when I was ready to give up. Their compassion taught me something invaluable: what it means to be loved and accepted—not by others but by myself.

If my story can offer even one person hope, courage, or strength to believe they deserve more, then every sleepless night, every tear shed, and every painful memory relived has served its purpose.

No one should live in fear! Everyone deserves a life filled with peace, love, and the knowledge that they are worthy of so much more.

AFTERWORD

One of the most agonizing aspects of my experiences at the hands of my abusers is how the police didn't help and the legal system was actually used against me. As I began to heal from the trauma, what struck me is how long it takes for change to occur. To give readers some context, I asked a friend to research the history of laws about domestic abuse, and she provided the following background.

A Brief History of Laws Regarding Domestic Abuse

In the 1800s, domestic abuse was widely considered a private family matter, and the law largely upheld a husband's right to discipline his wife. The "rule of thumb" doctrine, which permitted husbands to beat their wives with a stick no thicker than their thumb, was a commonly referenced, though unofficial, legal standard. There were very few legal avenues available for women to seek protection from abusive husbands.

Divorce laws were restrictive, and the courts typically did not intervene in cases of marital abuse unless the violence was extreme. Social norms were heavily influenced by patriarchal ideals, where men were seen as the heads of households and women were expected to submit. This cultural backdrop normalized certain levels of domestic control and abuse.

In the 1900s, divorce laws became more lenient in some states, and women had more opportunities to escape abusive marriages. However, divorce was still stigmatized, and economic dependence often kept women in abusive relationships. The Temperance Movement, which aimed to curb alcohol consumption, drew attention to the connection between alcohol abuse and domestic violence. Activists argued that alcohol contributed to wife-beating, helping to raise awareness about the issue of domestic abuse, albeit indirectly.

After World War II, domestic life was idealized, and traditional gender roles were reinforced, often at the expense of addressing domestic violence. Women were encouraged to maintain family harmony, and reports of domestic abuse were largely disregarded or minimized. The criminal justice system remained ill-equipped to deal with domestic violence cases. When law enforcement did respond to domestic disputes, the approach was often to mediate rather than arrest or prosecute abusers.

The feminist movement of the 1960s and 1970s was a turning point in bringing domestic violence to the forefront of public consciousness. Activists framed domestic violence as a violation of women's rights and pushed for changes in the legal system. This shift began with laws like the Equal Credit Opportunity Act of 1974, which prohibited discrimination based on gender in credit and banking practices. Before this, many banks required a husband or male relative to cosign for a woman's account, limiting her financial independence.

This shift also prompted the establishment of domestic shelters and crisis hotlines. The first domestic abuse shelter in the US was opened in 1974 in St. Paul, Minnesota. The shelter, known as Women's Advocates, provided a safe space for women and their children fleeing domestic violence. It marked a significant change in recognizing domestic abuse as a social issue requiring community intervention and paved the way for the establishment of similar shelters across the country.

The federal origins of the Violence Against Women Act trace back to the 1970s, when the Carter administration established the Office of Domestic Violence. This agency was part of the Department of Health, Education, and Welfare and was tasked with policy planning and interagency coordination to address domestic violence issues.

Research conducted in the late 1980s and early 1990s highlighted the widespread nature of domestic abuse, with statistics showing that one in four women experienced domestic violence. Still, the response to domestic violence varied widely from state to state, leading to inconsistent protections for victims.

Many areas lacked resources like shelters, counseling, or legal aid. This led to the growing recognition that existing state laws and policies were insufficient to protect victims and hold perpetrators accountable. Advocates, including survivors and support organizations, lobbied for stronger legal protections. These efforts contributed to a groundswell of support for comprehensive federal legislation.

In 1990, then-senator Joe Biden introduced the first federal legislation addressing spousal abuse during the 101st Congress. Biden emphasized the need to change cultural attitudes by making the problem visible to the public and by shifting accountability onto perpetrators rather than survivors: "We are helpless to change the course of this violence unless, and until, we achieve a national consensus that it deserves our profound public outrage."

Three separate public hearings revealed the severity of the issue, but the 1990 bill failed to pass. Senator Biden reintroduced the bill in 1991, but it stalled again. In 1993, Senator Biden introduced the Violence Against Women Act to the 103rd Congress, with support from 43 senators and President Bill Clinton, who had pledged to sign it. The Act finally passed with bipartisan support and was signed into law by President Clinton on September 13, 1994.

The Centers for Disease Control and Prevention (CDC) statistics show one out of every three women will be abused at some point in their life. A woman is more likely to be killed by a male partner (or former partner) than any other person. Approximately four thousand women die each year at the hands of their partners or former partners. This number does not include those who are injured or mentally damaged.

Take the First Step

My hope is after reading my memoir, you'll feel empowered to take that first brave step—to reach out for help and begin creating a plan to escape. You don't have to have it all figured out right away. Just begin. Your safety, your freedom, and your future are worth fighting for. Let my story be a reminder: you are not alone, and you are stronger than you realize.

Please refer to the About the Author page for contact information for resources to help you begin your plan to escape.

The Wall of Honor

On my website, **candicemorrowauthor.com**, you'll find *The Wall of Honor*—a sacred space dedicated to those whose lives have been touched by domestic violence.

Whether you're a survivor, mourning the loss of a loved one, or standing in solidarity, you are welcome to add a name to this wall. To protect privacy and ensure safety, I ask you only submit the first initial and state of the person you wish to honor.

Each initial represents a story of strength, survival, and remembrance. It is a way to say: You are seen. You are not forgotten. You are not alone.

Visit **candicemorrowauthor.com** to add your tribute. Together, name by name, we stand against domestic violence—and with every survivor.

ABOUT THE AUTHOR

Debut author and registered nurse Candice Morrow credits her nursing career with saving her life. Over the span of four decades, she has worked as a trauma nurse, owned a pharmaceutical home infusion company, and has traveled across the US training more than four thousand medical aesthetic providers.

Today, whether it's speaking engagements or conversations with strangers, she uses her voice to inspire others to break the silence about abuse and to help survivors heal and reacclimate into society. No one should have to live in fear, and she's living proof a life without fear is possible.

If you are being abused or if you suspect someone is being abused, please contact the National Domestic Violence Hotline: 1-800-799-SAFE (7233) or https://www.thehotline.org.

If you live outside the US, contact UN Women at https://www.unwomen.org/en. They provide a global directory by country with local hotlines, shelters, and support services.

Please dial 911 if you're in immediate danger or in a life-threatening situation.

Connect with the author:
Facebook: Author – Candice Morrow
Instagram: @candicemorrow.author
Website: https://www.candicemorrowauthor.com

www.ingramcontent.com/pod-product-compliance
Lightning Source LLC
Chambersburg PA
CBHW051615010526
44107CB00037B/1439/J